Transformation, Embodiment, and Wellbeing in Foreign Language Pedagogy

Also Available from Bloomsbury

Researching Language Learning Motivation,
edited by Ali H. Al-Hoorie and Fruzsina Szabó
Identity, Motivation, and Multilingual Education in Asian Contexts,
Mark Feng Teng and Wang Lixun
Social Networks in Language Learning and Language Teaching,
edited by Avary Carhill-Poza and Naomi Kurata
Language Education in the School Curriculum, *Ken Cruickshank,
Stephen Black, Honglin Chen, Linda Tsung and Jan Wright*
Language Learning Strategies and Individual Learner Characteristics,
edited by Rebecca L. Oxford and Carmen M. Amerstorfer
The Value of English in Global Mobility and Higher Education,
Manuela Vida-Mannl
Video Enhanced Observation for Language Teaching, *edited by Paul Seedhouse*
Study Abroad and the Second Language Learner, *edited by Martin Howard*

Transformation, Embodiment, and Wellbeing in Foreign Language Pedagogy

Enacting Deep Learning

Edited by
Joseph Shaules and Troy McConachy

BLOOMSBURY ACADEMIC
LONDON • NEW YORK • OXFORD • NEW DELHI • SYDNEY

BLOOMSBURY ACADEMIC
Bloomsbury Publishing Plc
50 Bedford Square, London, WC1B 3DP, UK
1385 Broadway, New York, NY 10018, USA
29 Earlsfort Terrace, Dublin 2, Ireland

BLOOMSBURY, BLOOMSBURY ACADEMIC and the Diana logo
are trademarks of Bloomsbury Publishing Plc

First published in Great Britain 2023
This paperback edition published 2024

Copyright © Joseph Shaules and Troy McConachy and contributors, 2023

Joseph Shaules and Troy McConachy and contributors have asserted their right under the
Copyright, Designs and Patents Act, 1988, to be identified as Author of this work.

Cover image: © L. Toshio Kishiyama/ Getty Images

All rights reserved. No part of this publication may be reproduced or transmitted
in any form or by any means, electronic or mechanical, including photocopying,
recording, or any information storage or retrieval system, without prior
permission in writing from the publishers.

Bloomsbury Publishing Plc does not have any control over, or responsibility for,
any third-party websites referred to or in this book. All internet addresses given in this
book were correct at the time of going to press. The author and publisher regret any
inconvenience caused if addresses have changed or sites have ceased to exist,
but can accept no responsibility for any such changes.

A catalogue record for this book is available from the British Library.

A catalog record for this book is available from the Library of Congress.

ISBN:	HB:	978-1-3502-5448-0
	PB:	978-1-3502-5452-7
	ePDF:	978-1-3502-5449-7
	eBook:	978-1-3502-5450-3

Typeset by Integra Software Services Pvt. Ltd.

To find out more about our authors and books visit www.bloomsbury.com
and sign up for our newsletters

Contents

List of Figures vi
List of Tables vii
List of Contributors viii

Introduction: Enacting Deep Learning in Foreign Language Pedagogy
Joseph Shaules and Troy McConachy 1

1. Deep Linguaculture Learning in Transformative, Holistic, and Contemplative-Reflective Forms *Rebecca L. Oxford* 15
2. Language Learning as a Transformative Experience of Resistance, Adjustment, and Change *Joseph Shaules* 39
3. Holistic Views of Language Learning in Metaphoric Conceptualizations *Martin Cortazzi & Lixian Jin* 61
4. Humanistic Motivation and Transformative Language Engagement *Zi Wang* 85
5. Developing Embodied Learning Activities to Teach English Causatives *David Wijaya* 107
6. Encouraging Deep Learning through an Interactive, Intercultural Approach to Shakespeare *Duncan Lees* 129
7. Reader Response, Aesthetics, and Deep Learning in the German Language-Culture Classroom *Chantelle Warner* 153
8. Exploring Pragmatic Resistance and Moral Emotions in Foreign Language Learning *Troy McConachy* 175
9. Positive Psychology Activities for Promoting Emotion Regulation and Wellbeing in Language Teacher Education *María Matilde Olivero, María Celina Barbeito, and Adelina Sánchez Centeno* 201

Index 223

Figures

1.1	Three Overlapping Approaches to Deep Linguaculture Learning	19
2.1	The Two Faces of Janus—Resistance and Engagement	48
2.2	Surface and Deep Resistance and Engagement	50
2.3	Plotting Language Learning as a Journey of Positive and Negative Feelings	54
3.1	Journeys of Learning Characterized in the Words of Metaphors from Students and Teachers in China	75
3.2	Teachers Guide Chinese Students' Journeys of Learning, as Expressed in Their Own Words in Metaphors	77
4.1	Xiaoming Motigraph	95
4.2	Cheng Yuanyi Motigraph	96
5.1	Action Chain (adapted from Langacker 1991: 283)	111
5.2	Linguistic Realization of An Action Chain (adapted from Gilquin 2010)	112
5.3	An Action Chain of Causativization (adapted from Gilquin 2010: 65)	113
5.4	A Kinegram of Someone Making Someone Else Do Something	119
5.5	A Kinegram of Someone Having Someone Else Do Something	120
5.6	A Kinegram of Someone Getting Someone Else to Do Something	121
5.7	A Diagram of the Passivized Causative Construction (adapted from Gilquin 2010)	122
9.1	Creation Process of the Self-confidence Booster Anthem	215

Tables

5.1 Descriptive Statistics 124
7.1 Curriculum Overview 162

Contributors

María Celina Barbeito is Associate Professor and Researcher at the National University of Río Cuarto, Argentina. She is a teacher in the English Teacher Education Program and Director of the Master's in Applied Linguistics program. She holds an M.A. in TESOL from the University of Arizona, USA. Celina has almost thirty-years' experience as a teacher, trainer, and researcher in the areas of learning strategies, beliefs, and emotions. She is currently interested in finding ways to help future English as a Foreign Language teachers enhance their wellbeing through the lenses of positive psychology.

Martin Cortazzi is Visiting Professor at the Department of Applied Linguistics, the University of Warwick, UK and at the City University of Macau, China. He has taught in primary and secondary schools and in universities, and trained teachers in all these contexts internationally. His research and over 200 publications focus on developing innovative qualitative research methods; applying linguistics in education and language teaching; cultures of learning and intercultural communication; and English language teaching materials.

Lixian Jin is Chair Professor in Applied Linguistics and Dean of Faculty of Humanities and Social Sciences at City University of Macau, China, after being Chair Professor and having worked at University of Nottingham Ningbo China for over four years and at a British university for twenty-three years. She has been awarded research grants and led many international research teams to study intercultural communication in leadership and business contexts. She has developed qualitative research methods to explore insights from participants. Her over 200 publications focus on researching cultures of learning, intercultural communication, metaphor, and narrative analysis and bilingual clinical assessments.

Duncan Lees is Assistant Professor in Applied Linguistics at the University of Warwick, UK, where he teaches a variety of courses relating to intercultural communication. His PhD on Shakespeare in Chinese higher education was funded by the Economic and Social Research Council, and drew on the thirteen years he spent teaching literature and drama at a university in southern China. His research interests include drama and intercultural language education, ethnomethodology/conversation analysis, and intercultural pragmatics.

Troy McConachy is Associate Professor in Applied Linguistics at University of Warwick, UK. His research focuses on intercultural learning in language education, particularly from the viewpoint of awareness, identity, ideologies and representations, and teacher education. He has published widely in international journals such as ELT Journal, Language Awareness, Journal of International and Intercultural Communication, Journal of Intercultural Communication Research, and Intercultural Education. He is Editor-in-Chief of the journal Intercultural Communication Education and co-editor of Cambridge Elements in Intercultural Communication.

María Matilde Olivero is Second Language Teacher Educator and Researcher at the National University of Río Cuarto, Argentina. Her main research interests include affective factors and peacebuilding approaches in language education, and teacher wellbeing. Matilde obtained her PhD in second language acquisition at the University of South Florida, USA. For the past years she has worked hard to expand the field of peacebuilding in language education through theoretical models, empirical research, and the design of teaching materials. Matilde has published extensively in her areas of expertise. She has recently co-edited Peacebuilding in Language Education: Innovations in Theory and Practice.

Rebecca L. Oxford (Professor Emerita and Distinguished Scholar-Teacher, the University of Maryland, USA) is a language learning specialist, peace specialist, educational psychologist, speaker (forty-three countries), and former language teacher. Of her fifteen books, seven concern language learning and five concern peace and spirituality themes. Her 2021 book is *Peacebuilding in Language Education* (Oxford, Olivero, Harrison, and Gregerson). With Jing Lin and others, she co-edits two book series: Spirituality, Religion, and Education and Transforming Education for the Future. She co-edited the sixty-nine-volume Tapestry series for ESL/EFL teaching and is a published poet and amateur artist.

Adelina Sánchez Centeno is an English as a Foreign Language teacher and researcher at the National University of Río Cuarto, Argentina, where she has worked since 2003. She holds an M.A. in applied linguistics from the same university. Her research explores beliefs and emotions about oral corrective feedback in EFL contexts and the impact of students' emotion self-regulation strategies on their language learning process. She has published papers, co-authored book chapters, and participated in national and international conferences. Adelina is currently working on a research project that involves the design and implementation of positive psychology-based classroom interventions to help future EFL teachers increase their wellbeing.

Joseph Shaules is Specially Appointed Professor at Keio University, Tokyo, Japan, and Director of the Japan Intercultural Institute. He also teaches in the Tsuda University Graduate Program in TESOL. His research and publications focus on cross-cultural adaptation, intercultural education, culture and cognition, the psychology of intercultural experiences, and linguaculture learning. Books include *Language, Culture and The Embodied Mind* (2019); *The Intercultural Mind* (2015); *Deep Culture* (2007). He is the host of The Deep Culture Podcast.

Zi Wang is currently Internationalization Coordinator at the University of Warwick, UK. Her research interests include motivation, language learning, and multilingualism. Her PhD project investigated Chinese learners' motivation to learn English and Japanese. She has published on language learning and translation studies. Her most recent first-authored publication is *Negotiating Identity Tensions in Multilingual Learning in China: A Situated Perspective on Language Learning Motivation and Multilingual Identity* (2021).

Chantelle Warner is Associate Professor of German Studies and a faculty affiliate of Second Language Acquisition and Teaching at the University of Arizona, USA. Since 2014, she has directed the German Language Program. She also co-directs the Center for Educational Resources in Culture, Language and Literacy (CERCLL), a National Language Resource Center at the University of Arizona. Dr. Warner's research focuses on affective, experiential, and aesthetic dimensions of language use and learning, foreign language literacy development, pedagogical stylistics, and critical multilingualism studies, and she has published and presented widely across these areas. Her current book project argues for an expansion of models of literacy development and related pedagogies in second language teaching and learning to better integrate not only a wider range practices and modalities, but also different aesthetic and feeling rules that tacitly shape our responses to different language uses.

David Wijaya is a PhD candidate in Applied Linguistics in the School of Languages and Cultures, University of Queensland, Australia. His research interests include applied Cognitive Linguistics, embodied pedagogy, thinking for speaking, second language Indonesian, and teachers' technological, pedagogical, and content knowledge (TPACK). He has published on applied Cognitive Linguistics (2018, 2021) and teachers' technological, pedagogical, and content knowledge (TPACK) (2021). His most recent publications are: *Exploring Language Teachers' Lesson Planning for Corpus-based Language Teaching: A Focus on Developing TPACK for Corpora and DDL* (2021) and *Investigating Indonesian EFL Learners' Knowledge and Use of English Periphrastic Causative Constructions* (2021).

Introduction: Enacting Deep Learning in Foreign Language Pedagogy

Joseph Shaules and Troy McConachy

Introduction

Language learning has long been seen as a way to enrich our lives and expand our minds. In the thirteenth century, the Sufi mystic Rumi is quoted as saying: "Speak a new language so that the world will be a new world." This reminds us that language learning is a psychologically powerful experience that can open up new worlds of experience to learners. This should come as no surprise. Language is central to the experience of being human—we use it to relate to those around us, to fulfill everyday needs, to express our essential uniqueness to others, and to affiliate with particular communities. Adjusting such fundamental elements of self is bound to be both eye-opening and a significant challenge. It requires not just mental effort, but also psychological resilience—time and effort to internalize foreign patterns into the self, willingness to engage in awkward exchanges, the courage to navigate unfamiliar communicative terrain, and openness to intercultural complexities. No wonder, then, that foreign language learning brings with it the potential for personal growth and change.

While few would deny this transformative potential, foreign language learning is often discussed primarily in instrumentalist terms—as a way to get a job or add value to a resume—as part of discourses that propel the tendency to see a foreign language as a commodity to be "acquired" (Ushioda 2017). This encourages language pedagogy that overemphasizes "the transactional, the transfer of information that link(s) language learning to career opportunities and the expansion of global exchange" (Ros-i-Solé 2016: 3). Yet this can lead to narrow definitions of "success" dictated by the market demand for quantifiable language proficiency and "functional" skills (Leung & Scarino 2016) and downplay the psychological demands and rewards inherent to the language learning endeavor. As Kramsch (2009) reminds us, however, the *experience* of learning a language "is neither successful or unsuccessful. It can be lived more or less meaningfully and can be more or less transformative, no matter what level of proficiency has been attained" (p. 4). So while proficiency objectives and functional needs are important goals in their own right, the transformative perspective reminds us of the importance of engaging the whole person in the learning process.

This volume seeks to refocus attention on the potential for personal enrichment spoken of by Rumi so long ago. It aims to connect with the humanistic current in language education and contribute to on-going discussions on the personally impactful nature of language learning at the theoretical and pedagogical level. It uses the notion of *deep learning* to capture understandings of language learning and approaches to pedagogy that emphasize: (1) the embodied nature of language learning and use; (2) the transformative nature of learning processes; and (3) the wellbeing of learners and teachers. The contributions to this volume will look at deep learning in connection with these three notions—embodiment, transformation, and wellbeing—as a way to generate discussions about how to promote humanistic goals of growth and development through language learning. With this in mind, this chapter will first look at the notion of deep learning more broadly and then describe the way deep learning is being conceptualized in this volume.

A Deep Learning Perspective

An interest in deeper, more personally meaningful elements of the learning experience is not new. Stevick (1976) long ago emphasized the psychological stresses that result from a foreign language that feels "imposed on us" and that threatens our sense of self-worth (Stevick 1980: 9). He, therefore, wrote of the need to attend to the learner as a whole person (see Oxford, this volume). A focus on the learner experience can also be found in methodologies such as Community Language Learning (Curran 1972) and Suggestopedia (Lozanov 2005). More recently, there has been increased interest in the psychology of language and learning, with many scholars now emphasizing the need to take a person-centered or ecological approach to issues such as language learning motivation (Dornyei & Ushioda 2009; Zi Wang, this volume), wellbeing (Mercer 2021), and identity (Block 2014). Language learning is increasingly seen as an embodied phenomenon that stimulates a range of emotions and is linked to learners' aesthetic, somatic, spiritual, and moral sensibilities (Oxford et al. 2021). Dewaele (2019) writes of the "lift-off" of emotion research in the field of second language learning, which has helped to highlight different dimensions of learners' subjective experiences of language learning. Prior (2019) refers to "an expanded focus from the experimental to the experiential side of human language and life and how it shapes and is shaped by diverse ways of communicating, knowing, doing, being, becoming, belonging, desiring, and feeling" (p. 517). The field has seen increased interest not only in the role of negative emotion such as the psychological stress of foreign language anxiety (Gkonou et al. 2017) but also on learners' experience of positive emotions such as joy, happiness, hope, and desire (Helgesen 2019; Macintyre et al. 2019).

More narrowly, the term *deep learning* is used in a variety of ways. The notion of deep learning is found in the field of educational psychology (Kirschner & Hendrick 2020; Smith & Colby 2007) where it is used to refer to more abstract, reflective, and contextualized understanding, as opposed to a superficial focus on facts and information (Halbert & Kaser 2006; Rhem 1995). Shaules, writing in the context of language and intercultural education, describes deep learning as "the integration of complex skills into the intuitive mind in a process that is meaningful and engaging for learners" (Shaules 2019: 60). He traces this usage to the notion of *deep culture*—the intuitive elements of culture that influence us largely without our knowledge (Shaules 2007). Tochon (2010, 2014) has developed what is described as a *deep approach* to language learning, which is informed by a semiotics perspective, and which focuses on student-directed projects that integrate language and culture thematically and holistically in a way that is socially significant. Further afield, the term deep learning is used to refer to pattern-recognition algorithms that allow computers to learn on their own, in domains such as facial recognition and language processing (Jones 2014). A conceptual thread which ties many of these usages together is that deep learning goes beyond superficial engagement with information to develop more implicit and holistic forms of knowing.

Foundations for Deep Learning: Embodiment, Transformation, and Wellbeing

The deep learning perspective in this volume concerns itself not with the quantification of learning but first and foremost with *the quality of the learning experience*. The notion of depth is used in two complementary senses: (1) experiences of learning that are *meaningful* to the individual learner, thus encouraging psychological engagement and increased potential for the experience of personal growth and transformation; and (2) pedagogy that takes into account *embodied* elements, particularly the affective, intuitive, somatic, aesthetic, and moral dimensions of learning, mind, and self. The deep learning perspective encourages an understanding of language learning as a complex, embodied process that not only results in increased knowledge or skills, but which also creates the potential for learners to enrich their sense of self and experience greater wellbeing. This refers not just to making learning more enjoyable—having a fun class or an engaging activity—but to a foundational recognition that language learning has a psychological impact on learners. As argued by Shaules in chapter two of this volume, language learning is disruptive to socio-cognitive habits and is thus both psychologically challenging and potentially rewarding. When the learning process does not go well, it can create psychological resistance and perhaps even trauma. The deep learning perspective encourages language educators to be more than language experts or classroom managers. They take on responsibility for helping learners navigate the personal, interpersonal, and intercultural challenges of language learning. They may be experts of language, but they are also caretakers of the heart who need an understanding of the embodied nature of language, body, and mind.

There can be no single "best" approach to achieving deep learning outcomes, given the highly complex, personal, and context-dependent nature of foreign language learning. This volume proposes, however, that there are three intersecting notions that should underpin the enactment of deep learning in language education: embodiment, transformation, and wellbeing. These ideas serve as a starting point for exploration and reflection—a way to focus our attention on key elements of learning that help orient pedagogy toward deeper more meaningful learning experiences.

Embodiment The notion of embodiment is central to the deep learning view and is supported by an empirical understanding of sociocognitive processes. Research in brain and mind sciences has shown that mental processes are integrated with the whole organism, rather than existing in some separate mental space (Farina 2021). Much of this research has focused on the notion of *embodied cognition*. Work in this area seeks to understand the role the body plays in cognitive processes and takes as a theoretical starting point that "cognitive processes are deeply rooted in the body's interactions with the world" (Farina 2021: 74). This represents a movement away from the idea that cognition is a phenomenon that takes place largely "in our head" in the realm of abstract thought, and/or as a form of information processing.

In line with this, there is increasing evidence that language is also much more than a symbolic code—its use is closely tied with physical, emotional, and moral functioning. Reflecting on shifting views of language in the field of Second Language Acquisition (SLA), Hall (2019) contends that converging evidence from fields including child language development, psycholinguistics, neurolinguistics, and cognitive linguistics supports a more dynamic, embodied view of language. She explains that:

> (i)nstead of a fixed property of human mind, language knowledge is revealed to be a complex, dynamic set of constructions that are developed from continual interaction between our neural and domain-general cognitive-emotional processes on the one hand and our varied, lifelong experiences in our social worlds on the other.
>
> (p. 23)

This view situates language not as a discrete cognitive function, but as integral to the functioning of the whole organism in its environment, as dependent on and interrelated to more general learning abilities, and as an embodied process that is inseparable from affect and the socio-biological structures of the body.

An understanding of the embodied nature of language learning has important pedagogical implications. As argued in Wijaya's chapter in this volume, the processes of understanding and creating meaning are grounded in our physical experience of the world, and thus language becomes intimately connected to sensory experience and body states, as well as metaphoric understanding of the physical and social world (see also Atkinson 2010; Bergen 2012). Embodiment is also closely linked to affect, including motivational states and emotion (Brookman 2016; Price et al. 2012). Research on dual process models of cognition has shed light on the respective roles of analytic and intuitive forms of cognition (Evans & Frankish 2009) and how they relate to decision-making and motivation in social and moral domains (Haidt 2012). Embodiment is thus closely related to the subjective quality of the learning experience—our intuitive "feel" for learning and using a new language. For example, McConachy's chapter in this volume argues that learners' moral intuitions are highly relevant to the learning of a new language and learners' attempts to reconcile existing assumptions about social relationships and understandings of "appropriate" language use in context, with those they are exposed to in the course of learning.

This increased understanding of the embodied nature of language, mind, and learning provides an empirical foundation for a humanistic emphasis on the whole learner. It also resonates with views of learning that originate outside of Western dualist traditions and which emphasize the integrated engagement of mind and body in the cultivation of knowledge and self-improvement (Li 2012).

Transformation An understanding of language learning as an embodied phenomenon draws attention to the transformative potential of the language learning experience. This refers most simply to the idea that language learning is not simply an additive process of increased knowledge or new skills—it is a complex, whole-body experience that is psychologically powerful and thus "causes the learner to change in some way—thinking, behaviour, acceptance of the other, values, mindset, and/or emotion" (Leaver 2021: 16). Leaver et al. (2021) elaborate on this by suggesting that "personal transformation involves cognitive, emotional, and cultural shifts occurring within the individual, that is, developing self-awareness, resolving disorienting dilemmas, identifying cognitive distortions, managing emotions, and integrating two (or more) cultures on their own terms" (p. 2). They further argue that the field of language education is currently undergoing a paradigm shift away from transactionally focused language education to education with a more transformative focus.

The transformative changes of language learning are powerful yet subtle. They are experienced not as a sudden overwhelming or shocking shift, but in the lived experience of adjusting to new ways of thinking, acting, and being. This transformative change can go unnoticed by the learner, however, because it is largely an intuitive, integrative process—what was experienced as foreign or awkward starts to feel natural and even an extension of the self. It happens moment-to-moment during language practice—e.g. an *A ha!* moment of linguistic or cultural insight; a feeling of "forgetting" that one is using a foreign language—but also cumulatively, as we gain the subjective feeling of "being" a foreign language user overall (Kramsch 2009). As Oxford (this volume) points out, transformative, holistic, experiential, and contemplative/reflective learning approaches emphasize the kind of deep learning that lends itself to this process of inner change. This reminds us that the transformative process of language learning is not a singular, uniform phenomenon or discrete cognitive change—it is complexly and uniquely personal to each learner. Indeed, it is the experience of personal growth itself. In line with this, Zi Wang (this volume) shows that language engagement and the experience of growth in academic, aesthetic, and ethical domains can generate a new foundation of self-confidence and self-awareness that stimulates humanistic motivation for language learning. Warner (this volume) argues for the importance of the aesthetic dimensions of language and literacy learning and shows how aesthetic reading can impact learner wellbeing in unexpected and transformational ways.

Wellbeing Accepting the premise that language learning is psychologically powerful focuses attention on the ethical responsibility of educators to attend to the learner's holistic needs and overall wellbeing. This is a notion that finds wide resonance in recent work on teachers' and learners' wellbeing in foreign language pedagogy and language teacher education (e.g. Barbeito & Sánchez Centeno 2021; Gkonou & Miller 2019; Mercer 2021). We concur with Mercer (2021) that addressing wellbeing in foreign language learning requires an integrated approach that incorporates both hedonic and eudemonic perspectives. That is, it focuses not only on the subjective experience of positive emotion (hedonic) but also on learners' aspirational tendencies and desires to pursue that which is personally meaningful (eudemonic).

In enacting deep learning, educators consider the need for language learning to be experienced as an intrinsically valuable experience—more than an accumulation of knowledge or skills. Cortazzi and Jin (this volume) explore the rich variety of metaphors used to make sense of this challenging yet rewarding learning journey, and argue that by understanding cultures of learning, educators can achieve more truly learner-centered pedagogy. Shaules (this volume) points out that language learning is psychologically demanding and can provoke negative outcomes—resistance—as well as increased wellbeing. In line with the humanistic tradition in Foreign Language Learning (FLL), he calls for educators to play a "counselling" role that supports learners as they adjust to the adaptive demands of the FLL experience. Rebecca Oxford (this volume) argues that deep linguacultural learning should be associated with a view of wellbeing that goes beyond the individual learner and considers how learners function within and contribute to society. Olivero et al. (this volume) also encourage us not to lose sight of teachers' own wellbeing concerns, arguing for the utility of positive psychology activities for helping teachers regulate their own emotions and wellbeing.

In short, the deep learning perspective in this volume emphasizes that language learning is an embodied phenomenon (not simply a form of mental manipulation or information processing) that involves a psychologically demanding process of development and change (it has transformational potential). As such, it entails an ethical commitment on behalf of language teachers to concern themselves not only with instrumental goals and measurable communicative outcomes, but also with the wellbeing of the learner as a whole person.

Aims and Organization of This Volume

This volume introduces pedagogical approaches and empirical studies that emphasize embodied engagement with language, the transformative potential of the language learning experience, and the importance of learner and teacher wellbeing. Chapters in this volume consider the enactment of deep learning from diverse theoretical perspectives, including positive psychology, embodied cognition, cognitive linguistics, motivational theory, literary theory, and moral psychology. Each chapter provides concrete discussion of ways that these theoretical perspectives can inform educators' approaches to deep learning, supported by critical synthesis of relevant theoretical literature, analysis of empirical data, or examples from particular teaching contexts. These diverse viewpoints are offered as a way to stimulate discussion of the many forms of pedagogy that can encourage deeper learning experiences.

The volume opens with a chapter by Rebecca Oxford which explores the nature of deep linguaculture learning in relation to key theories and theorists within three learning traditions: transformative learning, holistic learning, and contemplative-reflective learning. Oxford argues that each of these modes is valuable for deep linguaculture learning and emphasizes the need for the notion of wellbeing, both of individual learners and society at large, to act as an ethical framework for foreign language education. She argues that deep linguaculture learning helps develop the inner talents and strengths of learners, as well as inner wells of resilience. By creating communities of support, respect, and care, pedagogy focused on deep forms of learning fosters transformation not only in the learner, but also in the world at large. In this way, the transformative elements of learning are intimately related to the wellbeing of the learner and humanity more broadly.

In Chapter 2, Joseph Shaules highlights the Janus-faced nature of foreign language learning, arguing for the need to recognize the potential for language learning to be both psychologically challenging and rewarding. The chapter argues that the psychological challenges and rewards of FL learning are intimately related, and that cross-cultural adjustment theory provides a useful theoretical lens for understanding this interrelationship. In this view, the adaptive demands generated by the experience of foreignness in language learning are similar to the psychological dynamic of cross-cultural adaptation. Learners react to these demands in motivational terms—by resisting and/or engaging with the learning process. The chapter seeks to normalize a view of language learning as involving both engagement and resistance, and argues that transformative learning outcomes depend on how learners and teachers manage adaptive demands.

The third chapter, co-authored by Martin Cortazzi and Lixian Jin, considers the significance of language learners' metaphoric conceptualizations of language learning and how these provide insights into the deeply meaningful and embodied nature of the learning experience from the viewpoint of students and teachers themselves. The authors draw on an extensive corpus of metaphors provided by Chinese learners and teachers of English to highlight cognitive, affective, sociocultural, moral-spiritual, and aesthetic dimensions of learning, which they argue present a challenge to the view of language learning as the acquisition of skills. The chapter particularly highlights key metaphors revealing concepts of teacher cultivation, nurturing student wellbeing with care and concern, and students own change and transformation of the self. This exploration sheds light on the many ways that learners make sense of their language learning journey, the embodied nature of their own metaphoric understanding, and the psychological import that they imbue it with.

In the fourth chapter, Zi Wang puts forward a humanistic understanding of language learning motivation based on the experiences of Chinese learners of English and Japanese. The chapter highlights the potential for instrumentalist ideologies of language and language learning to obscure the possibilities for more humanistic goals in SLA research. It goes on to synthesize a number of key concepts in motivation research that are aligned with a broadly humanistic understanding of language learning. The data from Chinese learners shows that what the author terms "humanistic motivation" was emergent in learners' language engagement as they experienced a sense of personal growth in academic, aesthetic, and ethical domains. This contributed to increased self-awareness and helped transform learners' perceptions of themselves and their relationship with these languages. The chapter concludes with suggestions for how teachers can foster humanistic motivation in their own learners.

In Chapter 5, David Wijaya presents an approach to developing understanding of English causative constructions that draws on insights from cognitive linguistics and embodied cognition. This chapter calls for recognition of the close links between linguistic knowledge, bodily experience and bodily perception, and argues that embodied learning activities provide a potentially powerful way of promoting deep learning. The chapter offers a theoretical conceptualization of periphrastic causative constructions informed by cognitive linguistics and suggests how this could be fused with what the author sees as a deep approach to learning grammar. It seeks to move beyond the conceptualization of grammar as primarily a structural system governed by rules and abstract properties. The chapter presents a number of concrete pedagogical strategies that could be employed by teachers to teach causatives and other aspects of grammar in order to promote deep learning.

Chapter 6, written by Duncan Lees, argues that while using Shakespearean texts in the English classroom might seem impractical or counterproductive according to the instrumentalist logic of much foreign language education, their very "strangeness" can actually help teachers to encourage deeper learning. The chapter outlines a pedagogy that combines the collaborative, embodied, and playful techniques of active or "rehearsal room" approaches to Shakespeare with an intercultural perspective on language teaching and learning. Through practical examples drawn from the author's own classes with learners of English at universities in China and the UK, it shows how the processes of (de)familiarization and mediation involved encourage learners to reflect more deeply not only on Shakespeare's "strange" language, but also on their own linguistic and cultural assumptions and identities. This reflection encourages a richer, more meaningful engagement with the learning process as learners explore English learning as an intercultural experience.

In Chapter 7, Chantelle Warner looks at deep learning from the perspective of aesthetic experience and reader response in the German language classroom. While in linguistics "transactional" often denotes instrumental language use, in the reader response theories of Louise Rosenblatt it describes instead a deep, aesthetic relationship between reader and text. Using this tension as a starting point, this chapter explores the potential of a transactional approach to second language literacy in enabling learners to relate their aesthetic experiences to their emergent sense of themselves as multilingual subjects (Kramsch 2009). It argues that aesthetic reading can impact learner wellbeing in unexpected and transformational ways. A central focus of this discussion is a case study involving a creative writing composition in which the learner explores how her story and experiences intersect with the narratives she had read in class. The chapter concludes with tentative pedagogical principles for transactional literacy in language-culture teaching.

Chapter 8, authored by Troy McConachy, looks at the phenomenon of "pragmatic resistance," which is a term that represents learners' aversive reactions to target language pragmatic norms. Drawing on the author's own experience, published examples, and insights from moral psychology, the chapter argues for the need to see pragmatic resistance and pragmatic decision-making more broadly as an embodied phenomenon that is closely tied to individuals' intuitions about socially and morally desirable behavior. Whereas much existing work in the field tends to emphasize learners' rational decision-making as a basis for agency, this chapter posits an important role for moral emotions, particularly what are known as "other-condemning emotions" and "self-conscious emotions" in how language learners perceive and evaluate the appropriateness of language use in context. It argues for the importance of creating space for learners to explore difficult emotions triggered by language use that seemingly violates their own felt sense of right and wrong communicative behavior. The chapter then proposes a number of pedagogical strategies which promote mindful observation of bodily sensations, emotions, and thoughts that lead to negative evaluations of pragmatic differences.

The final chapter of the volume, co-authored by María Matilde Olivero, María Celina Barbeito and Adelina Sánchez Centeno, highlights the value of incorporating positive psychology activities based on holistic learning approaches into language teacher education programs as a way of enhancing teachers' emotion regulation and wellbeing. The chapter first reviews recent theoretical trends and empirical research on wellbeing and emotion regulation in language education as well as on holistic learning. This serves to frame the activities that are described next and to elucidate their underlying principles. It argues that in order for teachers to experience wellbeing throughout their careers and to care for the wellbeing of their language learners, it is paramount to incorporate a focus on wellbeing in language teacher education programs. It then offers several positive psychology-based activities that have been used in language teacher education courses with the purpose of helping future teachers regulate their emotions and enhance their wellbeing while learning to teach a foreign language.

As a whole, this collection of chapters challenges language teachers and teacher trainers to question instrumentalist views of language learning, to recognize the deeply impactful nature of the language learning experience, and to consider how language pedagogy can contribute to the development of the learner as a whole person. Each of them is informed by a view of language learning as an embodied, transformative process with powerful psychological consequences. Naturally, there are many roads to deep learning—each reflecting particular teaching contexts and the unique experiences and abilities of each educator. By reflecting on the various perspectives found in this volume, it is hoped that readers will be inspired to explore different aspects of the deep learning experience and contribute to an ongoing discussion of how to make FL learning the powerful, life-changing experience it has the potential to be.

Acknowledgments

We express our sincere thanks toward the following individuals external to the project who kindly agreed to review chapters: Sal Consoli, Jean-Marc Dewaele, Mike Fleming, Christina Gkonou, Geoff Hall, Noriko Ishihara, Jim King, Jeannette Littlemore, and Melina Porto. Your insightful comments and criticisms were valued by contributors and ourselves.

References

Atkinson, D. (2010), "Extended, Embodied Cognition and Second Language Acquisition." *Applied Linguistics*, 31 (5): 599–622.

Barbeito, M. C. and Sánchez Centeno, A. (2021), "Inner Peace and Emotion Regulation during Oral Production in ESL/EFL Teacher Education." in R. L. Oxford, M. M. Olivero, M. Harrison & T. Gregersen (eds), *Peacebuilding in Language Education. Innovations in Theory and Practice*, 63–79, Bristol: Multilingual Matters.

Bergen, B. K. (2012), *Louder than Words: The New Science of How the Mind Makes Meaning*. New York, NY: Basic Books.

Block, D. (2014), *Second Language Identities*. London: Bloomsbury Academic.

Brookman, A. (2016), "Learning from Educational Neuroscience." *The Psychologist*, 29 (10): 766–9.

Curran, C. A. (1972), *Counseling-Learning: A Whole Person Approach for Education*. New York, NY: Grune and Stratton.

Dewaele, J.-M. (2019), "When Elephants Fly: The Lift-off of Emotion Research in Applied Linguistics." *The Modern Language Journal*, 103 (2): 533–6. doi:https://doi.org/10.1111/modl.12576

Dewaele, J.-M., Chen, X., Padilla, A. M., & Lake, J. (2019), "The Flowering of Positive Psychology in Foreign Language Teaching and Acquisition Research." *Frontiers in Psychology*, 10 (2128): 1–13. doi:10.3389/fpsyg.2019.02128

Dewaele, J.-M., & MacIntyre, P. D. (2014), "The Two Faces of Janus? Anxiety and Enjoyment in the Foreign Language Classroom." *Studies in Second Language Learning and Teaching*, 4 (2): 237–74.

Dörnyei, Z. (2019), "Psychology and Language Learning: The Past, the Present and the Future." *Journal for the Psychology of Language Learning*, 1 (June): 27–41.

Dörnyei, Z., MacIntyre, P., & Henry, A. (eds). (2015), *Motivational Dynamics in Language Learning*. Bristol: Multilingual Matters.

Dörnyei, Z. & Ushioda, E. (eds). (2009), *Motivation, Language Identity and the L2 Self*. Bristol, UK: Multilingual Matters.

Evans, J. & Frankish, K. (eds). (2009), *In Two Minds: Dual Processes and Beyond*. Oxford, UK: Oxford University Press.

Farina, M. (2021), "Embodied Cognition: Dimensions, Domains and Applications." *Adaptive Behavior*, 29 (1): 73–88. doi:10.1177/1059712320912963

Gkonou, C., Daubney, M. & Dewaele, J.-M. (eds). (2017), *New Insights into Language Anxiety: Theory, Research and Educational Implications*. Bristol, UK: Multilingual Matters.

Gkonou, C. & Miller, E. R. (2019), "Caring and Emotional Labour: Language Teachers' Engagement with Anxious Learners in Private Language School Classroom." *Language Teaching Research*, 23: 372–87.

Haidt, J. (2012), *The Righteous Mind: Why Good People Are Divided by Religion and Politics*. New York: Pantheon Books.

Halbert, J. & Kaser, L. (2006), "Deep Learning: Inquiring Communities of Practice." *Education Canada*, 46 (3): 43–5.

Hall, J. K. (2019), *Essentials of SLA for L2 teachers: A Transdisciplinary Framework*. New York, NY: Routledge.

Helgesen, M. (2019), *English Teaching and the Science of Happiness: Positive Psychology Communication Activities for Language Learning*. Tokyo: Abax.

Jones, N. (2014), "The Learning Machines." *Nature*, 505 (7482): 146–8.

Kirschner, P. A. & Hendrick, C. (2020), *How Learning Happens: Seminal Works in Educational Psychology and What They Mean in Practice*. New York, NY: Routledge.

Kramsch, C. (2009), *The Multilingual Subject*. Oxford: Oxford University Press.

Langacker, R. W. (2008), *Cognitive Grammar: A Basic Introduction*. New York: Oxford University Press.

Leaver, B. L. (2021), "Transformative Language Learning and Teaching: The Next Paradigm Shift and Its Historical Context." In B. L. Leaver, D. E. Davidson & C. Cambell (eds), *Transformative Language Learning and Teaching*, 13–22, Cambridge: Cambridge University Press.

Leaver, B. L., Davidson, D. E. & Campbell, C. (eds). (2021), *Transformative Language Learning and Teaching*. Cambridge, UK: Cambridge University Press.

Leung, C. & Scarino, A. (2016), "Reconceptualizing the Nature of Goals and Outcomes in Language/s Education." *The Modern Language Journal*, 100 (S1): 81–95. doi:https://doi.org/10.1111/modl.12300

Li, J. (2002), "A Cultural Model of Learning: Chinese 'Heart and Mind for Wanting to Learn.'" *Journal of Cross-Cultural Psychology*, 33 (3): 248–69.

Li, J. (2012), *Cultural Foundations of Learning: East and West*. Cambridge and New York: Cambridge University Press.

Lozanov, G. (2005), *Suggestopaedia—Desuggestive Teaching Communicative Method on the Level of the Hidden Reserves of the Human Mind*. Vienna: International Centre for Desuggestology.

Macintyre, P. D., Gregesen, T. & Mercer, S. (2019), "Setting an Agenda for Positive Psychology in SLA: Theory, Practice, and Research." *The Modern Language Journal*, 103 (1): 262–74. doi: https://doi.org/10.1111/modl.12544

Mercer, S. (2021), "An Agenda for Well-being in ELT: An Ecological Perspective." *ELT Journal*, 75 (1): 14–21. doi:10.1093/elt/ccaa062

Oxford, R. L., Olivero, M. M., Harrison, M. & Gregersen, T. (eds). (2021), *Peacebuilding in Language Education: Innovations in Theory and Practice*. Multilingual Matters.

Price, T. F., Peterson, C. K. & Harmon-Jones, E. (2012), "The Emotive Neuroscience of Embodiment." *Motivation and Emotion*, 36: 27–37.

Prior, M. T. (2019), "Elephants in the Room: An 'Affective Turn,' or Just Feeling Our Way?" *The Modern Language Journal*, 103 (2): 516–27. doi: https://doi.org/10.1111/modl.12573

Rhem, J. (1995), "Deep/Surface Approaches to Learning: An Introduction." *The National Teaching and Learning Forum*, 5 (1): 1–5.

Rivers, D. J. & Houghton, S. A. (eds). (2013), *Social Identities and Multiple Selves in Foreign Language Education*. London: Bloomsbury.

Ros I Solé, C. (2016), *The Personal World of the Language Learner*. London, UK: Palgrave Pivot.

Shapiro, L. (ed.). (2014), *The Routledge Handbook of Embodied Cognition*. New York: Routledge.

Shaules, J. (2007), *Deep Culture: The Hidden Challenges of Global Living*. Clevedon, UK: Multilingual Matters.

Shaules, J. (2019), *Language, Culture and the Embodied Mind: A Developmental Model of Linguaculture Learning*. New York: Springer.

Smith, T. W. & Colby, S. A. (2007), "Teaching for Deep Learning." *The Clearing House: A Journal of Educational Strategies, Issues and Ideas*, 80 (5): 205–10. doi: https://doi.org/10.3200/TCHS.80.5.205-210

Stevick, E. W. (1976), *Memory, Meaning & Method: Some Psychological Perspectives on Language Learning*. Rowley, MA: Newbury House Publishers.

Stevick, E. W. (1980), *Teaching Languages: A Way and Ways*. Cambridge, MA: Newbury House.

Tochon, F. V. (2010), "Deep Education." *Journal for Educators, Teachers and Trainers*, 1: 1–12.

Tochon, F. V. (2014), *Help Them Learn a Language Deeply*. Blue Mounds, WI: Deep University Press.

Ushioda, E. (2017), "The impact of global English on motivation to learn other languages: Toward an ideal multilingual self." *The Modern Language Journal*, 101 (3): 469–82.

1

Deep Linguaculture Learning in Transformative, Holistic, and Contemplative-Reflective Forms

Rebecca L. Oxford

Introduction

The purpose of this chapter is to explore transformative, holistic (holistic-experiential and holistic-humanistic, which overlap greatly), and contemplative-reflective learning approaches. These contribute to *deep linguaculture learning*, to use Shaules' (2019) term. *Linguaculture* is the integration of language and culture (see Risager 2020). Our original linguaculture is the surrounding in which we live and move and have our being, and that original linguaculture is also inside us, shaping what we think, do, and feel. Unfortunately, many language teachers, language program administrators, and heads of schools, universities, and institutes think that learners need (or at least will accept) years of disembodied language instruction with a few sprinkles of cultural knowledge added to liven up the proceedings. Nevertheless, what learners really need, ultimately, is the full-bodied experience of deep linguaculture learning, in which the language and culture are both honored and united.

This chapter argues that deep linguaculture learning ultimately aims to contribute not only to individual learner wellbeing but also to the wellbeing of others and of society at large. I believe such learning can create communities of support, respect, and care; foster transformation in the learner and the world; address the whole learner; offer astounding experiences of language and culture, increasingly called linguaculture; and constantly provide reflection opportunities. In the process, the learner discovers unexpected inner talents and strengths. Challenges arise, fear or confusion emerges, and difficulty is in the air, yet the learner finds inner wells of resilience. None of this is done in isolation or loneliness. Much of the magic comes from relationships.

Ethically speaking, deep linguacultural learning should aim to enhance the wellbeing of learners and all others involved. Martin Seligman (2011: 16), the father of positive psychology, created the acronym PERMA to summarize his version of wellbeing: _p_ositive emotion, _e_ngagement, (positive) _r_elationships, _m_eaning, and _a_ccomplishment. PERMA is oriented to the wellbeing of an individual who engaged in some effort, has relationships with people, and seeks meaning, positive emotions, and accomplishment. PERMA offers a snapshot of personal wellbeing, and that's fine; yet to me it does not overtly signal deep concern for others' wellbeing, without which my own wellbeing cannot be complete. PERMA is the child of an individualist culture, as I am. Providing a balance to the individualistic focus is the South African tradition of *ubuntu*, which roughly means, "I can only be human through you" or "I am because we are." As explained by Archbishop Emeritus Desmond Tutu (1999), "*Ubuntu* […] speaks of the very essence of being human[:] … generous, … hospitable, … friendly and caring and compassionate…. It is to say, 'My humanity is caught up, is inextricably bound up, in yours.' We belong in a bundle of life. We say, 'A person is a person through other persons'" (p. 196). Individualistic cultural views of wellbeing are not wrong, but the spirit of *ubuntu* adds some necessary notes to the symphony. Linguaculture learning can be especially valuable for bringing people together in that *ubuntu* spirit.

In this chapter, deep linguaculture learning—deeply learning a linguaculture that is not one's own—is associated with a conception of wellbeing that means much more than one's own personal wellbeing. Here, the definition of *wellbeing* means caring about all people; giving compassion others and ourselves; listening mindfully, cherishing family and friends, and being kind to all; engaging in and/or supporting deep learning of any kind; exploring meaningfully; being curious; being increasingly flexible and willing to learn. Wellbeing for deep linguaculture learning also means participating in new ways of communicating and thinking; being open to new ideas; understanding that emotion and cognition are inseparable, as are language and culture. For some people, the above elements of wellbeing are obvious, but these elements do not seem to be on everyone's radar screen. However, anyone can work to develop these potentials and burnish them with use. Deep linguacultural learning can be a central part of this wellbeing process, and therein lies one of the greatest adventures of a lifetime.

The chapter first of all considers the nature of deep learning of linguaculture, and then goes on to highlight theories and theorists that have offered different perspectives on transformative learning, holistic-experiential/holistic-humanistic learning, and contemplative-reflective learning.

Theoretical Exploration

More on Deep Learning of Linguaculture

The idea that learning of linguaculture can be meaningfully understood through the notion of "deep learning" has been put forward recently by Joseph Shaules (2019), in an attempt to find common ground between language learning and culture learning. Shaules (2019) defined deep learning as "the process of embodying complex domains of socio-cognitive knowledge" (9). He made a distinction between explicit, conceptual *surface learning* (memorizing letters, sounds, words, sentences, and grammatical patterns, typically unconnected with a cultural context) to *deep* (intuitive, implicit) *linguaculture learning*. Through deep learning and with an attitude of engagement, the person's social, cultural, and linguistic boundaries enlarge. I believe this provides opportunities to encounter and interpret new perspectives, ideas, lifeways, and communications; expand social interactions and form new bonds; uncover personal strengths and emergent identities; and better understand one's original linguaculture while deeply learning the new linguaculture.

Language is part of culture and is simultaneously a crucial vehicle through which culture is expressed. All forms of language—spoken, written, paraverbal (e.g., voice tone, pitch, and pacing), and nonverbal (e.g., gestures and gaze)—embody culture. Art, music, and dance are often called "languages," and they, too, embody and express culture. Though a constant process of rich, stimulating encounters with aspects of linguaculture, the learner intuits—implicitly knows—the astounding complexity and depth of linguaculture. Language and culture are virtually unconnected in surface learning, but they become increasingly integrated at the deeper levels of implicit, intuitive learning (Shaules 2019). Consider this analogy. At the level of surface knowledge, language, and culture are like two islands in the ocean: separate, far distanced, not interacting. Each would look distorted or misshapen if seen from above. However, if divers go deeper and deeper into the waters of the ocean, they discover what had been hidden at the surface. At the level of deep knowledge, ocean divers encounter brilliantly colored, lustrous, thick webs of knowledge. These webs are wrapped and woven together so tightly that they seem to comprise a deep, underwater continent of linguaculture, in which language and culture are fully integrated, interwoven, inseparable, indivisible.

Merely adding culture objectives to existing language objectives does not lead to deep linguaculture learning (Shaules 2019); it risks creating long lists of impossible-to-meet objectives. If the hope is to integrate language and culture, none of the following is sufficient: tacking culture lessons onto language lessons and hoping for the best; planning for one day of culture learning to every four days of language learning; or piling up random layers of surface-level culture knowledge and language knowledge for no particular purpose. In a university Russian class, we gained extremely superficial knowledge of Russian words. Rote-memorizing culture facts was avoided, but the only course requirement was memorizing alphabetized sets of pages from an immense Russian-English dictionary and being tested each week, without any opportunity to use the memorized words. That resulted in the pile-up of surface-level knowledge, which perished rapidly without use. The random display of things to memorize would have been even larger if the teacher had additionally added context-free culture facts to memorize.

As per Shaules (2019), deep linguaculture learning involves a process of psychological adjustment, with learning triggered by adaptive demands. Many pressures occur all at once. Learners encounter the seeming strangeness of the language and the demands to internalize the new system of communication as soon as possible while simultaneously trying to adapt culturally and psychologically. Shaules (this volume) argues that these adaptive demands on the learner generate the potential for both resistance and engagement. Resistance can be characterized by a rejection of the learning experience as a whole or by more ambivalent motivational states. Resistance can also take the form of a psychological aversion toward particular features of language (McConachy, this volume). These ideas about resistance make a connection between the adaptive demands discussed by Shaules' chapter (this volume), and the current chapter's focus on wellbeing. When the learner is able to successfully negotiate and adapt to new experiences of foreignness and overcome the urge to retreat, the possibility for transformation and wellbeing emerges. The idea is that we need to recognize the potential for foreign linguaculture learning to be useful and psychologically challenging and to therefore place learner wellbeing at the forefront. This is a view which strongly resonates with my own.

Deep linguaculture learning can be usefully conceptualized in terms of its emphasis on learner transformation, its commitment to the holistic and experiential nature of learning, and its recognition of the need for contemplation (also known as reflection) as a key part of learning. As presented in Figure 1.1, deep linguaculture learning has important points of connection with these three different, yet overlapping, traditions of learning. Whilst these have come about through their own historical and theoretical trajectories, all have the potential to offer significant insights into the nature of deep linguaculture learning. In the following sections, I am to deal with each of them in turn, highlighting key theorists and other relevant work along the way.

There are similarities among these dimensions of learning. The differences are often in emphasis and details, with the purposes being similar. For instance, Shaules' (2019, 2020) works on deep linguaculture learning frequently refer to the other terms. Anthologies about transformative language learning and teaching (Leaver et al. 2021) and transformative learning (Cranton & Taylor 2012) employ words like experiential, holistic, deep, and reflective. Each learning approach has its own flavor, with certain flavors, compared with others, appealing to some learners and teachers more than to others. I turn first of all to transformative learning.

**Modes of Deep Linguaculture Learning
and Some Theorists Mentioned in This Chapter**

A. Transformative

Dirkx, Freire, Mexirow, Dirkx, Shaules, Taylor & Cranton, Vygotsky[1]

B. Holistic

Holistic Experiential[2]: Dewey

Holistic-Humanistic: Rogers, Stevick, Moskowitz

C. Contemplative-Reflective

David Boud, Tom Culham, Jing Lin

[1]Vygotsky is not usually considered a transformative learning theorist, but his metaphors show phases of transformation. [2]Kolb (2015) is an experiential learning theorist, but his work is not holistic, so he is not listed above.

Figure 1.1 Three Overlapping Approaches to Deep Linguaculture Learning

Transformative Learning

Transformative learning is learning that has a profound effect, "a deep shift in perspective, leading to more open, more permeable, and better-justified meaning perspectives" (Cranton & Taylor 2012: 3). Note the use of the word "deep" in the prior sentence. This underscores the fact that transformative learning involves far more than becoming open to other's viewpoints, gaining self-confidence, sorting vocabulary cards, or piling up new knowledge on the computer. It entails a significant shift in perceiving and experiencing the world. For Shaules (2019: 12), transformative linguaculture learning means that "new linguistic and cultural patterns are integrated at deep levels of the self—a new language becomes part of who we are, and a way to express our unique qualities." This represents an embodied understanding of transformation where the focus is not solely on change in cognitive structures but rather a broader expansion in ways of experiencing the link between language and experience (see Shaules, this volume).

Approaches to transformative learning are diverse, despite the shared goal of bringing about deep change. Cranton and Taylor (2012) emphasized the array of perspectives in transformative learning: individual change versus social change, autonomous learning versus relational learning, and rational versus extrarational (intuitive). As Lawrence and Cranton (2009: 316) suggest, "[n]o one theoretical perspective needs to mean others are excluded. That is, transformative learning can be both cognitive and imaginative; it can be collaborative and individually based; it can include depth psychology alongside a more practical reflective approach." No matter what form or fashion transformative learning takes, it can have a fundamentally similar outcome: the major shift in perspective mentioned above (Cranton & Taylor 2012).

Below I present different views of transformative learning that offer insights for deep linguaculture learning: Mezirow's approach, which he meant to be highly cognitive, and Dirkx's approach, which he intended to be strongly emotion-related, drawing on depth psychology. Realistically, cognition and emotion cannot be neatly sliced away from each other, and we should be very glad of that. Mezirow's approach was the "first wave" of transformative learning, while Dirkx's approach was the "second wave." Another chapter on transformative learning (see Oxford 2021) was the basis of this discussion of Mezirow and Dirkx and includes more details. In addition, I introduce below Stevick's "sacramental" approach, which is also intended to transform language learners.

Mezirow's Approach to Transformative Learning

Jack Mezirow's *cognitive-analytic approach* unintentionally, intrinsically supports Socrates' statement, "The unexamined life is not worth living," though this was not a maxim used by Mezirow. Individual transformative learning à la Mezirow involves numerous rational phases, with the initial phase always being a *disorienting dilemma*, a real problem or crisis in the life of a person that eventually, through phases, causes the rethinking of the person's unexamined meaning schemes or beliefs. This transformation aids the individual in gradually generating new perspectives that have been rationally, analytically, closely examined as a means of guiding actions. These transformed beliefs might not be the same for everyone, but they are to be consciously chosen, meaningful, and useful for shaping actions in the person's context.

At first, Mezirow described the phases as random and nonsequential, with phase-skipping possible by the individual (1978) and with the aim of transforming individuals' unexamined perspectives, as noted above. In the next decade, Mezirow (1981) settled on his favored approach, which included ten sequential, required phases, still involving constant rational analysis.

These are the ten phases in the perspective transformation as Mezirow delineated them in 1981: experiencing a disorienting dilemma or crisis, examining one's own assumptions, critically assessing the assumptions, recognizing dissatisfaction and its sources, exploring alternatives (i.e., new role options), planning a course of action, acquiring new knowledge, trying out new roles, building competence, and integrating the new perspective into one's life (Baumgartner 2012). As stated by Baumgartner, Mezirow's approach was criticized because it (1) was overly rational, ignoring emotions (except for anxiety) and intuition; (2) portrayed a unitary identity rather than recognizing an individual's multiple identities; and (3) failed to critically recognize an individual's social context, including ideologies, power, race, gender, and class. His response (Mezirow 2006) was to continue to ignore emotions and intuitions, though he stated that they might be considered; and to ignore social context as being political, though he said his transformative phases could become a basis for taking social action. In other words, Mezirow made no discernable, criticism-related changes in his approach. Furthermore, as noted by Oxford (2021), Mezirow's approach was clearly oriented to individualist cultures supporting personal autonomy, and the approach ignored Freire's (1970/2018) concept of collectivist cultures' group-based, liberatory autonomy.

I used Mezirow's model in two master's degree courses for EFL/ESL teacher education (see Oxford 2021). In these classes, culture was not treated as an add-on; I encouraged the future teachers to see language and culture as integrated, though I did not know the terms *linguaculture* or *deep linguaculture learning*. One of the master's courses was teaching EFL/ESL literacy, i.e., reading and writing but with aural/oral involvement. The other master's class focused on how to teach adult EFL/ESL learners. Both classes appreciated the disorienting dilemma in Mezirow's approach, because all students had experienced prior crises that they wanted to discuss. However, beyond the disorienting dilemma, only a subset of these future teachers found Mezirow's heavily rational, analytic, sequential approach to be overwhelmingly attractive. In my master's classes, this subset of "concrete-sequential" learners had to combine some of the model's phases because there was insufficient time to go slowly through all ten phases. A few highly enthusiastic members of this subset independently decided to interview current or former EFL/ESL adult learners from different countries about those learners' crisis-induced transformations.

Dirkx's Approach to Transformative Learning

The intuitive students in the same EFL/ESL teacher education classes preferred non-analytical, less sequential learning, so they were thrilled with Dirkx's emotional-integrative (imaginal) approach. Dirkx (2012) was influenced by Jung's (1957–79) depth psychology, which emphasizes relational, emotional, and largely unconscious individual issues and interpersonal, social interactions. Jung's psychology and hence Dirkx's transformative approach emphasize the personal unconscious and the transpersonal (collective) unconscious, which can both become conscious at the stage of individuation. Individuation, which not everyone achieves, involves becoming a transformed, integrated, unique person who can understand and reflect on personal, social, cultural, and universal memories and myths.

Dirkx's approach stresses transformative, "emotional soul work," because to him emotions are the "messengers of the soul." His approach encompasses imaginatively elaborating the meaning of emotions in one's life, not using reason to dissect emotions (Dirkx 2001; see also the discussion among Dirkx, Mezirow, and Cranton). He contended that the soul can be awakened, nurtured, and expressed in the classroom and even in cooperative online settings. Is the process ineffable and indescribable? No, because the subject matter and readings of assigned texts can stimulate dynamic discussion and engagement that brings submerged images, symbols, and emotions into the light. After such a discussion, the facilitator or teacher helps the students to debrief in four steps. The first step asks individual students to consider what was emotionally meaningful in the discussion and why; then to notice and describe an emotion-filled image that arose from the unconscious during the discussion; and next to identify the context, people, and relationships in the image. The second step is associating current experiences, especially in the group discussion, with similar past experiences when the image arose, thus leading to understanding the private myth of the individual. The third step is using popular culture, literature, and mythology to amplify the meaning of the original image, thus expanding the image from the personal to the transpersonal, collective myth. Finally, the fourth step engages the student in personifying the myth-bearing mage and then interacting with it in a two-way communication, which can be a written dialogue or an "empty-chair" roleplay between the person and the image to uncover the image's collective (including cultural) meaning. In sum, Dirkx's emotional-integrative (imaginal), depth-psychology approach uses emotion and imagery to move from the personal to the collective/cultural. Like Mezirow's approach, Dirkx's approach does not embody a critical theory of society's current ills, but unlike Mezirow's model, Dirkx's smoothly leads individuals from a personal focus into the broad and deep cultural context. This growth occurs in small, supportive groups.

The majestic psychospirituality of Dirkx's "emotional soul work" has a major association with deep linguaculture learning through the life and writings of Earl Stevick (1923–2013), whose work is primarily called holistic-humanistic (see later). Stevick (1990) wrote about the "sacramental" teaching of language and culture and the "sacred space" (classrooms) where it occurs. He was a well-known leader in the international humanistic language teaching movement. He worked for many years for the US Foreign Service Institute, part of the Department of State, where he wrote curricula for less commonly taught languages and helped ensure that diplomats would be as proficient as possible in the language and culture (now we would call it the linguaculture) of their next posting before arriving there. Among his many language teaching books are *Humanism in Language Teaching* (1990), *Teaching Languages: A Way and Ways* (1982), and *Memory, Meaning and Method: A View of Language Teaching* (1996). The confluence of emotion and cognition and of social relations and individualism made Stevick's examples of transformative teaching extremely powerful. Praise for him as a deeply wise language-and-culture teacher is abundant (see, e.g., Arnold & Murphey 2013). Aside from all his normal work, Stevick took time to mentor budding scholars like me. I benefitted from his gracious, detailed feedback on my first book (Oxford 1990).

Other concepts and processes that could correlate well with Dirkx's approach are mindful, empathic listening (Oxford 2020); deep education and radical amazement in Creation Spirituality (Oxford 2016), and pedagogy of the heart (Culham et al. 2019). Merriam and Bierema (2014) explained that education can include connections to self, to others, to the world, and to a higher being, a statement that Dirkx and Stevick would have approved of.

Vygotsky's Link to Transformative Learning

Lev Vygotsky (1978) considered himself a historical-cultural theorist. Others saw him as a child development specialist. Still others crowned him (long after his tragic death at age 37) as the first of the sociocultural theorists. For this chapter, Vygotsky can be considered a theorist of transformative-mediated learning. Vygotsky's learning model began with his research on child development, but it is relevant to transformative learning in all age groups. This model involves "mediated learning" with a more capable (more skilled, more knowledgeable) person as the mediator (guide), who strongly regulates or guides the learner at first, gradually releases that control when the learner needs less, and finally cedes control entirely when the learner is ready to self-regulate. Mediated learning does not involve smoothly shifting from one stage to another; instead, it involves several significant transformations or transitions from stage to stage across what Vygotsky (1978) called the "zone of proximal development" (ZPD). The ZPD is the metaphorical range of learning space that the individual can transit, first with assistance and later without it. The ZPD defines those functions that have not yet matured but are in the process of maturation.

In addition to the ZPD metaphor, Vygotsky used at least two other important metaphors to describe the developmental transformation process. One of these was the speech metaphor. The learner starts out being greatly dependent on the more capable person as mediator, who guides the learner through "social speech" interactions. In the next stage, the learner becomes somewhat more independent by using egocentric speech (oral self-guiding), while still partially needing the mediator. Transformation becomes complete by the third stage, when the learner self-regulates by means of the inner voice (private speech). Vygotsky also used a horticultural metaphor for the learner's transformation (Vygotsky 1978). In the first stage, the mediator-guide sows the seeds of the learner's development, but the seeds are hidden in the ground. Though transformation has begun, nothing yet can be seen. Transformation becomes evident in the second stage, when the "buds" and "flowers" show themselves but have not matured. At the third stage, the plant has matured so that the "fruits of development" are obvious.

These metaphors of learning, growth, and development are relevant to linguaculture learning. Surface learning occurs when the mediator-guide is in charge. At that point, language and culture probably seem very different from each other, and the learner is busy trying to do what the mediator, or teacher, wants the learner to do. The mediator helps the learner become more self-reliant, and eventually the learner, in Vygotsky's metaphors, becomes self-regulating, mature, and fruitful. When I compare Vygotsky's developmental, transformative learning model with Shaules' developmental, transformational, "surface-to-deep learning" linguaculture model, I see that the Vygotsky's learner at the self-regulating stage has much in common with Shaules' learner, in whom the linguaculture is implicitly, intuitively present and embodied.

Vygotsky's model describes the transformation of individuals through social mediation. His concepts of mediation (by a person or by books and other cultural "signs" and tools) have been socially, culturally, and educationally important; unfortunately, he did not live to see this happen. Thus, began the mediated learning movement, in both face-to-face and digital learning. Doolittle (1997) described Vygotsky's idea of the ZPD, in which the learner is guided by another until able to become self-regulated, as a foundation for cooperative learning. Vygotsky's writings became the basis for much subsequent work in sociocultural learning theories (e.g., John-Steiner & Mahn 1996; Kozulin 2002), and has had wide resonance in a range of disciplines. As Newman (2021: 4) explains:

> The work of Vygotsky is widely used in teacher education and other education-related literature, in discussion of sociocultural perspectives, and in relation to themes such as second language acquisition, the teaching of mathematics, and approaches to teaching and learning.

This was true at the universities where I taught. Vygotsky became a transformative folk hero to many future language teachers over my 35 years as a teacher educator. He was more popular than most other theorists in my classes in SLA and methods for language teaching. Although some of his very advanced theories were difficult, many of his ideas had profound effects. Future teachers (my students) readily grasped the ZPD construct and the transformation from social speech to private/inner speech (self-regulation). They were pleased to know that scaffolding, the practice of giving just the right amount and right kind of assistance and removing it bit by bit as the learner no longer needed it, was very similar to what Vygotsky described as the task of the "more capable other" (the teacher or mediator).

More Transformative Sources

Jones and Richards' (2016) book, *Creativity in Language Teaching*, explained that creativity offers a transformation in agency (a person's will, intent, and capacity to achieve specific, socially situated goals). The authors argued that creativity is not only transformative but is also central for language learning and teaching; that it is a potential of everyone, not just exceptional people; that it occurs in innovative use of language in regular discourse in authentic situations, not just in cleverness in artificial settings; and that it requires social interconnections through collaboration and "learning conversation." The book by Jones and Rivers depicted transformational creativity in language skills, in voices from the classroom, in multicultural texts, in technology use for language teaching, in narrative inquiry for language education, and as resistance. The anthology titled *Transformative Eco-Education for Human and Planetary Survival* (Oxford & Lin 2011) contains a wide range of transformative learning activities adaptable to language education.

Holistic-Experiential Learning and Holistic-Humanistic Learning

Holistic learning focuses on the whole person: cognitive, emotional, spiritual, physical, and social. Balance, peace, and positivity are products of holistic learning. It is participatory, creative, reflective, intuitive, spontaneous, and frequently artful (music, play, ritual). Holistic learning is described as the curriculum of character (Leggo 2018); the pedagogy of love and cultivation of the ability of the heart (Culham et al. 2019); and the combination of deep reflection and inner work, personally meaningful experience, and conscious concern for love, caring, peace, and justice (Miller et al. 2019). As Maslow (1971) described, holistic learning also offers the possibility of "peak experiences," resulting in a "cognition of being… [and] technology of happiness," as well as insight, transcendence, and self-actualization (p. 169).

John Dewey

Experience and Education, John Dewey's 1938 book, is an excellent explanation of what he, as a philosopher and educator, meant by deep, embodied, experiential learning. To my knowledge, he did not use the term "deep learning," although his writings exhibit something very much like deep learning. Dewey's importance is highlighted in Shaules' (2019) book on deep learning.

For Dewey, human beings learn through a transformative approach that is experiential, hands-on, holistic, experimental (not necessarily in the laboratory sense), and life-relevant. In his view, experience refers to the organism's embodied, physical, and mental self in meaningful interchanges with its physical and social environment. In Dewey's influential, experiential approach, students reflect on their experiences within self-and-environment interactions in order to grow and learn. Thus, experiential learning also entails an element of contemplative-reflective learning. Having a merely unreflective experience does not foster learning, in Dewey's view. I add that experience without contemplation-reflection can only shallowly aid remembering of something experienced and is not an aid to new cognition. Moreover, I contend that experience *sans* contemplation-reflection can bring emotions like foreboding, anger, sorrow, guilt, shame, pleasure, joy, contentment, excitement, or curiosity, but only a shadowy feeling or weak remnant of the experience stays.

Although Dewey is not famous for comments on emotion and reflection, two comments are very enlightening. According to Dewey (1933: 100, quoted by Felten et al. 2006), structured reflection helps learning arise from the chaos of experience: "The function of reflection is to bring about a new situation in which the difficulty is resolved, the confusion cleared away, the trouble smoothed out, and the question it puts is answered." Dewey (1934: 42 in Felten et al.) also said, "Emotion is the moving and cementing force. It selects what is congruous and dyes what it selected with its colour, thereby giving qualitative unity to material externally disparate and dissimilar." More information about Dewey's ideas concerning emotion is found in Solymosi and Shook (2014).

For Dewey, not only is reflection needed, but also learners need to feel ownership and a sense of control over circumstances and situations of learning. He felt that project work is an ideal for promoting learning goals, as well as goals of independent thinking and experimentation. In his educational philosophy, teachers and students would learn together experientially on projects. Project-based learning was Dewey's favorite form of holistic-experiential learning. He felt that projects should involve active exploration of real-world challenges and problems over significant periods, leading to deep knowledge, independent thinking, experimentation, and good works for communities and society. Beckett and Slater's (2020) edited volume showed that project-based language learning (PBLL) positively influenced language learning and development, discourse, engagement, collaborative learning skills, and many other aspects of language learning. The book includes PBLL case studies from many contexts and world regions. For instance, the book indicates that PBLL was successful in relation to translanguaging, advanced language learning, co-learning of linguistics, and technology-enhanced PBLL.

In Dewey's view, education is instrumentally, pragmatically transformative for the individual learner, helping all students realize their full potential. In addition, Dewey (1916, 1935, 1938, 1939) firmly believed that education transforms society and creates democracy, Dewey's *summum bonum* (in my words). A pragmatic education involves both developing personal consciousness and learning to share in social consciousness for promoting democracy and peace (Cohan and Howlett 2017) in the larger community, culture, and world. Dewey sought lasting world peace. For a time, believing that American engagement in the First World War would bring world peace, he supported that war. However, the war itself shattered his belief in the value of war, and the Second World War provided further confirmation that war could never bring peace. (This supports the idea of the famous peace theorist Johan Galtung 1996, in *Peace by Peaceful Means*.) Though Dewey gave up on war as a useful vehicle for peace, he never forsook his view that democracy was the model best suited to preserve peace.

Dewey would have told linguaculture learners and teachers to learn together, care for and respect everyone, see learning as a lifelong gift, find their identities in society, and work collaboratively for peace. He would have told them to bet their money on democracy, despite its complexities, because it is the only way to reach peace.

Continuing the holistic learning mode, we now move to Carl Rogers. He was the perfect person to begin the fields of humanistic psychology and humanistic education.

Carl Rogers, Holistic-Humanistic Psychologist and Educator

One of many interesting things about Carl Rogers (1902–87) is that he dropped out of Union Theological Seminary and soon enrolled at Columbia University, only a few blocks away, where he earned a doctorate in clinical psychology. Rogers' shift from one great institution to another one in close proximity allowed for a major change in his academic field and career emphasis. This change was providential for two international fields: psychology and education.

Rogers established a holistic psychology which he called "humanistic psychology." Perhaps the most famous elements of his therapeutic approach were "unconditional positive regard" for each person and "client-centered" treatment. This therapeutic approach, which is still popular today, helps the person find inner resources for self-understanding and for changing self-concept, behavior, and attitudes. The warmth, support, and optimism of humanistic psychology were carried into humanistic education, which Rogers also initiated. Humanistic education initially targeted adult learners but influenced education in general.

Rogers (1969) discussed principles of humanistic learning in his classic volume, *Freedom to Learn*, followed by Rogers and Frieberg (1994). He contended that the experience of being understood and valued gives the person the freedom to learn. Rogers' principles of humanistic learning include:

- *Significant learning*: This kind of learning occurs through experience when the student is in charge from the beginning to the end. Learner-initiated (not teacher-initiated) learning is lasting and pervasive. Significant learning occurs when threats to the self are minimized (see "Minimizing threats" below).
- *Basis for learning*: Learning is primarily based upon direct engagement with practical, social, personal, or research challenges, along with openness to change and learning to learn (strategic learning).
- *Evaluation of learning*: This is best done through student self-evaluation.
- *Features of each person*: Under the right conditions, each person can become self-actualized. Value is inherent in every person, and greatness lives in the human spirit.
- *Role of the teacher*: A person cannot teach another person directly. The teacher's role is to facilitate learning through (1) setting a positive learning climate, (2) clarifying purposes, (3) organizing and making available needed resources, (4) balancing intellectual and emotional components of learning, and (5) not dominating.
- *Minimizing threats:* Learning proceeds faster when threats to the self are low. Developing new attitudes and perspectives can be threatening to the self, so such learning is more readily assimilated when other threats are minimized. The structure and organization of self tend to relax their boundaries when free from threat but become more rigid under threat.

Carl Rogers' views were shared by Earl Stevick (mentioned under transformative learning) and Gertrude Moskowitz (1928–2021) in language education. Earlier I described Earl Stevick, an international leader of humanistic language teaching. Gertrude Moskowitz (1928–2021) was a humanistic language teacher educator, author, researcher, and frequent public speaker from Temple University (Pennsylvania). Imagination was her watchword, as seen in Moskowitz (1994). Among her four books is the volume *Caring and Sharing in the Foreign Language Class: A Sourcebook of Humanistic Techniques* (Moskowitz 1978), which contains 120 humanistic techniques for foreign language teaching. Her recent obituary (Miles 2021) noted, "Using the Flanders System of Interaction

Analysis and other progressive classroom learning practices, Dr. Moskowitz helped reshape traditional graduate school classes [for future language teachers] into personal, participatory, and student-centered exercises. And she did it, former students said, with a unique blend of determination and compassion." The Flanders system tracks quantitative and qualitative influences of teachers' verbal behaviors and the overall classroom climate. In my view, Moskowitz brought the brightness of her heart and mind to warm every classroom she entered and each teacher's life she touched.

Many language educators working today in different parts of the world share the ideals of Rogers, Stevick, and Moskowitz. Humanistic approaches to language education have resulted in colorful metaphors about language teachers: therapist, counselor, loving parent, gardener, suggester, liberator, facilitator, reflective listener, nurturer of souls, and assistant to language students as they burst their cocoons (Cortazzi & Jin 1996; Stevick 1982, 1990, 1996, 1990; Underhill 1989). Breen (1985) described language teachers and students as students as inhabitants of intricately complex "coral gardens," which they are exploring together. In a humanistic study, Oxford (2001) reported students' positive metaphors by which they described their favorite language teachers.

Contemplative-Reflective Learning

Transformative and holistic-experiential and holistic-humanistic education are fed by *contemplative-reflective learning,* also known as active reflection, contemplative practices, and contemplative inquiry. Emotions, particularly based on discrepancy and anomaly, can be a catalyst for reflective learning. Boud, Keogh, and Walker (1985) defined *reflection* as a general term for cognitive and emotional activities in which people engage to consider their experiences and come to new understandings. Boud is known for initiating the "Boud Reflection Model."

Contemplative learning encourages the learner's transformation, for which critical thinking (usually a critique of grave societal problems) is inadequate. Contemplative learning can include meditating with deep and slow breath, being mindful and present, using creative visualization, and adopting a sense of humility, gratitude, love, and respect for all beings and all things (Culham & Lin 2020; Zajonc 2009). In fact, Zajonc discussed meditation in contemplative learning as "knowing that becomes love." Additionally, contemplative learning can involve mental imagery, prayer, and walking in nature. Journaling is a written way to be contemplative, expressing emotions and thoughts about challenges to established identity patterns. Like journaling, contemplative poetry can reveal a range of emotions, such as grief, joy, contentment, anger, and disillusionment. Contemplative learning can also include participating in drama, art, and storytelling; conducting rituals and ceremonies; dancing spiritually; and reflecting mindfully with yoga or tai chi (Burggraf & Grossenbacher 2007; Oxford 2016; Zajonc 2009). Additionally, contemplative learning can involve art, such as painting, drawing, and collage; reflecting on colors, shapes, images, and symbols; and discussing experience of the artistic creation process (Malchiodi 2007; Meyer et al. 2018).

Both students and teachers can experience contemplative learning intentionally in a walking meditation (see the Rainbow Walk, Olivero et al. 2021). Freer forms of contemplation-reflection can involve engaging in unguided walks without any particular goals except being alone (or with a partner) and quietly reflecting. Contemplative learning can involve compassion: sending compassion to oneself; sending compassion to a beloved person to people in a different place or holding different ideas, or to every being around the world. All these contemplative/reflective experiences have been used in my courses and other's courses in language teacher education.

Vygotsky, whom we met in the section on transformative learning, was devoted to the concept of "seeing again" but instead of using "reflection," he employed the metaphor of "refraction." Veresov and Fleer (2016) maintained that refraction rather than reflection denotes an essential difference in how the environment functions in psychological development. They explain that reflection involves light waves following a direct linear path between the eyes of a viewer and a reflective surface such as glass, with the reflection returning to the viewer's eyes, without distortion. Refraction, in contrast, occurs as light passes through a medium, such as a prism, and is distorted according to its refractive index; specifically, light waves are bent, and images are not reflected but undergo change. For Veresov and Fleer (2016), Vygotsky's interest in refraction suggested that he believed the environment stimulates psychological development but does not determine it.

For Vygotsky, I assume, reflection would indeed have connoted a deterministic role of the environment, but he contended instead that the environment is refracted—imbued with meaning, assigned relevance—by individuals according to their psychology, not merely reflected uniformly in the mind. Veresov and Fleer (2016) argued that to understand this relation requires taking account of "what I am experiencing" (the ontological) and "how I am experiencing it," that is, my experience of the experience (p. 2). I add that for any given person, differences in interpretation of "what I am experiencing" and "how I am experiencing it" can vary dramatically depending on many internal factors, which can fluctuate.

Contemplative learning is transformational in helping learners reflect on (or to use Vygotsky's words, "refract," as with a prism) a different culture. Reflection and refraction fit deep linguaculture learning experiences when the learner processes these experiences afterward in speech or writing in the deep linguaculture being learned.

Conclusion

This chapter has discussed deep linguaculture learning in three potential modes. The first mode is *transformative learning* (Cranton 2009; Dirkx 2012; Mezirow 1981; Vygotsky 1978). Transformative learning changes our minds and hearts. It transforms who we believe we are and expands us in new, positive directions, though not without some growing pains as we grow and change. Ideally, transformative learning can move us cognitively, emotionally, and socially as we engage in deep linguaculture learning. The second mode is *holistic learning*, with its overlapping emphases: *holistic-experiential* (e.g., Dewey 1933; Maslow 1971) and *holistic-humanistic* (Moskowitz 1978; Rogers 1969; Stevick 1990). Holistic learning involves the whole being and fits deep linguaculture learning well. It is not tantamount to a 1,000-piece picture puzzle; instead, it is a deep, vast, guided journey on which learners discover the linguaculture and themselves. In holistic education, students can learn together with their teachers; experience unconditional positive regard; have a taste of the infinite in a peak experience and then engage in deep discussions about it; and feel the sacramental beauty of the spaces where deep linguaculture learning occurs; and can become more richly human and whole. The third mode is *contemplative-reflective* (Oxford 2016; Zajonc 2009), in which learners and teachers discover how contemplation, refraction/reflection, meditation, art, music, and movement can deepen human understanding and draw everything we have learned into the internally evolving linguaculture and accompanying self-awareness. These three broad learning orientations provide full-bodied, profound, and enjoyable experiences of deep linguaculture learning. In such experiences, a community grows and explores the linguaculture together. Participants become richer, fuller beings.

As mentioned in the Introduction, this chapter's ethical compass points away from a belief that individual wellbeing is enough. We live on a globalized planet. We are part of the whole world, and it is part of us. Deep linguaculture learning tells us that we do not totally consist of our job or our family, though they are crucially important. We are on a journey in which the wellbeing of all—not just a handful of individuals—is important. In the types of linguaculture learning described in this chapter, wellbeing is an assemblage, a holistic experience that cannot be broken into little pieces (Atkinson 2013). It belongs to all. Wellbeing, like deep linguaculture education, is not just for one or two of us, or for just our community, our nation, or our hemisphere. In principle, the deep linguaculture education, like unconditional positive regard, is the right of everyone, because we share the same humanity. We can help this principle become a daily reality as we enable students to increasingly embody and share deeply the linguaculture they are learning. We can enable communities around the world to adopt deep linguaculture education, although this will require much work.

We can connect philosophically, psychologically, and socially with the world through caring about the wellbeing of all and through embracing and embodying deep linguaculture education. To promote wellbeing for everyone, we need to offer in deep linguaculture education (and in all other areas of life) what we ourselves want to receive: respect, honesty, justice, compassion, love, kindness, wisdom, empathy, gratitude, caring, and sharing. Decades ago, I thought that Moskowitz's (1978) book title, *Caring and Sharing in the Foreign Language Class*, was a little too sweet for my taste. Now I know that "caring and sharing" make possible deep linguaculture learning and teaching as part of the wellbeing process. Deeply learning or teaching a linguaculture, including its people, places, colors, sounds, layers, and textures (not avoiding the scars of history), is part of the wellbeing process. Both deep linguaculture education and wellbeing are forces that this jittery and sometimes desperate planet needs. These forces can bring people together in new ways, introduce us to our best selves, and provide hope for greater peace.

Acknowledgments

I am profoundly grateful to Joseph Shaules and Troy McConachy for inviting me on the journey of writing this chapter. I was thrilled to explore the concepts of deep linguaculture learning with them. For me, it has been wonderful to enjoy this "newer world" with them. Thank you for caring and for sharing your guidance, as well as your great patience. I give my utmost appreciation to my dear husband Clifford Stocking, whose tolerance of my writing schedule knows no bounds.

References

Arnold, J. & Murphey, T. (2013), *Meaningful Action: Earl Stevick's Influence on Language Teaching*. Cambridge: Cambridge University Press.

Atkinson, S. (2013), "Beyond Components of Wellbeing: The Effects of Relational and Situated Assemblage." *Topoi*, 32: 137–44. doi:10.1007/s11245-013-9164-0

Baumgartner, L. M. (2012), "Mezirow's Theory of Transformative Learning from 1975 to Present." In E. W. Taylor & P. Cranston (eds), *The Handbook of Transformative Learning: Theory, Research, and Practice*, 99–155, San Francisco: John Wiley & Sons.

Beckett, G. & Slater, T. (eds). (2020), *Perspectives on Project-Based Language Learning, Teaching, and Assessment, Key Approaches, Technology Tools, and Frameworks*. New York: Routledge.

Boud, D., Keogh, R. & Walker, D. (1985), *Reflection: Turning Experience into Learning*. Abingdon, UK: RoutledgeFalmer.

Breen, M. P. (1985), "The Social Context for Language Learning: A Neglected Situation?" *Studies in Second Language Acquisition*, 7 (2): 135–58. doi:10.1017/S0272263100005337

Burggraf, S. & Grossenbacher, P. (2007), "Contemplative Modes of Inquiry in Liberal Arts Education." *Liberal Arts Online*. www.liberalartswabash.edu

Cohan, A. & Howlett, C. F. (2017), "Global Conflicts Shattered World Peace: John Dewey's Influence on Peace Educators and Practitioners." *Education and Culture*, 33 (1): Article 5. https://docs.lib.purdue.edu/eandc/vol33/iss1/art5

Cortazzi, M. & Jin, L. (1996), "Cultures of Learning in Language Classrooms." In H. Coleman (ed.), *Society and the Language Classroom*, 169–206, Cambridge: Cambridge University Press.

Cranton, P. (2009), *Understanding and Promoting Transformative Learning: A Guide for Educators of Adults*, 2nd edn. Hoboken, NJ: Jossey-Bass.

Cranton, P. & Taylor, E. W. (2012), "Transformative Learning Theory: Seeking a More Unified Theory." In E. W. Taylor & P. Cranton (eds), *The Handbook of Transformative Learning: Theory, Research, and Practice*, 3–20, San Francisco: John Wiley & Sons.

Culham, T. & Lin, J. (2020), *Daoist Cultivation of Qi and Virtue for Life, Wisdom, and Learning*. New York: Palgrave Macmillan.

Culham, T., Oxford, R. L. & Lin, J. (2019), "Cultivating the Ability of the Heart: Educating through the Pedagogy of Love." In J. P. Miller, K. Nigh, M. J. Binder, B. Novak & S. Crowell (eds), *International Handbook of Holistic Education*, 170–7, New York: Routledge.

Dewey, J. (1916), *Democracy and Education: An Introduction to the Philosophy of Education*. New York: Macmillan.

Dewey, J. (1933), *How We Think: A Restatement of the Relation of Reflective Thinking to the Educative Process*, new edn. Boston: D. C. Heath and Co.

Dewey, J. (1934), *Art as Experience*. New York: Minton, Balch & Co.

Dewey, J. (1936), "Authority and Social Change." *School and Society*, 44: 457–66.
Dewey, J. (1935), *Liberalism and Social Action*. New York: G. P. Putnam's Sons.
Dewey, J. (1938), *Experience and Education*. New York: Macmillan.
Dewey, J. (1939), *Freedom and Culture*. New York: G. P. Putnam's Sons.
Dirkx, J. M. (2001, Summer), "Images, Transformative Learning and the Work of the Soul." *Adult Learning*, 12 (3): 15–16.
Dirkx, J. M. (2012), "Nurturing Soul Work: A Jungian Approach to Transformative Learning." In E. W. Taylor & P. Cranton (eds), *The Handbook of Transformative Learning: Theory, Research, and Practice*, 116–30, San Francisco: John Wiley & Sons.
Dirkx, J. M., Mezirow, J. & Cranton, P. (2006), "Musings and Reflections on the Meaning, Context, and Process of Transformative Learning: A Dialogue between John M. Dirkx and Jack Mezirow." *Journal of Transformative Education*, 4 (2): 123–39.
Doolittle, P. (1997), "Vygotsky's Zone of Proximal Development as a Theoretical Foundation for Cooperative Learning." *Journal on Excellence in College Teaching*, 8 (1): 83–103.
Felten, P., Gilchrist, L. Z. & Darby, A. (2006), "Emotion and Learning: Feeling Our Way toward a New Theory of Reflection in Service-Learning." *Michigan Journal of Community Service Learning*, 12 (2): 38–46.
Freire, P. (1970/2018), *Pedagogy of the Oppressed*. 50th Anniversary Edition, 4th edn. New York: Bloomsbury.
Galtung, J. (1996), *Peace by Peaceful Means: Peace and Conflict, Development and Civilization*. International Peace Research Institute. Oslo: Sage Publications, Inc.
John-Steiner, V. & Mahn, H. (1996), "Sociocultural Approaches to Learning and Development: A Vygotskian Framework." *Educational Psychology*, 31: 91–206.
Jones, R. H. & Richards, J. C. (eds). (2016), *Creativity in Language Teaching: Perspectives from Research and Practice*. New York, NY: Routledge.
Jung, C. (1957-79), *Collected Works. Bolingen Series*. 20 vols. R. F. C. Hull (trans). Princeton, NJ: Princeton University Press.
Kolb, D. (2015), *Experiential Learning: Experience as the Source of Learning and Development*, 2nd edn. New York: Pearson Education.
Kozulin, A. (2002), "Sociocultural Theory and the Mediated Learning Experience". *School Psychology International*, 23 (1): 7–35. doi:org/10.1177/0143034302023001729
Leaver, B. L., Davidson, D. & Campbell, C. (2021), *Transformative Language Learning and Teaching*. Cambridge: Cambridge University Press.
Leggo, C. (2018), "The Curriculum of Character: Poetic Ruminations on Growing Old(er)." In J. P. Miller, K. Nigh, M. J. Binder, B. Novak & S. Crowell (eds), *International Handbook in Holistic Education*, 240–51, New York: Routledge.
Lyubomirsky, S. (2008), *The How of Happiness: A Scientific Approach to Getting the Life You Want*. New York: Penguin Press.
Malchiodi, C. (2007), *The Art Therapy Sourcebook*. New York: McGraw Hill.
Maslow, A. (1971), *The Farther Reaches of Human Nature*. New York: Viking.

Merriam, S. & Bierema, L. (2014), *Adult Learning: Linking Theory and Practice*. San Francisco: Jossey-Bass.

Meyer, M., Maeshiro, M. & Sumida, A. (2018), *Arting and Writing to Transform Education: An Integrated Approach for Culturally and Ecologically Responsive Pedagogy*. Sheffield, UK: Equinox.

Mezirow, J. (1978), "Perspective Transformation." *Adult Education Quarterly*, 28: 100–10. doi:10.1177/074171367802800202

Mezirow, J. (1981), "A Critical Theory of Adult Learning and Education." *Adult Education Quarterly*, 32 (3): 3–24.

Mezirow, J. (2006), "An Overview of Transformative Learning." In P. Sutherland & J. Crowther (eds), *Lifelong Learning: Concepts and Contexts*, 24–38, New York: Routledge.

Miles, G. (2021, Oct. 19. Updated Oct. 20.), "Obituaries: Gertrude 'Trudy' Moskowitz, Trailblazing Professor of Foreign-Language Education at Temple University, Dies at 93." *Philadelphia Inquirer*.

Miller, J. P., Nigh, K., Binder, M. J., Novak, B. & Crowell, S. (eds), (2019), *International Handbook in Holistic Education*. New York: Routledge.

Moskowitz, G. (1978), *Caring and Sharing in the Foreign Language Class: A Sourcebook on Humanistic Techniques*. Rowley, MA: Newbury House Publishers.

Moskowitz, G. (1994), "Humanistic Imagination: Soul Food for the Language Class." *The Journal of the Imagination in Language learning and Teaching*. http://www.njcu.edu/cill/vol2/moskowitz.html[12].

Newman, S. & Latifi, A. (2021), "Vygotsky, Education, and Teacher Education." *Journal of Education for Teaching*, 47:1, 4–17. doi:10.1080/02607476.2020.1831375

Oxford, R. L. (1990), *Language Learning Strategies: What Every Teacher Should Know*. Boston: Heinle & Heinle.

Oxford, R. L. (2001), "'The Bleached Bones of a Story': Learners' Constructions of Language Teachers." In M. Breen (ed.), *Learner Contributions to Language Learning: New Directions in Research*, 86–111, London: Longman.

Oxford, R. L. (2016), "Creation Spirituality as a Spiritual Research Paradigm Drawing on Many Faiths." In J. Lin, R. L. Oxford & T. Culham (eds), *Toward a Spiritual Research Paradigm: Exploring New Ways of Knowing, Researching and Being*, 199–232, Charlotte, NC: Information Age Publishing.

Oxford, R. L. (2020), "Teaching and Researching Listening Skills: Theory- and Research-Based Practices." In N. Polat, T. Gregersen & P. D. MacIntyre (eds), *Research-Driven Pedagogy: Implications of L2A Theory and Research for the Teaching of Language Skills*, 10–34, New York: Routledge.

Oxford, R. L. (2021), "Shaking the Foundations. Transformative Learning in the Field of Teaching English to Speakers of Other Languages." In B. L. Leaver, D. E. Davidson & C. Campbell (eds), *Transformative Language Learning and Teaching*, 23 -31, Cambridge, UK: Cambridge University Press.

Oxford, R. L. & Lin, J. (eds). (2011), *Transformative Eco-Education for Human and Planetary Survival*. Charlotte, NC: Information Age Publishing.

Olivero, M. M., Harrison, M. & Oxford, R. L. (2021), "Peacebuilding through Classroom Activities: Inner, Interpersonal, Intergroup, Intercultural, International and Ecological Peace." In R. L. Oxford, M. M. Olivero, M. Harrison & T. Gregersen (eds), *Peacebuilding in Language Education: Innovations in Theory and Practice*, 245–71, Bristol, UK: Multilingual Matters.

Risager, K. (2020), "Linguaculture and Transnationality: The Cultural Dimensions of Language." In J. Jackson (ed.), *The Routledge Handbook of Language and Intercultural Communication*, 109–23, 2nd edn. London and New York: Routledge.

Rogers, C. (1969), *Freedom to Learn*. Columbus, OH: Charles E. Merrill Publishing.

Rogers, C. & Freiberg, H. J. (1994), *Freedom to Learn*. New York: Pearson.

Seligman, M. E. P. (2011), *Flourish: A Visionary New Understanding of Happiness and Well-being*. New York: Atria/Simon & Schuster.

Shaules, J. (2019), *Language, Culture, and the Embodied Mind: A Developmental Model of Linguaculture Learning*. Singapore: Springer Nature.

Shaules, J., Fritz, R. & Miyafusa, S. (2020), "Measuring Resistance and Engagement: The Linguaculture Motivation Profiler." In P. Clements, A. Krause & R. Gentry (eds), *Teacher Efficacy, Learner Agency*, 92–9, Tokyo: JALT.

Solymosi, T. & Shook, J. R. (eds). (2014), *Pragmatist Neurophilosophy: American Philosophy and the Brain*. London: Bloomsbury.

Stevick, E. (1982), *Teaching and Learning Languages*. Cambridge: Cambridge University Press.

Stevick, E. (1990), *Humanism in Language Teaching*. Oxford: Oxford University Press.

Stevick, E. (1996), *Memory, Meaning, and Method: Some Psychological Perspectives on Language Learning*. 20th Anniversary Edition, 2nd edn. Boston: Heinle & Heinle.

Taylor, E. W. & Cranton, P. (eds). (2012), *The Handbook of Transformative Learning: Theory, Research, and Practice*. San Francisco: John Wiley & Sons.

Tutu, D. (1999), *No Future without Forgiveness*. New York: Image Book/Random House.

Underhill, A. (1989), "Process in Humanistic Education." *ELT Journal*, 43 (4): 250–60.

Veresov, N. & Fleer, M. (2016), "Perezhivanie as a Theoretical Concept for Researching Young Children's Development." *Mind, Culture, and Activity*, 23 (4): 1–11. doi:10.1080/10749039.2016.1186198

Vygotsky, L. (1978), *Mind in Society: The Development of Higher Psychological Processes*. Cambridge, MA: Harvard University Press.

Zajonc, A. (2009), *Meditation as Contemplative Inquiry: When Knowing Becomes Love*. Aurora, CO: Lindisfarne.

2

Language Learning as a Transformative Experience of Resistance, Adjustment, and Change

Joseph Shaules

Introduction

Foreign language learning (FLL) is a psychologically powerful, potentially life-changing experience. We see students get "hooked" on a new language; we see this lead to eye-opening foreign experiences and even a new sense of self. For some learners, FLL becomes a personal quest—a journey of discovery, transformation, and growth. At the same time, negative experiences are also common. Language practice is often stressful and learners often get frustrated, anxious, and flustered. This psychological impact on learners is both situational and cumulative—they have moment-by-moment affective responses—pleasure, interest, anxiety, curiosity, frustration—as well as long-term reactions to the process overall (Dewaele 2011). At the extremes, FLL may be a life-affirming adventure or something to be reviled.

These contrasting outcomes remind us of the high emotional and psychological stakes that FLL has for learner's wellbeing (Dewaele et al. 2019). For their part, educators face a dual challenge—helping learners manage what can be a stressful learning process, while also finding ways to help them experience FLL as an intrinsically rewarding endeavor. This dualism of challenge and reward speaks to what Dewaele and MacIntyre (2014) refer to as the "Janus-faced" psychological nature of FLL: it can be both anxiety producing and enjoyable; it can be stressful but carries within it the potential for enriching our lives. As educators, we need to help learners successfully navigate this psychological terrain of discouragement and promise.

This chapter presents a theoretical perspective that helps make sense of the Janus-faced psychology of FLL—the interrelated nature of its psychological challenges and rewards. It also seeks to encourage a view of FLL as a transformative experience. This refers most foundationally to the idea that FLL is not psychologically neutral—it involves a process of inner change and development in which learners must respond to the adaptive demands imposed by the experience of foreignness. FLL involves *adaptive* demands in the sense that the learner needs to modify mental habits and one's way of relating to the world. In essence, the psychological challenges and rewards of FLL are similar in important ways to the adjustment challenges faced by sojourners in a foreign environment. Having a positive learning experience that promotes growth and wellbeing is largely dependent on the learner's ability to successfully adjust to those demands.

This argument is informed by adjustment psychology, which seeks to understand the psychological responses to stressors and change. Adjustment psychology helps us understand how challenging experiences can lead not only to stress but also to growth and development (Matsumoto et al. 2006). This relates to a key premise of this chapter—that FLL is potentially both stressful and rewarding because it is psychologically disruptive—it involves changing deeply embodied habits of mind, behavior, and self. This chapter will draw on insights from the psychology of cross-cultural adjustment (CCA) to argue that the process of deep learning involved with FLL affects us at multiple levels of mind and self (Shaules 2019) and can trigger *resistance* (a psychological protective mechanism) and/or *engagement* (curiosity and openness to change). Importantly, the psychology of CCA teaches us that psychological resistance is a natural (though not desirable) reaction to experiencing foreignness (Shaules 2007).

The adjustment perspective can help us understand ways in which FLL can be experienced as transformational. As with adapting to life in a different country, integrating foreign elements into the self involves an evolution of experience (Bennett 1993). What felt alien, uncomfortable or threatening, becomes understandable and useful—a creative extension of the self (Shaules 2007). It may result in us developing a new sense of self as a foreign language user (Kramsch 2009). This transformation is complex—involving various aspects of the self; intellectual, emotional, somatic—yet is experienced holistically and intuitively. One develops a *feeling* for using a new language; one has *a-ha moments* of insight about cultural patterns or linguistic usage; one feels increasingly *comfortable* using the language, or increasingly *oneself* in interactions that previously felt awkward; or most simply, one feels "*into*" learning the language. Because this process is largely intuitive, however, learners may not consciously notice these subtle yet complex inner dynamics. Resistance to these adaptive demands may be construed simply as "not being motivated" and engagement and growth may be described simply as being "fascinated" with the language. Often, learners are not accustomed to thinking of FLL in terms of a meaningful personal challenge or the opportunity to have new experiences. They may have little sense for what they are getting into—how much time, commitment, and frustration is involved, or the potential for profound growth, exploration, and change. The adjustment perspective provides us with an approach to talking about FLL in these terms.

Language Learning as a Transformative Experience

An important starting point for understanding the stresses and growth potential of FLL is transformative learning (TL) theory. It was first articulated in detail by Jack Mezirow, an educator who became interested in the shifts in perspective experienced by women who chose to re-enter education (Mezirow 2000). Central to his work is the idea that when previously held assumptions, beliefs, and values are called into question, learners may undergo a paradigmatic shift in perception. Mezirow contrasts *informative learning* (changes in what we know) with *transformative learning* (changes in how we know). This is often discussed in terms of changes to one's frame of reference—shifts that occur as learners "revise their habits of mind" due to a disorienting dilemma and/or process of reflection and questioning. These shifts are transformative because learners are not only gaining new knowledge, "they are reinterpreting their sense of self in relation to the world" (Cranton 2016: 302). TL theory has also been influenced by the sociopolitical perspective of Paulo Freire, who saw pedagogy in terms of raising consciousness and fighting oppression (Freire 2000).

The TL approach has attracted the attention of foreign language educators. Leaver et al. (2021b) explore "the application of transformative principles to the study and teaching of world languages" (p. 1) and Leaver (2021) argues that TL is part of an emerging paradigm shift in FL education. Traditionally, language learning was thought about in terms of *transmission*—an information-based approach focused on knowing about language. More recently, this paradigm has shifted to *transaction* with an emphasis on skills and the ability to use language in real life. Leaver describes *transformation* as the next (emerging) paradigm in which pedagogy "causes the learner to change in some way—thinking, behavior, acceptance of the other, values, mindset, and/or emotion" (p. 15). Oxford (2021) argues that TL is "shaking the foundations" of foreign language education and calls for an integrated view of cognition and emotion that can lead to peak experiences of self-actualization. Others have explored TL in FLL in terms of curriculum design (Cambell 2021), cultural transformation and intercultural competence (Garza 2021), immersion programs (Davidson et al. 2021), learner autonomy (Little 2021), and faculty development (Nyikos 2021).

Theorizing about transformative learning often focuses on shifts in our experience of the world. That shift can involve different aspects of perception and the self: cognitive (e.g., how we conceptualize or think about something), emotional (e.g., how we react to a situation, or construe what we feel), sociopolitical (e.g., how we see issues of social justice), identity (e.g., how we experience or represent the self) (Cranton 2016; Leaver et al. 2021a). One common thread to much scholarship in TL as it relates to FLL is an emphasis on shifts in learners' sociopolitical perspective or consciousness. This has led to ambitious forms of pedagogy that emphasize authentic and unadapted materials, immersive in-country experiences, highly individualized programs, textbook-free classrooms, and fluid workspaces that lend themselves to scenario-based instruction, real-life experiences, and simulations (Leaver et al. 2021a). TL in FL education often treats language learning as an opportunity for critical reflection and shifts in learner perceptions. This is broadly in line with an interest in global citizenship and using language learning to encourage a critical perspective regarding issues of globalization and diversity (Byram et al. 2017). In short, the "transformation" that is taking place is often assumed to relate to an increased socio-political awareness or consciousness.

Transformation as an Embodied Process

This chapter takes the position that the nature of transformation in FLL goes significantly beyond a cognitive reframing. Rather, the embodied nature of language means that the learning of a new language has the potential to contribute to a complex recalibration of sensorial experience (new ways of thinking, feeling, sensing, and perceiving) and adjustments to the experience of self in the world; we must change our behavior, interact differently and relate to others in ways which take into account foreign norms, values, views of the world. We don't simply add to our behavioral repertoire; we must change deeply integrated habits of mind, feeling, behavior, and self. Scholarship in transformative learning often emphasizes epistemological breakthroughs—e.g., gaining a higher level of social or political consciousness. The adjustment perspective, on the other hand, sees transformation as a long-term disruptive process of ongoing, inner challenge, growth, and change. It requires more than a new frame of reference or critical perspective. It can be rewarding but is often stressful and can lead to positive, negative, and mixed outcomes.

The adjustment perspective emphasizes the responsibility of educators to help learners navigate the stresses and rewards of learning. This is particularly important because learners are often only vaguely aware of the transformative nature of FLL. As Paul (2014) points out, new experiences change our understanding of the world in ways that we cannot predict. In particular, any experience that involves adaptive change affects us in unpredictable ways: going back to school later in life, moving to a foreign country, having a child, adopting new religious beliefs, or taking up a new career. This frequently involves a "transformative choice" in which an individual decides to, essentially, take a leap into the unknown. He points out that the individual doesn't know the value of a new experience until they've had it—their "pre-experience information is dramatically incomplete (p. 49)"—yet they must still make a decision to move ahead. In the case of FLL, learners are being asked to invest themselves heavily in a long-term process of effortful change, yet it can be difficult or impossible to imagine what it feels like to succeed (how it feels, for example, to be bilingual). Thus, learners may be naïve about the time, effort, and adjustment involved and largely unaware of the potential for growth and satisfaction.

Within FLL scholarship more broadly, the transformative elements of the FLL experience are talked about in a variety of ways. Often, they are discussed in the context of learner identity—ways in which learning a foreign language involves expanding one's sense of self as an FL user (Kramsch 2009; Norton 2013), and of becoming an increasingly intercultural or multicultural person (Byram et al. 2017; Risager 2006). A willingness and desire to embrace a new sense of self is often seen as a critical element of language learning motivation (Clarke & Hennig 2013; Dörnyei & Ushioda 2009) and is seen as being closely related to learner autonomy (Murray et al. 2011). More generally, it's commonly understood that FLL is experienced as successful when it feels meaningful to the learner (Ros i Solé 2016). There is also scholarship which focuses specifically on transformative learning experiences in the context of FL education (Leaver et al. 2021a). Although much of this scholarship does not use the term "transformation" per se, it is widely recognized that FLL has a psychological impact and can affect learners at deep levels of the self.

The Psychology of FLL and Adjustment

The adjustment perspective builds on recent scholarship that emphasizes the psychology of learning (Dörnyei & Ryan 2015). There has been a trend away from seeing FLL as primarily a mental process that happens "in one's head" to a more embodied and psychologically complex view. This has included interest in the role of emotion in language learning (Dewaele 2019) and on the psychological wellbeing of the learner overall (Mercer 2021). It has included an exploration of how to decrease learner anxiety (Toyama & Yamazaki 2021) as well as how to increase learner engagement (Hiver et al. 2021). There has also been increased interest in applying insights from positive psychology to FL education (Dewaele et al. 2019). The field of positive psychology originated as a move away from a focus on pathology and toward an attempt to understand positive states, such as the experience of flow (Csikszentmihalyi 1997), as well as happiness and wellbeing (Seligman 2012). Educators have drawn on this to explore flow in the FL classroom (Egbert 2003) as well as ways in which the psychological insights from positive psychology can be applied to pedagogy (Helgesen 2019; Macintyre et al. 2019).

There has been significant interest in the psychologically challenging aspects of FLL, such as learner anxiety (Toyama & Yamazaki 2021), which is seen as the apprehension that results from learners not being proficient in the target language (Trang et al. 2013). For many individuals, language learning is anxiety inducing and this has been shown to inhibit linguistic achievement (Dewaele 2011). Dewaele and MacIntyre (2014) found that levels of anxiety remained high at the lower and intermediate ability levels, and only dropped off sharply for advanced learners, with a corresponding increase in language enjoyment. Older learners also reported lower levels of anxiety. This suggests a years-long process of dealing with anxiety as part of language learning. These stresses have also been explored from a humanistic perspective as well. Earl Stevick, for example, discusses the ways in which language learning can lead to feelings of being ignorant, powerless, and constantly evaluated, which can threaten a learner's sense of self-worth (Stevick 1980). Charles Curran (1972), a Catholic priest and counseling specialist who worked with the psychologist Carl Rogers, developed a counseling-learning approach to FL pedagogy. He saw the teacher's role as that of a counselor, and the student as the psychological client. He sought to use counseling techniques and take into account the learner's feelings about the learning experience.

As Carl Rogers recognized, helping learners manage stress and have positive learning experiences require that educators take on something of a "counseling" role—helping learners navigate the psychological terrain of their learning journey. In order to do so, educators need a clear understanding of the psychological dynamics at play. This is where insights from the psychology of *adjustment* can be of use. Adjustment refers most broadly to the psychological responses to stressors or change—how we adapt to, or protect ourselves from, challenging experiences, and grow or are damaged as a result (Carta et al. 2009). Inherent in the notion of adjustment is the imperative that all organisms have to meet needs, protect from threat, stay in equilibrium, and respond constructively of the demands of their environment. A demanding environment may damage an organism, but it can also stimulate growth—just as exercise can result in injury but can also lead to the development of stronger muscles. In humans, this dynamic extends to the psychological domain as well, as we adjust to the challenges we encounter throughout our lives—a demanding class in school, a new job, a move to a new city, a difficult relationship. When we adjust successfully, these challenges can lead to growth and development. When overwhelmed or unable to cope or protect ourselves, these challenges can lead to withdrawal, trauma, or psychological dysfunction.

FLL education can draw in particular on the psychology of cross-cultural adjustment, which is typically used to make sense of the stresses of being in foreign cultural environments (Matsumoto et al. 2006). Cross-cultural adjustment is seen as a dynamic process of responding to the demands of an unfamiliar socio-cultural environment (Kim 2001). It's largely accepted that cross-cultural adjustment has powerful psychological consequences. It can produce disorientation, stress, and culture shock (Ward et al. 2001). It stresses us because it is disruptive to the habits of perception and behavior that we rely on in everyday life (Oberg 1960). It can trigger discomfort and psychological resistance to foreign ways of acting and being (Matsumoto et al. 2006). Yet this process, while stressful, can also trigger transformative change and deeply meaningful personal growth (Shaules 2007). Indeed, developing a more intercultural perspective is often thought to *require* a challenging process of psychological change in which we integrate new ways of perceiving into our identity and worldview (Bennett 1993).

The psychological dynamic at work in cross-cultural adjustment is found in language learners as well. As with sojourners in a foreign environment, language learners face *adaptive demands*—a need to modify mental habits and ways of relating to the world. This includes not simply the demands of homework or classroom activities, but also the psychological demands inherent in attempting to change how we order our thoughts, relate to others, and express ourselves.

These demands are psychologically challenging because they involve adjusting habits of mind and self in ways that can make us feel uncomfortable, vulnerable, and incompetent. We must, in effect, construct a foreign language self even as we are stripped of our normal socio-communicative abilities. From this perspective, the FL classroom is, in psychologically important ways, the equivalent of spending time in a foreign land. Being deprived of the familiar patterns of communication and self that we normally rely on without thinking, and facing the need to internalize new ones, creates adaptive stresses. In short, it's not necessary to go abroad to experience a process of psychological adjustment—the psychologically demanding nature of FLL triggers it as well.

Thinking about FLL in terms of adjustment highlights the *foreignness* inherent in language learning. While the linguistic and cultural distance between languages can vary greatly, learning a new language is—to a greater or lesser degree—a foreign experience. While the term *foreign* may sound pejorative, Shaules (2017) argues that foreignness—referring to something that interferes with or is at odds with normal functioning—is precisely what learners must deal with as they make the psychological adjustments necessary to learn a new language. They must experiment with the unfamiliar—produce new sounds, search for words, arrange their thoughts in new ways, make countless mistakes and suffer through awkward interactions. This perspective is consistent with the notion of *linguaculture*, the idea that language and culture are part of a larger whole (Risager 2015), and thus using a new language requires navigating unfamiliar cultural terrain as well. A new language is not simply a value-neutral code or information system, it is experienced as something *foreign* because it is at odds with the usual habits of mind and self. In line with this, Gardner (2010) argues that learning a foreign language is unlike any other subject in school because it involves integrating elements of another cultural community into one's repertoire of the self—it is a foreign experience.

For some people, the words "foreign language learning" are associated mostly with a mental experience of linguistic processing—the ability to decipher and internalize a linguistic code. Those who (implicitly or explicitly) accept this view are more likely to see the outcomes of learning in instrumental terms. It may be harder to see that FLL has consequences far beyond the manipulation of linguistic patterns—it involves the integrating of a new "system of mind" and developing linguistic and social multi-competences, such as the ability to shift between different styles of communication or cultural worldviews (Cook & Li 2016). The psychological impact of multilingualism has also been associated with greater tolerance for ambiguity (Dewaele & Li 2013) and openness (Dewaele & Botes 2019). FLL is transformative because it involves so much more than learning new lexical items. It requires a leap into an experiential unknown that impacts us at deep levels of the self, yet that process may not be obvious to all learners.

Helping learners see the transformative potential of FLL involves encouraging a subtle yet profound shift in their perceptions of the learning process—from seeing it primarily as a mental or academic pursuit, to a more psychological view of FLL as a personal process that touches us at many levels of self. It can be stressful but can lead to great satisfaction and personal growth. For us to do so, we must ourselves try to make sense of the psychological complexities and transformative aspects of the FLL experience.

The Two Faces of Janus—Resistance and Engagement

From the adjustment perspective, FLL is transformative because it involves a demanding process of inner change as we integrate foreign elements into the self. This implies that disruptive stress is a natural—indeed, largely unavoidable—element of the learning process. As with any organism confronted by a demanding environment, learners react either with (1) *engagement*—valuing, opening up, and attempting to integrate new elements into the self, and/or (2) *resistance*—a self-protective psychological retrenchment. At the core of this dual motivational dynamic is a process of value expectancy and affective appraisal (Schumann 2004)—we are willing to invest energy and make change when it feels valuable, yet resist demands that feel coercive, and resist expending energy if it feels wasted or counterproductive.

It is in the dual dynamic of engagement and resistance that we find the two faces of Janus—the potential pleasure and satisfaction of FLL, coupled with the potential for distaste and rejection. The negative face of Janus—the idea that we may psychologically resist learning experiences—is found not only in cross-cultural adaptation scholarship (Shaules 2007), but also in the field of educational psychology (Alcorn 2013), and is now beginning to be explored in FL education (Shaules 2017, McConachy, this volume). Similar ideas can be found in research grounded in the approach-avoidance perspective in FLL motivation (Henry & Davydenko 2020), as well as the idea that learners have multiple and competing "selves" which are at play in their motivational dynamics (Lanvers 2016), and the notion of the "anti-ought-to self" in which the learner "is motivated by the opposite of what the external pressures demand" which reflects a *Don't tell me what to do!* attitude toward learning (Thompson 2017: 39).

There is, of course, also a positive face of Janus. Foreignness can also spark interest and curiosity—as when we are stimulated or fascinated by foreign experiences, or get "hooked" on learning a new language. For some, this process of adjustment will feel stimulating and eye-opening—it will lead to more active *engagement* with learning (Hiver et al. 2021; Mercer & Dörnyei 2020). Engagement is associated with approach motivation (Rutherford & Lindell 2011), a seeking of something that is perceived to have value. It can also be seen as a form of integrative motivation (Gardner 2010), which is associated with a desire to take into the self the characteristics of a foreign language. From the adjustment perspective, engagement is related to cross-cultural adaptation, when a sojourner modifies aspects of the self to be in better alignment with the cultural patterns of a foreign environment (Shaules 2007). In everyday terms, we might simply say that a learner is "into," interested in, or motivated by the language they are learning.

The dual nature of engagement and resistance can be represented as in Figure 2.1. The psychological demands of FLL (its adaptive demands) are disruptive and provoke resistance and/or engagement as the learner adjusts to these demands. This reflects the idea that FLL is fundamentally not a psychologically neutral process and implies that negative reactions to the demands of learning are to be expected. This represents an important assumption, since learners may feel that they *should* always be motivated to study and learn, even though it's difficult or impossible to always stay engaged. The adjustment view normalizes

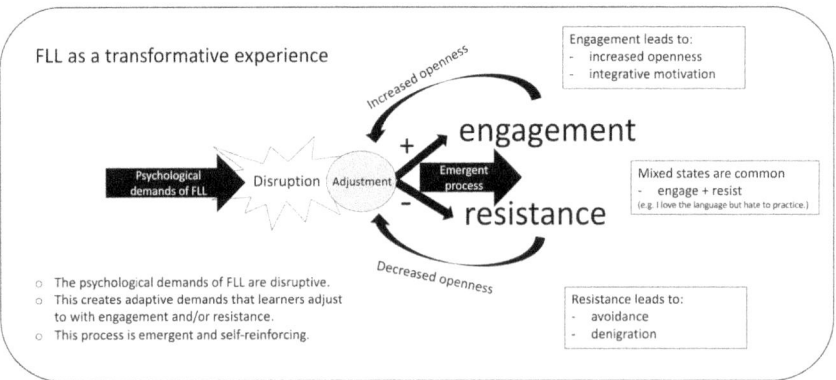

Figure 2.1 The Two Faces of Janus—Resistance and Engagement

resistance—it sees it as something that must be recognized and managed. And because resistance and engagement are considered emergent properties—they are a reaction to the challenges of learning—they are not thought to reside within the learner as a finite or essential quality. And while it's recognized by specialists that motivation is dynamic (Dörnyei et al. 2015), it's not uncommon for teachers and learners to talk about "having" or "losing" motivation. In contrast to this, the adjustment perspective emphasizes the idea that motivation is a dynamic process—a state which can be nurtured in an ongoing way—rather than something that is solely within the learner.

Surface, Deep, and Mixed States

Because approach and avoidance motivation involve distinct motivational systems (Rutherford & Lindell 2011), the adjustment perspective on offer here accepts that resistance and engagement can and do co-exist—learners may feel both a desire to learn yet resist the demands of learning as well. Shaules (2007) has explored these *mixed states* as they relate to cross-cultural adaptation. He describes sojourners who are happy to adapt to surface elements of life in a foreign country—food, transportation systems—but who resist deeper elements of change (e.g., they don't learn the local language; are critical of local cultural values). He describes this as mixed state because it involves contradictory reactions to adaptive demands—often surface adaptation together with deeper forms of resistance. This is captured in the quip of one British sojourner who declared "I love France but I hate the French." Presumably, loving "France" relates to the wine, food, and forms of French culture, whereas "the French" referred to deeper elements of French cultural norms and communication styles.

Such comments are not uncommon with language learners, as when we hear *I love Italian but I hate my Italian class*. This perspective also helps explain why learners may say one thing (*I want to be a fluent English speaker*) but do another (*I never to my homework*). This hints at the complexity of this adjustment dynamic, in which openness to and interest in learning (engagement) often coexists with aversive responses (resistance) to the challenges of learning. Those with the greatest desire to learn may even feel frustration more acutely due to slow progress. Learners may consciously think of the FL as important and fun (surface engagement), yet also feel frustration and a lack of desire to make effort or practice (deep resistance). The psychological dynamic of these complex motivational states can be represented as in Figure 2.2.

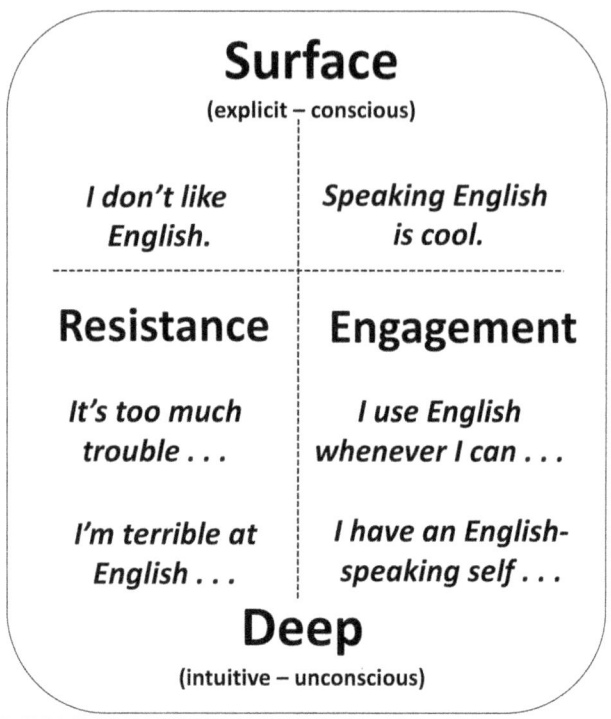

Figure 2.2 Surface and Deep Resistance and Engagement

A Case Study in Adjustment and Transformation

Using terminology like *resistance, adaptive demands* and psychological *adjustment* may create the impression of extreme emotional states or intense psychological disruption. Often, however, the dynamic of resistance and engagement operates at subtle levels of the self. One example of this played out recently over the loudspeakers on Tokyo subways. One of the companies running the subway system decided to change its policy regarding in-train announcements in English (Iki 2021). Rather than using automatic recordings of "native" speakers, train conductors were encouraged to announce coming stops in English themselves. The decision was based on feedback from foreign customers, who felt that "perfect" recorded announcements implied that train staff couldn't be approached in English. Even rudimentary interactions in English were reassuring to international travelers.

According to news reports, the policy at first met with resistance from conductors who felt their English was inadequate for the transmission of such important information. To overcome this hesitation, the company did not rely on English-language training or mandate change. Instead, it took a more purely psychological approach, creating a peer-based information campaign focused on changing how the conductors perceived using English. Conductors who had already made the switch to using English on the job shared their experiences, including the positive interactions they had with foreign passengers. Instead of talking about English in terms of information which had to be transmitted "correctly," it was presented as a way to help appreciative passengers—something conductors could brag to their grandchildren about. Thanks to this campaign, increasing numbers made the switch and reported satisfaction in using English in their work.

While not a research study, this story illustrates the different elements highlighted by the adjustment perspective, and also serves to show how the adjustment process can result in a transformative learning experience.

Adaptive Demands and the Leap into the Unknown

By asking conductors to begin making train announcements in English, the company was placing *adaptive demands* on them. Conductors faced a choice—either to continue to use Japanese or take the *leap into the unknown* of attempting to use English. Using English was a new experience for many conductors, and we can imagine that they felt pressured and uncertain about how to handle the request. The adaptive demands, in this case, relate to the psychological pressure that is experienced when faced with such choices. This reminds us that attempting to use a foreign language—even for linguistically "simple" tasks (e.g., making train announcements)—can have important psychological consequences. Even rudimentary foreign language use can be highly stressful and/or deeply meaningful. From the transformative perspective, conceiving of a linguistic task as "simple" because it requires only limited linguistic knowledge is fundamentally misconceived. Similarly, learners in the classroom setting face a series of choices each time they walk into the classroom, are given a homework assignment, called on in class, or put into a pair for language practice. They too must decide how much to invest in this leap into the foreign unknown of using a new language.

Resistance. The hesitation of at least some of the conductors also reveals a natural tendency to *resist* the uncertainty, vulnerability, and responsibility (the psychological demands) of using a foreign language. Resistance is not necessarily experienced as a strong emotional reaction—it could simply be felt as a reluctance to try new things, a distaste for doing homework, or the hesitation to fully engage in a practice activity. Given that resistance is the equivalent of a self-protection mechanism to adaptive stresses, lowering resistance requires providing support and security. In this case, conductors were not forced to use English against their will by company policy. Instead, they had the example of their colleagues as role models and were encouraged to see how meaningful English use could be. A more heavy-handed approach (e.g., mandatory trainings) might have *increased* resistance to English.

Engagement. If resistance is a form of psychological self-protection, then engagement is an opening up to the challenges of learning. This requires, most fundamentally, that learners find the endeavor meaningful. This story reminds us of the psychological importance of creating opportunities for meaningful use of the language. In this case, conductors were encouraged to see English announcements as a way to provide an important service to customers, and to take on a challenge that they could be proud of. Having meaningful learning contexts (in this case, real-life train announcements) may increase both the potential stresses of language use, but also the potential rewards. Because of this, attempting to create a psychologically "neutral" environment in the classroom, or trying simply to make activities "fun," might not increase engagement much if the effort is not connected to meaningful outcomes.

Transformation. The experience of the conductors reminds us that FLL involves a change to the experience of the self—it is an act of *becoming* a foreign language user, not simply a skill that must be perfected. This highlights the difference between mental effort—memorizing the phrases needed to make train stop announcements—and the psychological *adjustment* necessary to integrate language into one's sense of self (e.g., feeling comfortable using English to announce train stops). Assumptions about learning also influence how we experience the learning process. Japan is well-known for its exam-driven approach to foreign language education. Because of this, conductors were more likely to think of language learning in terms of "correct" usage and "perfect" pronunciation. By shifting their perception of language use, the information campaign opened them up to a different experience of language use. From the adjustment perspective, this "different experience" is a transformational element of foreign language learning—an evolution and development in the way that the foreign language is experienced, and by extension the degree to which it is increasingly experienced as a natural element of the self.

Pedagogical Reflections

For this author, embracing the idea that the language learning involved a process of psychological adjustment took time. For many years, I taught intercultural communication as one subject and thought of the English teaching I did as largely separate. I researched the adaptive processes of long-term expatriates but did not relate that to what I did in the FL classroom. At a given moment, however, I realized that the psychological resistance to foreignness I encountered when studying cross-cultural adaptation was remarkably similar to the motivational struggles that my language students were facing. Long-term expatriates who failed to learn the local language spoke of language learning in terms that were remarkably similar to "unmotivated" students of English at my university. Often, they said that it was very important, yet found it difficult to become deeply engaged in learning. They resolved to make future progress yet often seemed stuck or discouraged. Typically, these struggling learners had only a superficial sense for how language learning could benefit them. They often spoke of it in transactional terms (English as a way to get things done, travel more effectively, advance in one's career). They regularly made self-critical comments, such as *I'm a terrible language learner* or *I know I shouldn't be so lazy.*

Language Learning as a Journey

These realizations had a gradual but significant impact on my pedagogical choices. I started speaking of language learning as a developmental journey that must be navigated, rather than a set of skills which must be accumulated (see also Chapter 3, this volume). I place an emphasis on awareness activities that help learners become aware of, and thus better manage, their personal reactions to the challenges of that journey. I may, for example, begin the semester with activities in which learners reflected on their "relationship with English" by plotting their negative and positive feelings/experiences on a graph (Figure 2.3). This and other reflection activities encouraged them to actively manage their feelings and frustrations, and to see resistance to the challenges of language learning

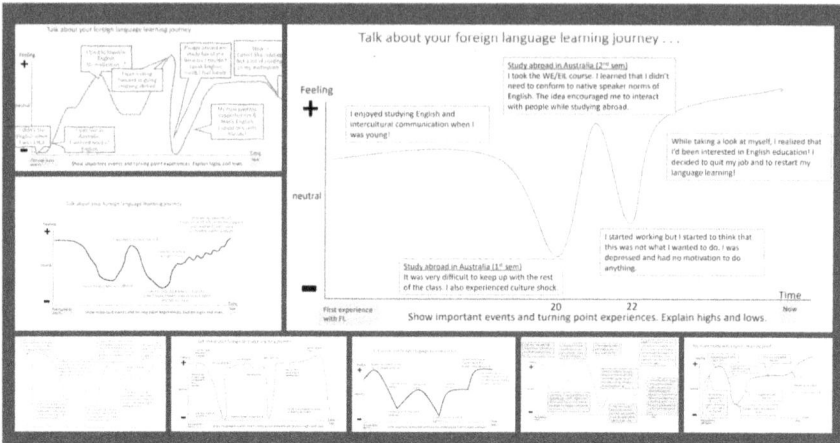

Figure 2.3 Plotting Language Learning as a Journey of Positive and Negative Feelings

as a normal part of the learning process. Activities that made learners nervous (e.g., giving presentations in front of their peers) were described in terms of getting comfortable as an English user—like a mock tournament that helps us get ready to use the FL out in the world. I did not focus on trying to get students to have "fun" (e.g., by playing games). Instead, I increasingly emphasized FLL as a life choice and a challenging journey on which the challenges go hand in hand with its satisfactions.

The adjustment perspective has helped me make sense of the complex motivational states in my students that I previously found contradictory—e.g., having good intentions yet failing to try hard; liking a foreign language but feeling like a failure as a learner. I have come to believe that negative learning experiences are not simply a momentary anxiety response. Resistance is a form of psychological self-protection that can turn off learners to language learning long term. It can also make learners become self-critical—blaming themselves for their failures (e.g., *I'm terrible at English; I'm a lazy student*). When this happens, the language learning process has brought about destructive change rather than positive transformative. Ideally, helping learners recognize that resistance is a natural part of the learning process may help them gain autonomy and self-efficacy, something that is an important element of the transformative learning experience (Little 2021). Also I now less often speak of motivation in binary terms (e.g., motivated vs. unmotivated) or of learners "having" or "losing" motivation—as though it was an object or precious substance.

Personal Growth and Transformation

The adjustment perspective has made it easier for me to talk to students about the very real challenges they face as they seek to improve, and the deeper rewards of foreign language learning that await. It has helped me see that the experience of personal growth that comes from FLL is importantly related to the challenging nature of the whole endeavor. Most foundationally, growth comes from the fundamental accomplishment of not giving up and making progress over the long term. There may not be awe-inspiring moments, but that doesn't mean transformational change hasn't taken place. In the moment, the satisfactions of FLL may be experienced at the micro level of learning—remembering the word you need; feeling happy about one's FL presentation; using a new language in a foreign country for the first time. It's only in retrospect and upon reflection that many learners may be able to articulate the feeling of having *become* a user of that language or the new worlds of experience this has enabled. For many successful learners, the desire to keep going is driven by a deeper interest in the social and cultural world of that family of speakers. Even when learning an internationalized language, such as English, Russian, or Swahili, FLL involves engaging with intercultural contexts and having foreign experiences.

As I experience it in my own teaching, the key element of developing pedagogy that emphasizes growth and transformational experience is finding ways to make the challenging aspects of FLL meaningful for learners. The adjustment perspective reminds us how enormously effortful and stressful FLL is, and it's not surprising that learners may not see the immediate value of making such an investment. With this in mind, I try to help learners become more aware of their own inner processes of stress, challenge, and change. I don't sugar-coat the learning choices they face. I tend not to say that FLL is or can be "fun" (although it may be sometimes). Rather, FLL takes time, effort, and emotional investment. Success often requires a fundamental shift—away from thinking about FLL simply as a subject in school and repositioning it as an important life choice. Once this happens, learners are in a much better position to navigate their learning journey in their own way and find the destination that will give them the most satisfaction. The adjustment perspective has made me more comfortable discussing FLL as a life challenge, rather than simply a way to get a job or order food abroad. At the same time, because it recognizes that resistance to learning is normal, and that the whole process can be psychologically challenging, I find myself more sympathetic toward learners who, for whatever reason, struggle to engage fully with learning.

Conclusion

This chapter has discussed the psychology of FLL from the perspective of adjustment and transformation. The implications of the views expressed here relate to multiple areas of concern in FLL—the psychology of learning, learner wellbeing, motivation, autonomy and efficacy, language (learning) awareness, foreign language identity, and so on. It is hoped that the ideas presented here can stimulate discussion about the value of a more holistic, embodied, and growth-oriented view of the learner. As a philosophical stance, it's easy to agree that FLL can and should lead to learner growth and transformative experiences. Yet this creates pedagogical challenges as well. It forces us to take into account the learner in all their complexity and take responsibility for the psychological impact of the learning experience. It reminds us that FLL is no more and no less than a life challenge and that we owe it to learners to treat it as such.

References

Alcorn, M. W. (2013), *Resistance to Learning: Overcoming the Desire-Not-to-Know in Classroom Teaching*. New York: Palgrave Macmillan.

Bennett, M. J. (1993), "Towards Ethnorelativism: A Developmental Model of Intercultural Sensitivity." In M. R. Paige (ed.), *Education for the Intercultural Experience*, 21–71, Yarmouth, ME: Intercultural Press.

Byram, M., Golubeva, I., Han, H. & Wagner, M. (eds). (2017), *From Principles to Practice for Intercultural Citizenship*. Bristol: Multilingual Matters.

Cambell, C. (2021), "Open Architecture Curricular Design: A Fundamental Principle of Transformative Language Learning and Teaching." In B. L. Leaver, D. E. Davidson & C. Campbell (eds), *Transformative Language Learning and Teaching*, 43–50, Cambridge: Cambridge University Press.

Carta, M. G., Balestrieri, M., Murru, A. & Hardoy, M. C. (2009), "Adjustment Disorder: Epidemiology, Diagnosis and Treatment." *Clinical Practice and Epidemiology in Mental Health*, 5 (1): 15.

Clarke, M. & Hennig, B. (2013), "Motivation as Ethical Self-Formation." *Educational Philosophy and Theory*, 45 (1): 77–90.

Cook, V. & Li, W. (eds). (2016), *The Cambridge Handbook of Linguistic Multi-Competence*. Cambridge Handbooks in Language and Linguistics. Cambridge: Cambridge University Press.

Cranton, P. (2016), *Understanding and Promoting Transformative Learning*. Sterling, VA: Stylus Publishing.

Csikszentmihalyi, M. (1997), *Finding Flow: The Psychology of Engagement with Everyday Life*. New York: Basic Books.

Curran, C. A. (1972), *Counseling-Learning: A Whole Person Approach for Education*. New York: Grune and Stratton.

Davidson, D. E., Garas, N. & Lekic, M. D. (2021), "Transformative Language Learning in the Overseas Immersion Environment: Exploring Affordances of Intercultural Development." In B. L. Leaver, D. E. Davidson & C. Campbell (eds), *Transformative Language Learning and Teaching*, 109–19, Cambridge: Cambridge University Press.

Dewaele, J.-M. (2011), "Reflections on the Emotional and Psychological Aspects of Foreign Language Learning and Ese." *Anglistik: International Journal of English Studies*, 22 (1): 23–42.

Dewaele, J.-M. (2019), "When Elephants Fly: The Lift-off of Emotion Research in Applied Linguistics." *The Modern Language Journal*, 103 (2): 533–6.

Dewaele, J.-M. & Botes, E. (2019), "Does Multilingualism Shape Personality? An Exploratory Investigation." *International Journal of Bilingualism*, 24: 811–23.

Dewaele, J.-M., Chen, X. A., Padilla M. & Lake, J. (2019), "The Flowering of Positive Psychology in Foreign Language Teaching and Acquisition Research." *Frontiers in Psychology*, 10 (2128): 1–13.

Dewaele, J.-M. & Li, W. (2013), "Is Multilingualism Linked to a Higher Tolerance of Ambiguity?" *Bilingualism: Language and Cognition*, 16 (1): 231–40.

Dewaele, J.-M. & MacIntyre, P. D. (2014), "The Two Faces of Janus? Anxiety and Enjoyment in the Foreign Language Classroom." *Studies in Second Language Learning and Teaching*, 4 (2): 237–74.

Dörnyei, Z., MacIntyre, P. D. & Henry A., eds. (2015), *Motivational Dynamics in Language Learning*. Bristol: Multilingual Matters.

Dörnyei, Z. & Ryan, S. (2015), *The Psychology of the Language Learner Revisited*. New York: Routledge.

Dörnyei, Z. & Ushioda, E. (2009), "Motivation, Language Identities and the L2 Self: A Theoretical Overview." In Z. Dornyei and E. Ushioda (eds), *Motivation, Language Identity and the L2 Self*, 1–8, Bristol: Multilingual Matters.

Egbert, J. (2003), "A Study of Flow Theory in the Foreign Language Classroom." *The Modern Language Journal*, 87 (4): 499–518.

Freire, P. (2000), *Pedagogy of the Oppressed (30th anniversary edition)*. New York: Continuum.

Gardner, R. (2010), *Motivation and Second Language Acquisition*. New York: Peter Lang Publishing.

Garza, T. J. (2021), "Cultural Transformation: Virtual Communities, Autonomous Contact, and Intercultural Competence." In B. L. Leaver, D. E. Davidson & C. Campbell (eds), *Transformative Language Learning and Teaching*, 89–97, Cambridge: Cambridge University Press.

Helgesen, M. (2019), *English Teaching and the Science of Happiness: Positive Psychology Communication Activities for Language Learning*. Tokyo: Abax.

Henry, A. & Davydenko, S. (2020). "Thriving? Or Surviving? An Approach–Avoidance Perspective on Adult Language Learners' Motivation." *The Modern Language Journal*, 104: 363–80.

Hiver, P., Al-Hoorie, A. H. & Mercer, S. (eds). (2021), *Student Engagement in the Language Classroom*. Bristol: Multilingual Matters.

Iki, M. (2021), "'This train is…': Bit by Bit Progress Towards Live Train Announcements" (*"Disu turein izu" nikusei annai kotsu kotsu*). In *Asahi Shimbun*, 9, Tokyo: The Asahi Shimbun Company.

Kim, Y. Y. (2001), *Becoming Intercultural: An Integrative Theory of Communication and Cross-Cultural Adaptation*. London: Sage.

Kramsch, C. (2009), *The Multilingual Subject*. Oxford: Oxford University Press.

Lanvers, U. (2016), "Lots of Selves, Some Rebellious: Developing the Self Discrepancy Model for Language Learners." *System*, 60: 79–92. doi:10.1016/j.system.2016.05.012.

Leaver, B. L. (2021), "Transformative Language Learning and Teaching: The Next Paradigm Shift and Its Historical Context." In B. L. Leaver, D. E. Davidson & C. Cambell (eds), *Transformative Language Learning and Teaching*, 13–21, Cambridge: Cambridge University Press.

Leaver, B. L., Davidson, D. E. & Campbell, C. (eds). (2021a), *Transformative Language Learning and Teaching*. Cambridge: Cambridge University Press.

Leaver, B. L., Davidson, D. E. & Campbell, C. (2021b), "Introduction." In B. L. Leaver, D. E. Davidson & C. Campbell (eds), *Transformative Language Learning and Teaching*, 1–9, Cambridge: Cambridge University Press.

Lee, N. (2004), "The Neurobiology of Motivation." In Schumann, J. H., Crowell, S. E., Jones, N. E., Lee, N., Schuchert, S. A. & Wood, L. A. (eds), *The Neurobiology of Learning: Perspectives from Second Language Acquisition*, 23–42, New York: Routledge.

Little, D. (2021), "Language Learner Autonomy and Transformative Classroom Practice." In B. L. Leaver, D. E. Davidson & C. Campbell (eds), *Transformative Language Learning and Teaching*, 176–83, Cambridge: Cambridge University Press.

Macintyre, P. D., Gregesen, T. & Mercer, S. (2019), "Setting an Agenda for Positive Psychology in SLA: Theory, Practice, and Research." *The Modern Language Journal*, 103 (1): 262–74.

Matsumoto, D., Hirayama, S. & LeRoux, J. A. (2006), "Psychological Skills Related to Intercultural Adjustment." In P. T. P. Wong & L. C. J. Wong (eds), *Handbook of Multicultural Perspectives on Stress and Coping*, 387–405, New York: Springer.

Mercer, S. (2021), "An Agenda for Well-being in ELT: An Ecological Perspective." *ELT Journal*, 75 (1): 14–21.

Mercer, S. & Dörnyei, Z. (2020), *Engaging Learners in Contemporary Classrooms*. Cambridge: Cambridge University Press.

Mezirow, J. (ed.). (2000), *Learning as Transformation: Critical Perspectives on a Theory in Progress*. San Francisco, CA: Jossey-Bass.

Murray, G., Gao, X. & Lamb, T. (eds). (2011), *Identity, Motivation and Autonomy in Language Learning*. Second Language Acquisition. Bristol: Multilingual Matters.

Norton, B. (2013), *Identity and Language Learning*. Bristol: Multilingual Matters.

Nyikos, M. (2021), "Incremental Drivers of Transformative Learning among World Language Preservice Teachers." In B. L. Leaver, D. E. Davidson & C. Campbell (eds),

Transformative Language Learning and Teaching, 195–204, Cambridge: Cambridge University Press.
Oberg, K. (1960), "Culture Shock: Adjustment to New Cultural Environments." *Practical Anthropology*, 7 (4): 177–82.
Oxford, R. L. (2021), "Shaking the Foundations: Transformative Learning in the Field of Teaching English to Speakers of Other Languages." In B. L. Leaver, D. E. Davidson & C. Campbell (eds), *Transformative Language Learning and Teaching*, 23–31, Cambridge: Cambridge University Press.
Paul, L. A. (2014), *Transformative Experience*. Oxford: Oxford University Press.
Risager, K. (2006), *Language and Culture: Global Flows and Local Complexity*. Clevedon: Multilingual Matters.
Risager, K. (2015), "Linguaculture: The Language-Culture Nexus in Transnational Perspective." In Farzad Sharifian (ed.), *The Routledge Handbook of Language and Culture*, 87–99, New York: Routledge.
Ros I Solé, C. (2016), *The Personal World of the Language Learner*. London: Palgrave Pivot.
Rutherford, H. J. V. & Lindell, A. K. (2011), "Thriving and Surviving: Approach and Avoidance Motivation and Lateralization." *Emotion Review*, 3 (3): 333–43.
Schumann, John H. (2004), "The Neurobiology of Motivation." In John H. Schumann (ed.), *The Neurobiology of Learning: Perspectives from Second Language Acquisition*, 23–42, New York: Routledge.
Seligman, M. (2012), *Flourish: A Visionary New Understanding of Happiness and Well-being*. New York: Free Press.
Shaules, J. (2007), *Deep Culture: The Hidden Challenges of Global Living*. Clevedon: Multilingual Matters.
Shaules, J. (2017), "Linguaculture Resistance: An Intercultural Adjustment Perspective on Negative Learner Attitudes in Japan." *Juntendo Journal of Global Studies*, 2: 66–78.
Shaules, J. (2019), *Language, Culture and the Embodied Mind: A Developmental Model of Linguaculture Learning*. New York: Springer.
Stevick, E. W. (1980), *Teaching Languages: A Way and Ways*. Cambridge, MA: Newbury House.
Thompson, A. S. (2017), "Don't Tell Me What to Do! The Anti-ought-to Self and Language Learning Motivation." *System*, 67: 38–49.
Toyama, M. & Yamazaki, Y. (2021), "Classroom Interventions and Foreign Language Anxiety: A Systematic Review with Narrative Approach." *Frontiers in Psychology*, 12 (80). doi: 10.3389/fpsyg.2021.614184.
Trang, T. T. T., Baldauf, R. B. & Moni K. (2013), "'Foreign Language Anxiety: Understanding Its Status and Insiders' Awareness and Attitudes." *TESOL Quarterly*, 47 (2): 216–43.
Ward, C., Bochner, S. & Furnham, A. (2001), *The Psychology of Culture Shock*. Hove, East Sussex: Routledge.

3

Holistic Views of Language Learning in Metaphoric Conceptualizations

Martin Cortazzi & Lixian Jin

Introduction

For effective language teaching and teacher professional development, the ability of language teachers to reflect on their own personal conceptions of "language learning" and how their learners' conceptions and expectations may differ from their own is crucial. Student conceptions of learning may be quite different from influential concepts and theories derived from the psychology of language learning or second language acquisition (e.g., Cook 2016; Ellis & Shintani 2014; Mitchell et al. 2019; van Patten et al. 2020). In particular, notions of learning and teaching inspired by Western SLA research and popular methodologies may contrast with "cultures of learning" in other parts of the world, which have their own preferred ways of learning, sets of expectations, experiences, and preferred patterns of classroom engagement (Jin & Cortazzi 2019). As we have argued in previous work, recognition that the conceptualization and enactment of learning and teaching are culturally variable generates the need for *learning-centered* approaches (e.g., Cortazzi & Jin 1996, 2002; Jin & Cortazzi 1998, 2019) in which emphasis is placed on learning from and consciously extending repertoires of cultural ways of learning.

Often research orientations to language learning are top-down, taking theory toward practice, and even specific accounts of conceptualizations of language learning (e.g., Seedhouse et al. 2010) rarely actually ask learners themselves about this, although this could yield a complementary bottom-up view. Without some knowledge of how learners conceive of language learning as part of the beliefs and values which they bring to classroom interaction, it is difficult to adopt a truly learner-centered (e.g., Nunan 1984) or learning-centered approach (e.g., Hutchison & Waters 1987). With such knowledge teachers are in a stronger position to relate pedagogically to student attitudes toward language learning and to build on the evident ideas which learners already have.

In this chapter, we aim to elaborate the significance of learners' views of language learning based on thousands of analyzed metaphors about "journeys of learning." These are elicited from sets of Chinese participants as learners and advanced users of English: in schools, in universities in China, as international students in Britain, as well as teachers of English in Chinese universities. The chapter also elaborates a model of five "meta-functions"—cognitive, affective, socio-cultural, moral-spiritual, aesthetic—derived here from the sets of Chinese participants' metaphors. Unlike similar functions mentioned in educational philosophy or curriculum theories, these are significant because they are derived inductively, bottom-up, from hundreds of students and teachers.

The chapter will focus on learners' conceptualizations of foreign language learning with three main purposes in mind. It will show that language learning for participants is cognitive, social, and emotional, but it also has moral and aesthetic features which all together represent a holistic view of language learning which engages the whole person. First, the metaphors show a range of characteristics that reflect students' perspectives of their language learning experiences (including hardship and many mixed emotions of a journey) and qualities held to be necessary for success (such as patience and persistence in making constant efforts, and determination to overcome difficulties). Parallel to this are teachers' roles as characterized in journey metaphors (for instance to show care and concern for student wellbeing, to cultivate and nurture students' whole development and serve as an all-round guide). Such examples may help teachers reflect on their own context and develop similar qualities and roles for students. Teachers may reflect on both these and on their own metaphors and consider how such notions may enrich their own language teaching.

Second, we show how a metaphor analysis can be applied to ascertain conceptualizations of learning. Through details of clusters of metaphors related to journeys of learning, teachers are encouraged to explore related metaphors with students. The metaphors analyzed here may offer information, insights, and imagination for students to make explicit their own ideas, experiences, and expectations about journeys of learning. Such an activity can be framed by a cultures of learning approach in which teachers and learners reciprocally develop their own and each other's repertoires of cultural views of learning and teaching, moving toward a cultural synergy.

Third, we show how many students (and teachers) in China already have holistic, humane ideas, and ideals which emphasize personal and social growth through foreign language learning (see also Chapter 4 of this volume). These emerge strongly in their metaphors. Some metaphors express learning as related to bodily experience, other metaphors relate to learning in the head, heart, and soul. To generalize these features, we outline a model of five meta-functions which are derived from the participants' metaphors of journeys of learning. The model as a holistic conceptualization of journeys of language learning can be applied to language teaching generally or provide a framework for teacher training and professional development.

In the sections following, we first outline the concept of cultures of learning and the related idea of cultural synergy, which we see as a framework for investigating metaphors and for metaphor teaching and learning activities. We then present some introductory ideas about metaphors and an overview to indicate what journey metaphors tell us. This is followed by a section showing a brief rationale for a metaphor approach, with details of participants and the metaphor analysis related to journeys of learning. Subsequent sections explore the journey metaphors to show metaphors as embodiment reflecting travel experience and other characteristics emerging from the metaphor data, including how learners see a transformation of the self and features of their holistic growth, and how teachers show care and concern as "a friend," "parent," or "cultivator." The model of five meta-functions is outlined with metaphor examples; these are seen further in Figures 3.1 and 3.2. The chapter concludes with possible directions for teacher reflection to engage further with conceptualizations of learning through metaphors. We suggest mini-tasks for students (and teachers) to gain insights and inspiration through metaphors. The chapter thus provides material for professional development through which teachers can reflect on whether and how these detailed features of learning journeys are part of their current practices or might be included in future teaching.

Understanding Cultures of Learning

The term "culture of learning" can refer in a general way to students' cultural background toward learning or, within an institution, to a particular ethos of designed practices for learning, perhaps with a learner-centered focus. However, the emphasis here is on how learning is culturally constructed (Yuan & Xie 2013). This means that cultural practices for learning are built up gradually, usually implicitly, through family and community socialization practices. For example, learning can be predominantly through observation and imitation, or through listening to stories and proverbs. These ways may differ from institutional expectations in schools and colleges. Hence, in different communities, students may have distinct cultural preferences for ways of knowing and ways of speaking (including marked preferences for how to learn a foreign language). Recognizing this, many teachers now make efforts toward recognizing and involving indigenous pedagogies in order to develop culturally responsive teaching practices. This is a direction for professional development for teachers with aboriginal learners in Australia (Craven 1999), Maori students in New Zealand (Metger 2015; Pihama et al. 2015) and among Native American groups in the United States (Cazden et al. 1985), and Canada (Battiste & Barman 1995; Canadian Council on Learning 2009). These indigenous pedagogies favored by learners often give particular importance to metaphors, images, and symbols as media for significant learning; beyond classroom skills they emphasize learning as a holistic process for individual and community wellbeing.

In the context of language learning, the notion of "culture of learning" provides a framework for understanding learners' (or teachers') preferred classroom practices and culturally taken-for-granted beliefs relating to ways of learning, communicating, interacting, and evaluating what happens in classrooms. As shown in our work with Chinese learners (e.g., Cortazzi & Jin 1996; Jin & Cortazzi 1993, 1998), a culture of learning may be shared— or not—between teachers and most learners. For example, some Chinese learners may not share "Western" language teachers' expectations for classroom interaction, questioning and discussion, or even ideas about what characterizes "good" teachers or learners. A further issue is that students and teachers can be largely unaware of each other's cultures of learning, or feel unappreciative and uncomfortable about them (Cortazzi & Jin 1996, 2002). By articulating the assumptions and expectations associated with different cultures of learning, we can counter perceived stereotypes of "Chinese" students as passive, relatively quiet and apparently unquestioning, who reportedly engage little in classroom interaction in the ways expected by "Western" teachers (Yuan & Xie 2013). Thus, we ascertain the inside views of Chinese and other cultures of learning (Cortazzi & Jin 2002; Jin & Cortazzi 2008, 2019).

The "cultures of learning" concept is increasingly important in contexts of diversity and internationalization when language learners and teachers encounter other peoples, cultures, ways of thinking, and ways of learning. Our position is that it is vital for language teachers—and students—to learn *about* other cultures, their ways of using language, and their general ways of learning applied to foreign language learning. By reflecting on details, teachers can learn *from*, *with*, and *through* students regarding their beliefs and values about "learning" and "teaching." "Cultures of learning" is thus a reciprocal process for teachers and students to learn from each other about ways of learning, including through different metaphors of "journeys of learning." In the idea of "cultural synergy" (Jin & Cortazzi 1995), this mutual seeking to learn from participants creates a larger notion of holistic learning, as students and teachers continually transform learning-and-teaching by learning from, and experiencing, other ways of learning.

We pluralize the term "cultures" to indicate diversity within overall recognition of Chinese characteristics of learning. China (population 1.41 billion) has the world's largest education system and the greatest number of learners and users of English as a foreign or second language. China sends the largest cohorts of international students and teachers to many other countries (and increasingly receives international students). Hence, metaphor models from Chinese participants may have wide relevance. Chinese cultures of learning blend socially transmitted values and practices of learning with modern innovations (Jin & Cortazzi 2019). Cultural trends do not apply to all individuals: within an identifiable culture of learning there are contextually varied ways of learning. Any culture is dynamic, flexible, adaptive, and it includes diversity.

Metaphors and Journeys of Learning

Cultures of learning can be seen in widely adopted metaphors about learning. In language teaching, very different orientations are expressed if language itself is regularly represented in an instrumental metaphor as "a tool" or more socially as "a bridge" to link communities or more culturally as "a mirror" to reflect cultures (Cortazzi & Jin 2021). A metaphor is an analogy. It is an essential way of thinking. A metaphor typically compares something complex, abstract, or hard to explain with something more familiar, readily experienced, and accessible. A metaphor can be a mental frame of reference. When the same metaphor is consistent and common within a community, it represents a shared network of meanings (Cortazzi & Jin 2021; Jin & Cortazzi 2019). It is an indicative guide to how people think and act. So exploring alternative metaphors can lead teachers to focus on different ways of thinking about language learning: some metaphors are familiar, some are overlooked, others offer refreshing insights. Metaphors can orientate us to lines of action, so when teachers have a variety of metaphors of "learning" in mind, they can shift frames to adapt flexibly to different learners and changing contexts. When teachers draw on learners' own metaphors, they can empower learners by starting from familiar ground. When teachers help learners to expand the range and depth of an available repertoire of considered metaphors, they are likely expanding learners' understanding about language learning.

The *"journey of language learning"* is a key metaphor, self-chosen by many of our research participants, expressed in their own voices. As an advance summary, we briefly elaborate the "journey" in a mosaic of related images which are central to many learners' conceptualizations. The "journey" is more than a process of acquiring and refining skills, although linguistic skills are inherently part of the picture. Our data obtained from many learners—and teachers—suggest that the journey involves visualized movement, progression, change, and often transformation of the whole person. It involves personal cultivation, nurturing, and growth. For success, it demands apparently endless striving through patient and persistent efforts. These determined efforts are vital for learners to survive many threats to wellbeing, to emerge as winners in a context which some see as a competitive marathon or a journey of war. For most, with teacher guidance and care, the journey is onwards and upwards to realize goals of excellence and attain heavenly ideals. For some, the journey seems like misery, torture, or a punishing descent into hell. For many, exercising a strong will, working hard continuously and maintaining self-belief in attaining eventual success will, they think, carry them forward. Their destination is imagined as a bright future of success to find a treasure of wealth, happiness, and fulfilled dreams.

Such conceptions by Chinese participants are elaborated in "journeys of learning" with corresponding teachers' roles (see Jin & Cortazzi 2011, 2020). In the following sections, we report a remarkable range and depth of conceptions of learning. Some features of these metaphors are also seen to be common in our studies in Malaysia (Cortazzi & Jin 2020b) and Iran (Cortazzi et al. 2015), which suggest some metaphors are apparently widespread, but we also see culturally specific nuances (e.g., in our data, language learning as "making war" or "fighting a battle" is mentioned in far more frequently and with greater elaboration in Lebanon than in China, Iran, or Malaysia).

Metaphor Analysis for Understanding "Journeys of Learning"

Metaphor expressions are commonplace in ordinary language and in educational discourse, frequently occurring in classroom teaching and teacher discussions about language teaching. In the next sections, we highlight key findings from large metaphor datasets obtained from foreign language students and teachers in China. These include 3,325 metaphors for "learning" from 1,081 students of English in China, mostly given in English, supplemented with 471 metaphors from 258 experienced Chinese teachers of English, with 623 metaphors from 303 Chinese students studying in Britain, and 283 metaphors from 144 students in Chinese schools. These are complemented with findings from analyses of 3,465 metaphors for "teachers" from 1,781 Chinese students, and 541 metaphors from 258 Chinese teachers. As shown below, the metaphor data illustrated here align closely with public ideas about learning in China, as part of Chinese cultures of learning.

The method used to analyze these metaphors extends recognized practices in cognitive linguistics but with socio-cultural applications to language pedagogy (see Cortazzi & Jin 2020a, b; Jin & Cortazzi 2020). In the metaphor expression "Learning is a journey" the hard-to-pin down concept of "learning" (known as the "target") is compared to the familiar experience of "a journey" (the "source" of the comparison). We ask students (or sometimes teachers) to complete proforma sentences, like "*Learning is ...*," using their own metaphors to express their own ideas without further prompting. In responding, participants have a completely open choice: some say "learning is a butterfly" or "a bottomless well." The participant explanations (known as "entailments") are equally open-ended: there is an enormous choice of appropriate reasons for metaphors. Metaphors are concise comparisons, often with different interpretations in entailments ("the bottomless well" might be an endless source of life-giving water or a dry prison for a person who falls in). Rather than impose outside interpretations, we ask participants to explain their own metaphors by giving their own reasons. Our metaphor analysis attends closely to patterns of the sources and entailments, and provides representative quotes in participant's own words to maintain their own voices.

Eliciting metaphor data is parallel to getting responses in questionnaires or interviews, but often participants making their own metaphors are more involved emotionally and imaginatively. Students' metaphors may be commonplace, conventional, or creative and deliberative. However, the metaphors are not arbitrary, nor simply decorative devices. Metaphors are held to relate intimately to cognition as part of our conceptual system (Lakoff & Johnson 2003) because they employ analogical processing as a fundamental way of thinking. Importantly, within cognitive linguistics (Gibbs 2017; Lakoff & Johnson 1999) many metaphors are shown to be fundamentally embodied, representing images of physical experience of the human body, but they extend this through elaborated abstract concepts to shape our understanding of the world (Littlemore 2019). Everyday examples show strong analogical correspondence between bodily orientation in space with some concepts of time (the future is "in front of us," but the past is "behind" us), assessment of quantity (an increase means "going up"; a decrease is "going down"), and quality (when things improve, they "go up" but deterioration is "on a downward slope"). This body experience also conceptualizes some emotions (happiness is "a rise in spirits"; depression is "feeling low"). However, journeys of learning are not only cognitively or affectively oriented: many metaphors show different cultural nuances (Kövecses 2005). Since we analyze large databases from within different communities, our approach is more socio-culturally aligned to foreign language learning. Notably, we inductively identify moral-spiritual and aesthetic functions of metaphors, which are largely absent in cognitive metaphor theory (Cortazzi et al. 2015; Cortazzi & Jin 2020a, b).

Embodiment in Learning Journeys: Travelling, Climbing, and Sailing

Embodiment is common in everyday metaphor and it is widespread in our datasets. The journeys of learning are represented in physical terms relating to travel. Typically, in a dataset of 337 journey metaphors there are entailments about the length, time, distance, circumstances, and conditions of travel, barriers, and difficulties to overcome, plus the effort required, the emotions experienced en route, and ideas and feelings about reaching a goal or destination (e.g., Jin & Cortazzi 2011, 2019). Often, journey metaphors carry ideas of adventure, exploration, and search. Embodied features are seen in physically oriented ideas which evaluate learning experiences: forward movement is considered positive or good; upward movement is an increase in quantity and improved quality. Together forward-and-upward represent the image of progress and development, associated with positive emotions of success (conversely, downwards, or backward movement implies difficulty or failure). Achievements and setbacks of language learning are often characterized in spatial oppositions of embodied metaphors: "it is full of ups and downs." These represent emotions associated with the success and failures experienced in learning journeys. This spatial orientation and directionality of movement is extended emotionally and spiritually: "heaven" is a learning destination ahead, a higher positive place or condition; "hell" is negative, down below, an experience of learning to be endured or avoided. Some metaphors have sacred implications. They reflect how learning is "a ladder, a way leading to heaven but also to hell," "it's a road with thorns, the road to paradise, it's too painful for us to walk forward but at the end of the road there's a paradise filled with flowers," "it's a pilgrimage: the road is too long and painstaking, but you may arrive at a holy place in the end."

The body-image of intense physical movement is represented in 176 "climbing" metaphors: "language learning is climbing a mountain." Students elaborate this in their entailments: "you have to strive to move forward," "as you step forward, it means you are improving," "with each small step you reach a new height," "we climb higher and higher towards the peak of knowledge." Embodiment is evident in the movement, directionality, and the felt image of physical climbing. This is easily overlooked in metaphors in daily life: the images are cognitively held in language to express abstractions (Littlemore 2019). This commonly expressed cognition complements the literal embodiment in language classrooms which has been researched by examining in detail participant's gaze, gesture, facial expression, and physical movement in interaction (Hall & Looney 2019). The "mountain climbing" metaphors stress the need for persistent physical effort, "we can only reach the summit with great effort"; "sometimes you go forward, sometimes backwards, but we just need to climb unremittingly." However, this is a compelling worthwhile activity: "if you give up in the middle you will get nothing," "it is difficult but you must do it," "when you get to the top with so much sweat, you know it is really worth it." Both the process and result are associated with salient emotions, "climbing with both hardship and happiness"; "the process of climbing is bitter but the happiness you get after you arrive at the top cannot be substituted." The language learner who keeps "climbing" progressively obtains a panoramic vision, "the higher you are, the more beautiful the scenery you'll see."

While "journey" and "travel" metaphors for learning seem common among language learners elsewhere, a particular metaphor has strong resonances for Chinese students: for fifty-three participants, "Learning is sailing against the current." Again, this expresses physical movement with a forward upstream direction but, crucially, it depicts the learners' hard, unceasing effort "rowing" against opposing forces which threaten to overwhelm those who do not work hard for immediate improvement. Students describe this as a binary choice with consequences: learning is "taking a boat upstream: if you don't make progress, you'll fall behind," it is "fighting against the river: if you can't go upwards, you'll go downwards." However, this is not an open choice; students repeat the exhortation for more clearly directed effort: "if you stop going ahead, you will be pushed back by the current," "if you refuse to press on you will go back," "you will go backwards, if you don't go forwards." There is implied competition: "you'll fall behind if you don't make efforts"; "not advancing means losing." Other metaphors of "learning is a path" or "an escalator" confirm the need for responsible action to make the right choice: "learning is a moving stairway whether it goes up or down is up to you"; it's "a two-way path, one leads to success, the other to failure."

The Socio-cultural Status of Metaphors

A critic might downplay these metaphors as "simply" cognitive constructions or "just" examples of participants' imaginations. They may seem detached from actual practices of student learning. However, four points of validation confirm their socio-cultural orientation and value for language learning research and language teaching. First, some metaphors are salient sayings within a Chinese cultural tradition which is quoted by parents and teachers, e.g. "learning is sailing a boat against the current"; "a teacher is an engineer of the soul" (Jin & Cortazzi 2008: 190–5). Second, some metaphors are reiterated in Chinese policy documents and invoked in teacher development programs (Jin & Cortazzi 2011: 117–9), e.g. "a teacher is a gardener" or "a cultivator of talents." Third, some are seen enacted in the physical classroom stance of Chinese teachers and students, visible evidence for which is in classroom photographs (Hall & Looney 2019; Jin & Cortazzi 2008: 179–84). Teachers commonly adopt a straight-upright bodily position and a fixed manner of holding a book at arms-length for reading, reciting, or choral speaking (some students are taught to re-enact this). Thus, some teachers teach from the book, as a source of knowledge, and by the book, as a process. This embodies the metaphor, "a teacher is a book" (one Chinese translation of "to teach" is *jiao shu*: "teach the book").

Fourth, some metaphor meanings are confirmed in notices in English displayed in Chinese university corridors and school classrooms. These public exhortations align closely to our metaphor data to illustrate socio-cultural values. Examples observed in six different institutions include: "No pain, no gain: let us work hard together!" "Cultivate virtues; study diligently: there is no end to learning!" "Never give up hope, and hope will never give up on you," "All things are difficult before they are easy." "Keep in mind that as a teacher of classes, you are also an educator of the students, an instructor of their lives and a leader of their moral virtues." A bilingual poster reminds everyone that teachers are "guides": "Strengthen the professional ethics of teachers: be a guider for students' characters, for student's knowledge, for students' innovative thinking, for students' dedication"; "Be a good teacher with ideals and beliefs, moral sentiments, knowledge, and a benevolent heart."

These four points illustrate the strong alignments of the metaphors discussed here with more recent socio-cultural ideas within foreign language education in China, e.g., to develop student attitudes, personalities, values, and qualities of character (Liu & Wu 2015).

Facing Adversity in Competitive Journeys toward a Destination

Further details of learning journeys give insights into how these Chinese participants think and feel about language learning. The participating English teachers in China see the journey of learning as "an endless road," "the boundary is ever-increasing," "the more you learn, the less you see the end." Many students echo this: language learning is "a journey that can never end"; "no matter how high you climb there is more to climb." Teachers (as ex-students) recognize the hardship and toil of learning journeys: "you will face many difficulties and obstacles, risks, twists and dangers," "you may find treasures or you may lose everything, including your life." Students agree and elaborate the emotions: "We're walking on a road of thorns, we get bloodstained and depressed through loneliness but we can hear the leisurely birds singing and see the yearned-for rising sun," "it's the unique road of overcoming adversity and becoming a genius, it is hard and dangerous, there are no short cuts."

Participants, both students and teachers, reiterate the need for persistence despite difficulties; they emphasize how learners must continue determined efforts to overcome obstacles. Teachers advise: "You always conquer one difficulty then another comes; keep going, it takes a lot of effort but it is worth struggling;" "diligence is the path to the mountain of knowledge." Again, students elaborate emotionally: "it is months of enduring hardships, waking in the clouds, walking in the fog, walking in the desert, you must have persistence until you reach the sunshine," "you must spare no effort, it needs unremitting efforts," "our attitude determines the result—you have to stick to working hard to make your dream come true."

Chinese students often portray learning as a fierce competition, "there are always many competitors around you and people are always rushing to the goal." Chinese school students confirm this, facing the notoriously competitive "*gaokao*" national university entrance exam; so do Chinese students studying competitively in Britain in English-medium contexts alongside life-long users of English. Learning is "a long-running marathon," "a grueling competition: you can win only by training hard, with patience, determination and confidence"; "in this competition race, everyone tries their best to be first: if you give up learning just for one day, you'll fall behind others." The metaphors emphasize student needs for endurance, a strong-will, and endless determination to maintain an unceasing effort "to overtake others and surpass them on the road." The highly selective competition for educational opportunities through English is symbolized by quoting a saying: "Learning English is an army crossing a dangerous river over a one-log bridge": "On this bridge you just have only the one direction and must keep going this way or you will fall off."

A salient feature of the journey is the envisaged successful destination. Many learners imagine "a bright future in a job" by "crossing the bridge to success," "to real the ideal end-point, the climax of success," 'the road to success, full of tears and mirth; the process is bitter, the result is sweet.' This is "the process to enrich yourself," "you can climb from a lower social position to a higher one," "to realize your dreams." The "bridge" is further characterized as "the bridge between the past and the future," "a bridge for students from the countryside to come out of the mountains and create a nice life," "the bridge between a dream and reality, connecting ideals and reality." For other Chinese students in Britain, what matters is the process of the learning journey, "the result is not so important, I enjoy the process of travelling"; "we enjoy the process of the journey, not the destination we arrive at."

Learners: Transformation of the Self and Growth

Our dataset shows that many students see the learning journey as a process of self-change and developing self-knowledge based on accessing truth. Learning is "to walk forward on the road of pursuing truth," "the path to change your life, the way to get wisdom." For some, this "way" or "path" may have philosophical or spiritual resonances of Chinese heritage worldviews within Taoist, Confucian, Buddhist, and Islamic traditions. In metaphors, students assert: "the way of learning is the process of seeking oneself," "the way to know your true self," "the path to our heart," "the way to perfect oneself." This may feature enlightenment: "the sudden comprehension that you have are like the flowers that bloom suddenly in your heart." It may recall features of Confucian traditions of teaching (Jin & Cortazzi 2008, 2020): it is "a walk along the road travelled by our ancestors," because "teachers help us grow up healthily in the edification of Confucianism."

Elements of developing personal growth through learning include empathy, associated with gaining intellectual, social, and cultural insights: it is "walking on the road of other people's mentality," "a way to enter others" inner world, "a wide road to ideals, it can tell you how to live better." Other metaphors indicated philosophical reflection and moral improvement: "Learning is searching for your true self," "pursuing the value of life," "searching for the secret of the world and to become a true person." Such transformation is not easy: "it's a rugged road: I am a worm not knowing the way out"; "walking on a road of thorns, we get bloodstained and depressed through loneliness." Some students understand how suffering is inevitably part of the journey: "the process is bitter—the result is sweet," "you will gain only if you have pain," "It's rowing upstream with a sail that seeks to release us from suffering; I can't reach the other side of the sea until I take all the pains." Teachers confirmed this, "Learning is a journey in which it is true that no pains, no gains."

Learner growth is seen less directly in sixty-two metaphors for teachers as "engineers of the human soul." This long-standing image in Chinese education is shared among older teachers but given here by students. The metaphor shows teachers helping to construct individual and collective futures through "soul-development": "the teacher makes tall buildings of students' souls, of the human character, building with knowledge, not bricks, and makes the human soul". Ultimately this is self-transformation by learners' own efforts when they follow teacher blueprints, "the teacher is the designer of the building of the human soul, an engineer who designs but students realize the design by themselves." The transformative soul-construction in "engineering" metaphors features moral aspects ("helping us to tell the difference between evil and goodness") associated with how teachers "cleanse" wrong-doing, as linked to re-cycling and sustainability. The teacher is: "a sanitation engineer who cleans out rubbish and waste and lets us be healthy," "a cleaner of heart and soul contributing to the clean and healthy environment, classifying the rubbish and re-cycling it to something new: without this, there is no development of cultures and civilization," "a sustainer of the human soul, who with great moral quality educates us" and "brings wisdom to our souls."

Learner growth is elaborated through 205 metaphors of "the teacher is a diligent gardener" by all four groups of participants. In this complex metaphor, teachers "cultivate," "nurture," "nourish," "protect," and "take care of" student growth so that they "bloom and thrive." For participants, the cultivation is obviously intellectual, including language skills. However, cultivation includes care for physical and mental wellbeing, with moral and spiritual features. "Cultivation" in the Confucian tradition has resonances of self-cultivation of knowledge-informed reflective thinking, with upright behavior and moral integrity (Jin & Cortazzi 2020). Here, students see learners as "flowers" or "plants": "teachers grow flowers of knowledge," "teachers water us with knowledge and experience," "growing our minds." In these metaphors, teachers "cut," "trim," and "prune" the students, "to get rid of our bad habits in learning," they "cultivate students; they make us grow straight… healthy and clever… to be good people," "cultivating students" characters, to make students more perfect, by "transmitting principles of good behaviour, our shortcomings disappear." The teacher "as a knowledge-sower" and "a sower of the human soul" can have a transformational effect to "transform something ordinary into something spectacular." Such transformation is visualized centrifugally for the planet: "they teach people to grow and to be spiritual which would influence them for their whole life, through the whole generation, and then the country and the whole world."

Language teaching as "cultivation" entails teacher sacrifice through transformative hard work. Students recall teacher-gardeners who "exhaust themselves in toiling to help their students to grow up," "to the extent of forgetting food and sleep." These teachers "use their own sweat to pour onto flowers, making themselves suffer," "pouring their blood and sweat to us to make us into beautiful flowers," "using pouring sweat to cultivate the flowers of the motherland"; "we are the flowers of the motherland; they create our learning with beauty."

Teachers: Caring for Learner Wellbeing

Many further metaphors focus on how teachers show a humanistic concern for student wellbeing. Essentially, such metaphors frame language teaching as "to cultivate the person" (in Chinese, "*yu ren*," "teach the person"). Thus, "a teacher is a parent" in ninety metaphors: "a nice parent: who offers me great care, concerned for our growth, demanding us to learn seriously," "a kind-hearted mother: she instructs our study and cares about our thought," and "our sacred mother, who gives us warmth and strength when we feel lonely."

More generally, "a teacher is a friend" in 132 metaphors: evidently this is similar to a parental caring and sharing relationship. It has strong social and emotional functions. To expect teachers to be "friendly" is common everywhere; however, for Chinese participants the teacher as "a friend" shows greater closeness with a warm sharing of heart-to-heart feelings and being a role model who cultivates the whole person. Students explain: "My teacher is a friend who cares about students and guides them, who shares happiness with them, caring about our health." "Teachers share joy and sorrow with us; they communicate with their students to share happiness and sadness; we can share feelings and ask for help and support, by talking or spending time with them you can feel warm." "Teachers are our friends, solving our difficulties and sharing our sorrows; when we feel sad, we can open our heart to them." Two teachers elaborate the relationship: "A language teacher is a true friend who can give you help when you are in trouble, who helps us with our study problems and the life difficulty.... I think most of us will love teachers who are not only teachers but also friends, and caring (sometimes our enemy)":

> A language teacher is a friend in my heart, who can talk heart to heart with students and become their friend, not only teaching us knowledge but more importantly teaching us how to become a person through the model of their behaviour, caring for us and looking after us, and cultivating our ability to survive in society, teaches us many things not just language, a guide in study, but a friend in life.

Key characteristics of the learning journey are summarized in Figure 3.1, which uses participants' expressions from their metaphors.

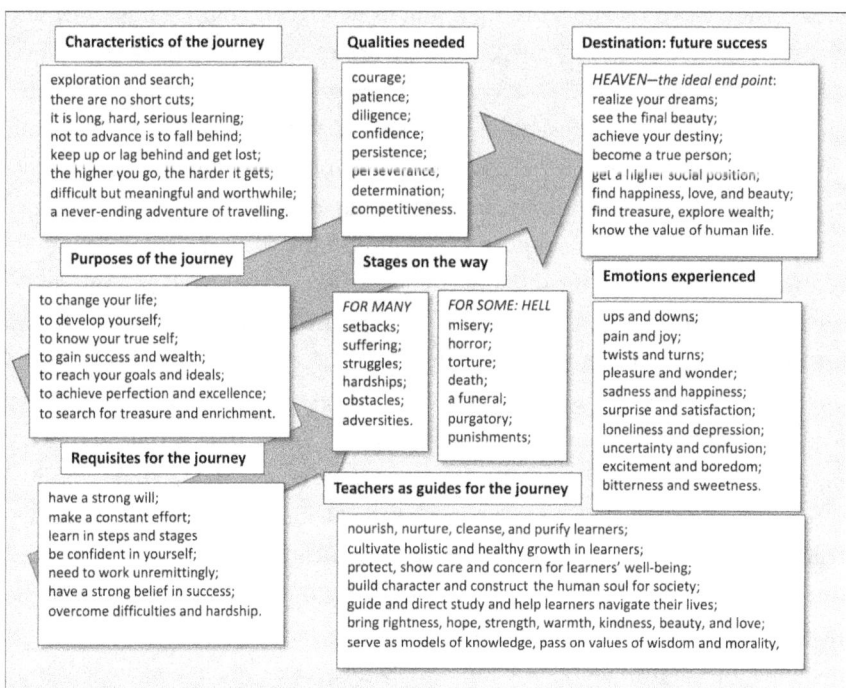

Figure 3.1 Journeys of Learning Characterized in the Words of Metaphors from Students and Teachers in China

A Holistic Model of Metaphors

Figure 3.1 provides an overall visual representation of a holistic model of learning journeys based on the evidence presented, with many other metaphors in datasets. This integrates participants' ideas of the purposes, destinations, and characteristics of the journey, together with the qualities students need, and the emotions experienced. As can be seen in Figure 3.1, participants view learning as not only being cognitive, social, and emotional, but also as having moral and aesthetic features. Viewed collectively, these represent a holistic view of learning which engages the whole person (see also Chapter 4, this volume).

The holistic roles of teachers in these journeys emerge strongly. In addition to being "a friend" concerned with learner "wellbeing" (as above), a teacher is "a guide" in 137 metaphors. Cognitively, one teacher explains: "a teacher is a guide in the ocean of knowledge, guiding us in the future direction, taking us to the light, cultivating the professions and explaining problems." Another teacher adds a moral function of modelling learning and exemplifying knowledge, "teachers guide our methods of learning, tireless, giving us basic knowledge, teaching skills, in everyday life they should be a model using their own behaviour to motivate all of us, therefore they should have high ability, knowledge and skills is required in their language teaching profession and having a high moral standard is required, too." Other teachers elaborate; "A teacher is a navigator of life, when we feel confused they will lead us to the right direction without forgetting to protect us"; "as a tourist guide, this is an important but difficult role especially for an English teacher, a guide taking us to the destination, a runner leading us, to pass on values and guide us professionally towards an honourable future, telling us how to be upright people." Some students in such "tour guide" metaphors clarify socio-cultural and aesthetic functions: "Language teachers are tour guides: they take us to many beautiful views in different countries and cultures"; "they teach students much about society and how to survive"; "they lead students to enjoy the beauty of knowledge ... to enjoy the beautiful scenery of life"; "they take us to the beauty spots and leave it to ourselves to feel beauty." As guides, some language teachers seem explicit about cultures of learning; they teach students how to learn, "they always enlighten their students to think and learn; as a navigator they guide us to find the right path of learning despite the mass of knowledge; they can conduct us to find our own way of learning." In combinations of such meta-functions (see Figure 3.2), a whole-person pedagogy is implied: "A language teacher is a navigator: they guide us to the correct road and to happiness in life, they not only help us in our studies but teach us how to be a well-educated person as well."

In Figure 3.2, the five meta-functions of "learning is a journey" are presented as categories which subsume hundreds of specific metaphors. They give generalized insights into holistic views of language learning based on Chinese cultures of learning. The meta-functions related to metaphors for teachers can be compared for different nuances between those of participants in China (Jin & Cortazzi 2020), Malaysia (Cortazzi & Jin 2020b), and Iran (Cortazzi et al. 2015). In Figure 3.2, we list examples (quoting metaphor sources and entailments) to show meta-functions common to both the "learning journey" and "language teachers" who guide students in their journeys.

For curriculum and learning theorists, learning has different major functions: some cognitive functions centrally relate to knowledge and understanding; some affective functions relate to student emotions and motivation; social and cultural functions relate to living in society and transmission and innovation within cultural heritages. Some theorists seek to combine cognitive, affective, social, and cultural foundations of learning (Illeris 2016, 2018; Joyce et al. 2008; Wells & Claxton 2002) and some theorists add ethical, moral, and spiritual dimensions (Bigger & Brown 2012; Eaude 2008; Lucas & Claxton 2010; Lucas et al. 2013) and argue for the role of aesthetics (Abbs 2012) as part of embodied learning

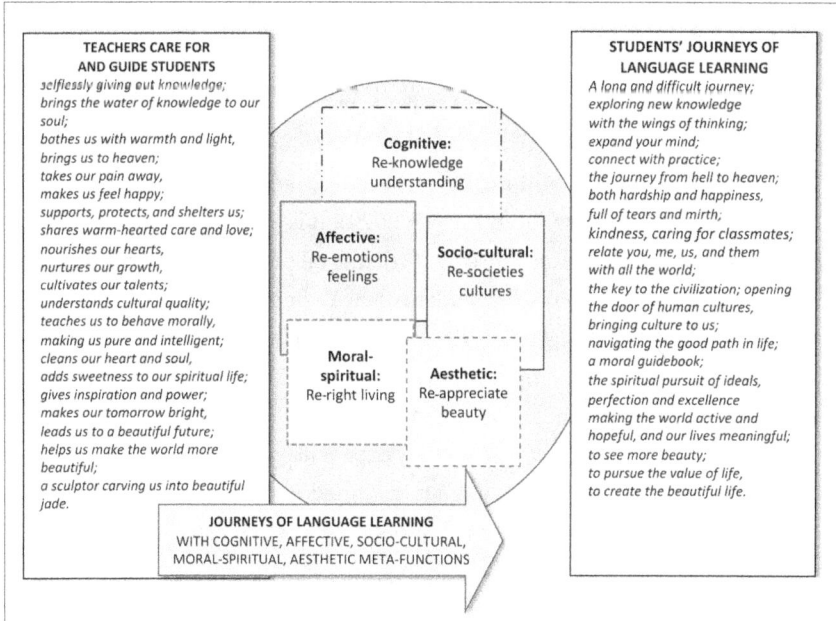

Figure 3.2 Teachers Guide Chinese Students' Journeys of Learning, as Expressed in Their Own Words in Metaphors

(Bresler 2004). In parallel, humanistic orientations specific to language teaching, as well as positive psychology, emphasize conjoining cognition and emotions for learner wellbeing and whole-person development (Arnold 1999; Gabryś-Barker et al. 2016; MacIntyre et al. 2016), which are further linked to cultural shifts and transformative learning (Leaver et al. 2021; Shaules 2019). However, these meta-functions in Figure 3.2 are specifically part of the conceptualization of language learning, or "*journeys of learning*," they are held by student and teacher participants in China, most of whom are unlikely to be familiar with these ideas of "Western" curriculum theorists or whole-person language teaching scholarship.

Applications toward Developing Cultures of Learning in Synergy

Our suggestions for applications are framed within a cultures of learning approach aimed at developing an enhanced synergy. In this view, a learner-centered approach must attend seriously to learners' ideas about learning, known here through their metaphors (students presumably already learn about teachers' professional concepts of language learning—implicitly through activities, if not explicitly through explanations). The cultures of learning approach is reciprocal; it seeks to engage teachers and students in a mutual endeavor to learn more about each other's perspectives on learning, exemplified here through metaphor viewpoints.

"Cultural synergy" is a concept for pedagogic interaction in internationalized and multicultural language learning contexts. This means more than recognizing or respecting differing cultures, communities, and practices of learning (Cortazzi & Jin 2002; Jin & Cortazzi 1995, 2020). It is learning-centered in that it constitutes *learning about learning* from the cultural perspectives of participants. Metaphors give insight into this. Students learn about language learning from teachers (or from fellow learners). Reciprocally, teachers can learn more about learning by attending explicitly to students' cultures of learning, both as a point of professional development and for practical pedagogy. Teachers might use their own metaphors to explain clearly how they expect learners to learn, and the ways in which they themselves teach, with an informed rationale. Similarly, students are encouraged to share metaphors to show their particular visions of learning portrayed in journeys of learning. Making and sharing metaphors provides a practical vehicle to do this. Synergy recognizes mutual accommodation between participants (but not necessarily accommodating half-way) to attain a more holistic harmony.

Synergy implies developing repertoires of metaphors for learning, derived from groups of learners, teachers, and others. Synergy highlights ways in which cultural interaction engenders something new that is more than the sum of the separate parts. In this sense, internationally, learners and teachers can develop conceptualizations of learning and teaching through metaphors from China (and vice versa for Chinese conceptualizations drawing on others' metaphors). Thus, if teachers and learners interact with these metaphors, they can ask: What insights and implications are there for us in the cultures of learning shown in Chinese participants' metaphors? Can we engage positively with these ideas to extend our own repertoires of metaphors within our cultures of learning?

Pedagogical Suggestions

Teachers, teacher trainers, and language educators can use metaphors to reflect systematically on the question of "What is language learning?" They can examine their own metaphors for journeys of learning and teacher roles within such journeys. Their metaphors might be personal (to the individual), or professional (as encountered in training), or research-based (as disseminated through theories of language learning and pedagogy), or institutional (as found in official documents and reports or as heard in collegial discussion), or cultural (as investigated here). The examples here encourage imaginative elaboration of metaphors through entailments and the clustering of metaphors. Particular questions might arise from evident features of learning journeys: how can student difficulties and suffering be alleviated? How can teachers try to ensure the practical realization of student ideas and ideals?

Teachers can ascertain the learning journey metaphors held by their own students, or related metaphor conceptualizations (about language in general or particular foreign languages, about specific language skills, or about given communities of language speakers and contexts). Teachers can select some key metaphors (language learning is "crossing a bridge," "climbing a mountain," or "sailing a boat") and ask students what they think most people would understand by these; what difference does it make if we think about learning through these metaphors; what feelings or social and cultural implications are involved? The examples presented here might serve as stimuli for metaphor-making in class, which engages students' imagination and creativity. Students might find this easier if they draw their journey of learning, or make posters, or cartoons, or construct a personal time-line, with notes on appropriate stages, depicted people, contexts, and emotional "highs and lows."

Features of journeys of language learning might be discussed in class, using examples from the Figures presented here. Students in groups might engage in a mini-task to interview a few members of the public who speak another language about "learning a foreign language is a journey." Interviewers ask which languages people have learned and what their experience was like, and especially what people understand by the journey metaphor. Related questions might be "Is foreign language learning a journey through hell to heaven? Is it a journey towards fulfilling your dreams? How does it help you to become a better person?" The results are then put together to make posters or electronic presentations with oral commentary and conclusions. Similarly, pre-service or novice teachers might make collaborative charts based on enquiries with students and their personal-professional experience. A major aim of the above is to consider the implications of clusters of metaphors and to compare and evaluate features which recognize strengths and limitations within familiar contexts and their application to other contexts internationally. Ethnic and minority group students, or those from international contexts, should find their voices are especially valued in such activities.

The model of five metaphors with the associated metaphor elaborations merits reflection, further research, and imaginative application. It can be "a tool" (or "a textile loom," a framework for weaving multi-colored fabrics) for reflection on the language curriculum and specific programs. These surely include cognitive, affective, social-cultural elements, but how far do moral-spiritual and aesthetic functions fit in? Could all five be more integrated and better-balanced for more holistic and transformative language learning? In applied linguistics programs at university level, metaphor functions might be taken into account with reference to textbook and materials design, levels, and stages of language learning. What might follow if a moral-spiritual or aesthetic dimension receives emphasis? How would a teacher relate forthcoming teaching of given materials to a holistic perspective for student wellbeing? The model can be extended to examining local contexts, international comparisons, and expanding the five meta-functions with geographical, historical, political, or economic meta-functions.

From the learning journey metaphors, in a synergetic approach, both students and teachers, locally and internationally, can learn *from* cultures of learning by gaining knowledge *about* them. Understanding how others learn culturally is part of a holistic view of learning. Classroom participants often learn implicitly *with* cultures of learning, sometimes peripherally, but this can be made more explicit by discussing key practices through metaphors. Since there are many ways to learn, teachers and students can develop a repertoire of ways from professional sources and from indigenous and other cultural pedagogies to learn *through* different cultures of learning. This may happen for international students studying abroad or with international teachers working in different cultural contexts. "Cultural synergy" therefore implies that teachers and learners can develop repertoires of ways of teaching and learning which extend and complement previously enacted ways. Close attention to metaphors of learning journeys can be one practical approach toward this.

Conclusion

The metaphors shared here cumulatively help to broaden conceptualizations of language learning. They suggest a series of alternative ways to envisage what learning a foreign language is like and how it feels for Chinese students and teachers or wider international contexts. The metaphors provide resource materials for teacher reflection and potential professional development in teacher discussion groups. For a learner-responsive pedagogy, it is vital to know *about* and know more *through* learners' and teachers' metaphors. Sharing teacher and learner metaphors can move us toward cultural synergy to inform interaction and influence practices which encompass ideas, ideals, and imagination. The study here contributes specific metaphor examples for teaching metaphor within a cognitive linguistic approach to classroom pedagogy (Holme 2009), but this can be made deeper and broader through five meta-functions. The metaphor meta-functions identified here apply to many features and facets of language learning—an insight which, shared with learners, may promote learners' confidence to engage with and talk about more holistically oriented learning. It is worth exploring how far language learning students understand, appreciate, and develop the involvement of their cognition, emotion, social-cultural, moral-spiritual, and aesthetic competences. Teachers can ask students about their metaphors through elicitation and share their own. Teachers, together, might use metaphors to make explicit the cultures of learning in their institution before they engage learners more explicitly within the institution for more conscious metacognitive engagement. Thus, knowledge and understanding of metaphors and meta-functions can contribute as key models of cultures of learning to develop practices of cultural synergy. This takes journeys of learning further, with many more metaphor paths to explore.

References

Abbs, B. (2012), *Aa Is for Aesthetic: Essays on Creative and Aesthetic Education.* London: Routledge.

Abbs, P. (2012), *Aa Is for Aesthetic: Essays on Creative and Aesthetic Education.* London: Routledge.

Arnold, J. (ed.). (1999), *Affect in Language Learning.* Cambridge: Cambridge University Press.

Battiste, M. & Barman, J. (eds). (1995), *First Nations in Canada—The Circle Unfolds.* Vancouver: University of British Columbia.

Bigger, S. & Brown, E. (2012), *Spiritual, Moral, Social and Cultural Education: Exploring Values in the Curriculum.* London: Routledge.

Bresler, L. (ed.). (2004), *Knowing Bodies, Moving Minds: Towards Embodied Teaching and Learning.* Dordrecht: Springer Science.

Canadian Council on Learning (2009), *The State of Aboriginal Learning in Canada: A Holistic Approach to Measuring Success.* Ottawa: CCIL.

Cazden, C., John, V. & Hymes, D. (eds). (1985), *Functions of Language in the Classroom.* Columbia: Teachers College Press.

Cook, V. (2016), *Second Language Learning and Language Teaching*, 5th edn. London: Routledge.

Cortazzi, M. & Jin, L. (1996), "Cultures of Learning: Language Classrooms in China." In H. Coleman (ed.), *Society and the Language Classroom*, 169–206, Cambridge: Cambridge University Press.

Cortazzi, M. & Jin, L. (2002), "Cultures of Learning: The Social Construction of Educational Identities." In D. C. S. Li (ed.), *Discourses in Search of Members*, 49–78, New York: University Press of America.

Cortazzi, M. & Jin, L. (2020a), "Elicited Metaphor Analysis: Approaching Teaching and Learning." In S. Delamont & M. Ward (eds), *Handbook of Qualitative Research in Education*, 2nd edn, 486–503, Chichester: Edward Elgar.

Cortazzi, M. & Jin, L. (2020b), "Good Teachers: Visions of Values and Virtues in University Student Metaphors." *KEMANUSIAAN Asian Journal of Humanities*, 27 (2): 145–64.

Cortazzi, M. & Jin, L. (2021), "Metaphorical Conceptualizations of Language: Networks of Meanings and Meta-functions." *International Journal of Education and Literacy Studies*, 9 (1): 2–14.

Cortazzi, M., Jin, L., Kaivanpanah, S. & Nemati, M. (2015), "Candles Lighting up the Journey of Learning." In C. Kennedy (ed.), *English Language Teaching in the Islamic Republic of Iran*, 123–39, London: The British Council.

Craven, R. (1999), *Towards an Appropriate Pedagogy for Aboriginal Children.* Sydney: Allen & Unwin.

Eaude, T. (2008), *Children's Spiritual, Moral, Social, and Cultural Development*, 2nd edn. Exeter: Learning Matters.

Ellis, R. & Shintani, N. (2014), *Exploring Language Pedagogy through Second Language Acquisition Research*. London: Routledge.

Gabryś-Barker, D. & Galajda, D. (eds). (2016), *Positive Psychology Perspectives on Foreign Language Learning and Teaching*. Cham: Springer.

Gibbs, R. W. (2017), *Metaphor Wars: Conceptual Metaphors in Human Life*. Cambridge: Cambridge University Press.

Hall, J. K. & Looney, S. D. (eds). (2019), *The Embodied Work of Teaching*. Bristol: Multilingual Matters.

Holme, R. (2009), *Cognitive Linguistics and Language Teaching*. Basingstoke: Palgrave Macmillan.

Hutchinson, T. & Waters, A. (1987), *English for Specific Purposes: A Learning-Centred Approach*. Cambridge: Cambridge University Press.

Illeris, K. (2016), *How We Learn: Learning and Non-learning in School and Beyond*, 2nd edn. London: Routledge.

Illeris, K. (2018), *Contemporary Theories of Learning: Learning Theorists... in Their Own Words*, 2nd edn. London: Routledge.

Jin, L. & Cortazzi, M. (1993), "Cultural Orientation and Academic Language Use." In D. Graddol, L. Thompson & M. Byram (eds), *Language and Culture*, 84–97, Clevedon: Multilingual Matters.

Jin, L. & Cortazzi, M. (1995), "A Cultural Synergy Model for Academic Language Use." In P. Bruthiaux, T. Boswood & B. Du-Babcock (eds), *Explorations in English for Professional Communication*, 41–56, Hong Kong: City University.

Jin, L. & Cortazzi, M. (1998), "The Culture the Learner Brings: A Bridge or a Barrier?" In M. Byram & M. Fleming (eds), *Language Learning in Intercultural Perspective*, 98–118, Cambridge: Cambridge University Press.

Jin, L. & Cortazzi, M. (2008), "Images of Teachers, Learning and Questioning in Chinese Cultures of Learning." In E. Berendt (ed.), *Metaphors of Learning: Cross-cultural Perspectives*, 177–202, Amsterdam: John Benjamins.

Jin, L. & Cortazzi, M. (2011), "More Than a Journey: 'Learning' in the Metaphors of Chinese Students and Teachers." In L. Jin & M. Cortazzi (eds), *Researching Chinese Learners: Skills, Perceptions and Intercultural Adaptations*, 67–92, London: Palgrave Macmillan.

Jin, L. & Cortazzi, M. (2019), "Investigating Chinese Cultures of Learning through Elicited Metaphor Research." In C.-R. Huang, Z. Jing-Schmidt & B. Meisterernst (eds), *The Routledge Handbook of Applied Chinese Linguistics*, 131–48, London: Routledge.

Jin, L. & Cortazzi, M. (2020), "Reaching for the *Gold Standard*: Metaphors and Good University Teachers." *Chinese Journal of Applied Linguistics*, 43 (2): 131–49.

Joyce, B., Calhoun, L. & Hopkins, D. (eds). (2010), *Models of Learning—Tools for Teaching*, 3rd edn. Buckingham: Open University Press.

Joyce, B., Weil, M. & Hopkins, D. (2018), *Models of Learning - Tools for Teaching*, 3rd edn. Buckingham: Open University Press.

Kövecses, Z. (2005), *Metaphor in Culture, Universality and Variation*. Cambridge: Cambridge University Press.

Lakoff, G. & Johnson, M. (1999), *Philosophy in the Flesh*. New York, NY: Basic Books.

Lakoff, G. & Johnson, M. (2003), *Metaphors We Live by*, 2nd edn. Chicago: The University of Chicago Press.

Leaver, B. L., Davidson, D. E. & Campbell, C. (eds). (2021), *Transformative Language Learning and Teaching*. Cambridge: Cambridge University Press.

Littlemore, J. (2019), *Metaphors in the Mind: Sources of Variation in Embodied Metaphor*. Cambridge: Cambridge University Press.

Liu, D. & Wu, Z. (2015), *English Language Education in China: Past and Present*. Beijing: People's Education Press.

Lucas, B. & Claxton, G. (2010), *New Kinds of Smart: How the Science of Learnable Intelligence Is Changing Education*. Maidenhead: Open University Press.

Lucas, B., Claxton, G. & Spender, F. (2013), *Expansive Education: Teaching Learners for the Real World*. Maidenhead: Open University Press.

MacIntyre, P. D., Gregersen, T. & Mercer, S. (eds). (2016), *Positive Psychology in SLA*. Bristol: Multilingual Matters.

Metger, J. (2015), *Tauira: Maori Methods of Learning and Teaching*. Auckland, NZ: Auckland University Press.

Mitchell, R., Myles, F. & Marston, E. (2019), *Second Language Learning Theories*, 4th edn. London: Routledge.

Nunan, D. (1984), *The Learner-Centred Curriculum: A Study in Second Language Teaching*. Cambridge: Cambridge University Press.

Pihama, L., Tiakiwi, S. J. & Southey, K. (eds). (2015), *Kaupapa Rangahau: A Reader*, 2nd edn. Hamilton, NZ: Te Kotaki Research Institute.

Shaules, J. (2019), *Language, Culture, and the Embodied Mind, a Developmental Model of Linguaculture Learning*. Singapore: Springer.

Seedhouse, P., Walsh, S. & Jenks, C. (eds). (2010), *Conceptualizing Language Learning*. Basingstoke: Palgrave Macmillan.

Van Patten, B., Keating, G. D. & Wulff, S. (2020), *Theories in Second Language Acquisition*, 3rd edn. New York: Routledge.

Wells, G. & Claxton, G. (eds). (2002), *Learning for Life in the 21st Century*. Oxford: Blackwell.

Yuan, Y. & Xie, Q. (2013), "Cultures of Learning: An Evolving Concept and an Expanding Field." In M. Cortazzi & L. Jin (eds), *Researching Cultures of Learning: International Perspectives on Language Learning and Education*, 21–40, Basingstoke: Palgrave Macmillan.

4

Humanistic Motivation and Transformative Language Engagement

Zi Wang

Introduction

Against the backdrop of globalization, the field of language education has witnessed increasing ascendence of instrumentalist views of language and language learning propelled by neoliberal ideologies associated with global capitalism. In the global economy, there is the tendency for a person to be perceived as a bundle of skills and for language to be commodified as a soft skill and seen as a form of capital (Heller 2010; Holborow 2012). Such a neoliberal emphasis on the value of a language "in terms of its usefulness in achieving specific utilitarian goals, such as access to economic development or social mobility" (Wee 2008: 32) has given rise to market-driven language education agendas (Leung & Scarino 2016) and marginalized humanistic approaches toward language education. The marginalization has the potential to constrain our thinking about the transformative potential of language learning and the fact that many language learners and teachers are motivated to achieve more than just the acquisition of skills (e.g., Muir 2020; Pinner & Sampson 2021; Ushioda 2020).

Indeed, the field of language education has seen a growing number of calls for more humanistic understandings of language learning that see the learner as a whole person and recognize the potential for students to experience personal growth (e.g., Kramsch 2009; Leaver et al. 2021; Leung & Scarino 2016; Ros i Solé 2016; Shaules 2019; The Douglas Fir Group 2016).

Recently, motivation research has also come to place more emphasis on taking a humanistic view, which involves understanding the subjective world of the language learner and the ways that learning motivations are shaped by learners' personal understandings of language as a means for self-transformation and personal growth in multiple dimensions of life (e.g., Clarke & Hennig 2013; Harvey 2017; Ushioda 2011; Wang et al. 2021). Such a view helps illuminate how learners make sense of their engagement with various aspects of the language learning process (Dörnyei 2019) and dynamically shape and regulate their language learning motivation in relation to their broader life motivation (Harvey 2017). From a pedagogical viewpoint, motivation research carried out within a humanistic view also has the potential to provide implications for teachers who aim to create learning environments which encourage learner motivation and self-transformation (Ushioda 2017). Therefore, this chapter adopts a broadly humanistic perspective to answer the following questions and discuss pedagogical implications:

1. How do learners experience transformation in their language engagement?
2. How is learners' language learning motivation influenced by their transformative experience?

It is worth noting that engagement is used in this chapter as a broad term to refer to a person's personal and subjective experience of language-mediated tasks and activities, which is line with Dörnyei's (2019) understanding of language learning experience from an engagement perspective.

Taking a Humanistic View of Language Learning Motivation

In this section, I discuss a number of humanistically oriented perspectives and concepts in language learning motivation. One key defining element of a humanistic view of motivation is an understanding of the learner as a "thinking and feeling human being with an identity, a personality, a unique history and background" (Ushioda 2009: 220), as captured within Ushioda's person-in-context relational view of emergent motivation. This view recognizes that learners can make personalized use of a language such as "to expand and express our identity or sense of self… to… broaden our experiences and horizons…" (Ushioda 2011: 204). In this sense, it foregrounds the centrality of learner agency, individual meaning making, and the potential for learners to experience a growth orientation that goes beyond satisfying instrumental goals. "Investment" is an additional concept that has humanistic resonance: it refers to a learner's "choice to participate in a social practice"—language learning—and "involves understanding the material and symbolic context in which this choice is made" (Darvin & Norton 2021: 5). The mostly clear humanistic dimension of investment is the importance attributed to learners' subjective social positioning and their self-empowerment through participation in face-to-face communities, as well as imagined communities in the wider world (Norton & Pavlenko 2019).

The ideas of "motivation as ethical formation" and "motivation as ideological becoming" also have a strong humanistic orientation in their emphasis on learner agency, subjectivity, and the personal meaningfulness of language learning within a learner's life (Clark & Hennig 2013; Harvey 2017). "Motivation as ethical formation" is proposed by Clark & Hennig (2013) based on the Foucauldian concept of ethical self-formation which stresses the subject's freedom to become and develop in the historical and social context. They suggest that motivation can arise from a learner's understanding of language learning as a means to transform themselves intellectually, emotionally, and spiritually and to pursue their "ultimate goals of being and becoming in the world" (Clark & Hennig 2013: 88). To continue Clark and Henning's line of discussion and to expand it into a learner's broader life, Harvey (2017) looks at motivation through the lens of Bakhtin's ideological becoming and proposes "motivation as ideological becoming." She sees ideological becoming as "a process of learning to be in the world, of finding one's own voice" (Harvey 2017: 71) through dialogic interactions in the languages of oneself and the other, which is bound to a learner's personal and social growth (Harvey 2016, 2017).

Discussions of the key concepts above have helped bring into focus the intersection of the social and the individual in motivation, and also point to the importance of capturing the meaningful and transformative elements of language learning from learners' own perspective (see also Cortazzi & Jin, this volume). This chapter aligns with the work above in that it takes a person-in-context relational view of motivation, with emphasis on subjectivity, agency and meaning making, and seeks to understand the emergence of learners' aspirations toward personal growth in their language engagement.

In the following sections, I discuss the motivational journeys of three Chinese learners of Japanese drawn from my doctoral research, highlighting different ways in which these learners experienced transformations in their language engagement and how their language learning motivation took on a humanistic orientation.

Overview of the Study

This chapter draws on data from a larger longitudinal qualitative dataset collected as part of my doctoral project which aimed to investigate learners' motivational experiences in multilingual learning. This involved three rounds of in-depth semi-structured interviews (from September 2018 to July 2019) and monthly online communication (from September 2018 and still ongoing) with nineteen Chinese university students who were majoring in Japanese while continuing to study English. They were in their late teens or early twenties during the period of data collection. In the interviews, the participants were asked about their language choice, language perceptions, language engagement experience and life plans, and also asked to plot their motivational trajectories on a blank graph with the x axis being time and y axis being level of motivation from 0 to 10, to stimulate their retrospection and facilitate their narration of their personal experience (Henry 2015). A metaphor, or rather simile, elicitation task "Learning Japanese is like…, because…" was also used in the final round of interview as a supplementary means to approach the participants' perspectives and beliefs (Cameron & Low 1999). In the online communication, the participants were asked monthly to rate their current language learning motivations from 0 to 10 and briefly explain why, which allowed them some space for real-time introspection. The interviews were audio-recorded, transcribed verbatim, and analyzed together with the communication data.

A narrative analysis approach was adopted to look at the content of learners' subjective experience and look for salient themes in their stories (Barkhuizen 2015; Duff 2017). I read the data several times carefully and noted the pattern; for participants whose Japanese learning motivation emerged out of their language engagement, they also experienced personal transformation(s) of some sort in the process. In the course of analysis, I identified themes in relation to types of language engagement experience, namely language engagement as academic experience, as aesthetic experience, and as ethical experience. Then I examined and triangulated the data concerning their language engagement experience specifically to co-construct a narrative of the emergence of motivation along with the personal transformations. For this chapter, I selected three participants Xiaotang, Xiaoming, and Cheng Yuanyi (pseudonyms) as the focal cases, because their personal stories work as powerful illustrations of the transformative potential of language learning. Below I include a vignette for each participant to provide a summary of their background information and their personal journey relevant to this study:

> **Xiaotang** was admitted to the Japanese programme rather than to her first choices such as law. In the beginning of university, she was having a difficult time learning Japanese but gradually built up her self-confidence. At the same time, she failed to transfer to study law and had to stay in her current degree programme.
>
> **Xiaoming** slightly disfavored fandom of Japanese anime in junior high school, but later became a fan himself in senior high school when he felt socially isolated. Then, he started learning Japanese himself and carried on to read Japanese literature. He applied to major in Japanese at university and was successful in his application.
>
> **Cheng Yuanyi** held negative attitudes toward Japan in junior high school for historical and political reasons. In senior high school, he felt lonely and started watching Japanese anime, which changed his previous attitudes toward Japan. He taught himself Japanese and considered emigrating to Japan. He applied to major in Japanese at university and was successful in his application.

Experiencing Transformation and Motivation: Three Stories

In this section, I highlight three types of subjective experiences identified in the participants' engagement with Japanese language and culture in relation to their transformation and motivation. I use Xiaotang's experience to illustrate how a learner's self-confidence can be transformed and their motivation enriched to involve future life goals in their process of engaging in language learning as an academic activity. Then, I draw on Xiaoming's case to show how a learner's aesthetic engagement with language and culture can contribute to their enhanced self-understanding as well as give rise to motivation to learn the language. Lastly, I refer to Cheng Yuanyi's story to demonstrate how a learner can reshape their understanding of language, culture, and nation and reposition themselves socially and develop their motivation through their ethical experience of language engagement.

Boosting Self-confidence in Academic Experience

Involuntarily positioned as a Japanese major, Xiaotang started university with a lack of motivation to learn Japanese. Japanese was not among her first choices in university application but her grade in the College Entrance Exam was not high enough for her to be admitted to other programs that she applied for such as Chinese, history, and law. With an initial expectation that "Japanese looks a lot like Chinese, and I thought it would be easy to learn," she realized that Japanese was actually difficult and considered the beginning of her Japanese learning a "low (motivation) period":

1. Upon entering university, I was like we would learn from scratch anyway and I could have some fun first. Then in October, I realized the others were so good and that I needed to work hard. As my learning continued, I felt I was so bad and did not want to learn. I felt so bad and frustrated. I felt frustrated and at the same time I wanted to take the University Transfer Exam, so I decided to put Japanese on hold.

It can be seen from the above extract that her lack of perceived competence in Japanese caused feelings of frustration and undermined her motivation to learn Japanese. At the same time, she was kept busy with her plan to transfer to study law at another university. However, as she carried on with her study in the Japanese department, she was engaged in self-reflection which deepened her self-understanding and helped with her self-confidence, as can be seen from the extracts from our communication data below listed in chronological order:

2. Japanese (motivation) nine (out of ten): I am often criticized by the teacher and my proficiency is much lower compared to my classmates. I don't think it should be like this. I think I actually have some gift in language learning. I am indeed not working hard enough or being efficient in learning. I need to work hard from now to prove that I have the competence and to surprise others, hahaha… (November 2018)
3. Japanese (motivation changed) from six to nine: I failed the mid-term. I was disappointed at my ability to learn Japanese. My learning motivation was definitely affected to some extent. However, from my experience in junior high and senior high, I have known that I am the type of student that is slow at first and gets better and better later, so I still have confidence in myself. I have been trying different ways of learning after consulting my teachers and other classmates to adapt myself. (December 2018)
4. Japanese (motivation) nine: Nothing special, just learning as previously. But recently the teacher praised me for my progress, so I am pleased and want to keep making progress… (April 2019)

5. Japanese (motivation) seven: The mid-term results are satisfactory and I have to some extent got the hang of Japanese. I am preparing for the (University Transfer) Exam, so I am putting Japanese on hold as long as I can keep up. (May 2019)
6. Japanese (motivation) nine: Since my Japanese learning came on track, I haven't felt it is as difficult. The more I learn, the more confident I feel. I am not in pain, so I start to love learning. I also got encouragement and affirmation from teachers… (June 2019)

The above five extracts displayed her change in self-confidence over a seven-month time span from November 2018 to June 2019. In extracts (2) and (3), her sense of incompetence in Japanese was reinforced by the criticism she received in class, her negative comparison with her peers, and her failure in the mid-term exam in the first term. During her unpleasant learning process, she started to reflect on herself as a learner in terms of her language learning potential and her own learning style and proactively regulated her learning. As her study continued, she began making progress, getting good exam results, and receiving positive feedback, which helped build her self-confidence.

She developed her self-confidence not only as a language learner, as demonstrated previously, but also as a whole person, as was said by herself in the final round of interview:

7. Interviewer:… How has learning multiple languages influenced your personal growth or development?

> Xiaotang: First of all, it has enhanced my self-confidence. I used to think that I knew nothing and hadn't learned much. Now I think, wow, if I tell people from outside (our department) that I can speak Japanese, they will think I am cool. Then I think my existence is meaningful and has value. About my future career development, I think it has provided me with more thoughts.

As can be seen in extract (7), she developed a stronger sense of confidence in herself in the process of learning Japanese. There was another comment from her that "a language is a distinctive strength. If I can (speak it), I feel that I have a skill and that helps boost my self-confidence." Therefore, being able to speak Japanese gave her a sense of distinctiveness and further contributed to her sense of meaning and value as a human being existing in the world.

In this way, Xiaotang transformed from the formerly unconfident person to the more confident person while progressing in Japanese learning. Along with her increased sense of competence in Japanese, the boost in self-confidence extended from her perception of herself as a learner of Japanese to her perception of herself as a person and facilitated the integration of Japanese into her future career plan. As can be summarized from the three rounds of interview, the main focus of her future plan changed from taking the University Transfer Exam to study law, to doing research on law or Japan studies, and then to researching Japan-related topics after failing to transfer. Her perception of Japanese was expanded from Japanese mainly as a subject of study shown in extracts (1) to (6) to include Japanese as a means to be distinctive from others and as a possible part of her future career in extract (7). In summary, alongside her increased self-confidence and failed attempt to transfer, Xiaotang's Japanese learning motivation developed from a focus on the current learning engagement to also include her future plan.

Enhancing Self-understanding in Aesthetic Experience

Xiaoming's motivation to learn Japanese started from his need for emotional support and self-expression in his transition from junior high school into senior high school. He originally held a negative attitude toward Japanese anime because in junior high "there were some classmates who were talking about anime all the time and I found that really annoying," but his later contact with anime upon his matriculation into senior high changed his previous attitude toward anime and initiated his Japanese learning motivation:

8. They (My classmates) had their small groups when they entered senior high and I was excluded. Then I felt extremely lonely and had contact with anime. Then I found there was something very healing in anime. My first anime was *Natsume's Book of Friends*[1] and I found it very heart-warming… In my first year of senior high, I was in that environment and found those things less aversive, so I planned to start learning Japanese. My initial motivation was because of anime. Later I found that anime alone was not enough… I wanted to learn Japanese and use Japanese to express my thoughts so no one around me would understand what I was saying and then I could be free to express my thoughts. Whether in writing or in speaking, no one would judge me. This was my second motivation… I think Japanese literature, through its language and my understanding, conveyed the sense (of detachment) to me. That was in line with my state of mind

in that tough time of senior high... At that time, I was thinking, I would probably learn some Japanese literature in the future, because it was in line with my state of mind. That was another change of my purpose, and my purpose has remained that way...

The above extract is Xiaoming's answer regarding his choice to major in Japanese at university. When he went to senior high school and felt lonely in the new environment, he watched *Natsume's Book of Friends* and derived emotional and social support from the "healing" and "heart-warming" anime. He later further commented on the aesthetics of Japanese language: "the pronunciation of Japanese is very healing"; "I was touched by the whole sound system and that made me think that it might be nice to learn Japanese." The same adjective "healing" was used to describe firstly Japanese anime and then Japanese language, suggesting that he might have projected his aesthetic appreciation of and emotional attachment with Japanese-mediated cultural products onto the Japanese language. After some contact with Japanese anime, he sought out more engagement with Japanese language by learning the language and reading the literature. Also, in times of his interpersonal struggle, he desired to express himself in a language other than Chinese, his mother tongue which he shared with his peers, and English, a foreign language which he couldn't speak well. Japanese as a potential alternative already present in his entertainment thus became his new target medium for self-expression.

As his contact with Japanese culture—including anime and literature—increased and his Japanese language learning progressed, he came to appreciate the aesthetic aspect of Japanese language and culture, perceived a sense of detachment and personally identified with it. The two extracts below are elaborations of his perception of the sense of detachment:

9. In the process of practicing, I noticed that there is something special about the Japanese language. That is, if you literally translate some expression with a fixed grammar into Chinese, you will know there is an idea in it, an idea of detachment. For instance, "this is what it is" in Japanese is "to iu kotodesu"... I think this expression contains a sense of detachment and I think it was in line with my state of mind back then.
10. Back in senior high, I was among the minority and I thought and did things differently from others, so I was isolated... My personality was that I preferred to be on my own and not to bother others or be bothered by others... so in Japanese literature such as Haruki Murakami's, there

are few characters in a long story. I think the sense of detachment is very obvious... which was in line with my state of mind. Reading (Japanese) literature has greatly influenced my personality and thinking...

In extracts (8)–(10), Xiaoming situated his Japanese learning motivation in the context of his social isolation and stressed the congruence between his state of mind and the perceived sense of detachment in Japanese language and culture. Such identification with the perceived essence of Japanese for Xiaoming was a process of getting to know himself better and deeper through engaging in Japanese listening, speaking, reading, and writing in the form of watching anime, reading literature, admiring the language, and expressing himself. In this sense, he was able to manage the difficult transition through his engagement in Japanese language and culture and self-transformation was taking place in the process: "the sense perceived in Japanese had a quite big influence on my mind in terms of how I got used to being on my own and going my own way without being influenced by others."

Xiaoming gave a simile of learning Japanese being like "looking in the mirror" and stressed its contribution to his self-understanding in terms of his state of mind, his desires, abilities, weaknesses, and plans:

11. Through learning Japanese... I know my desire and what I really like. Then, I see what competence I have. Maybe I am not as good as others at maths or English, but I learn Japanese more quickly than others, which means I have the competence and potential. In this way, I know about myself. Also, I see my weaknesses... Also, through learning Japanese, I reflect on my plans or something like that. For example, things not considered before are reflected in Japanese learning, such as whether I will depend on Japanese (for a living)... and in what state I am now and in what state I want to be in the future. I am gradually coming to be aware of those that emerge in my Japanese learning, so I think it is like looking in the mirror.

In summary, Xiaoming perceived congruence between his own state of mind and his essentialized perception of Japanese language and culture and enhanced his self-understanding in transition. His aesthetic experience in language engagement gave rise to his Japanese motivation and kept it high throughout his learning process from senior high to university, as is made explicit in extract (8) and shown in the motigraph presented in Figure 4.1. From the Japanese learning motivational trajectory, it can be seen that his self-reported motivation was consistently at a high level only except when he had to prepare for the high-stake College Entrance Exam at the end of his senior high days.

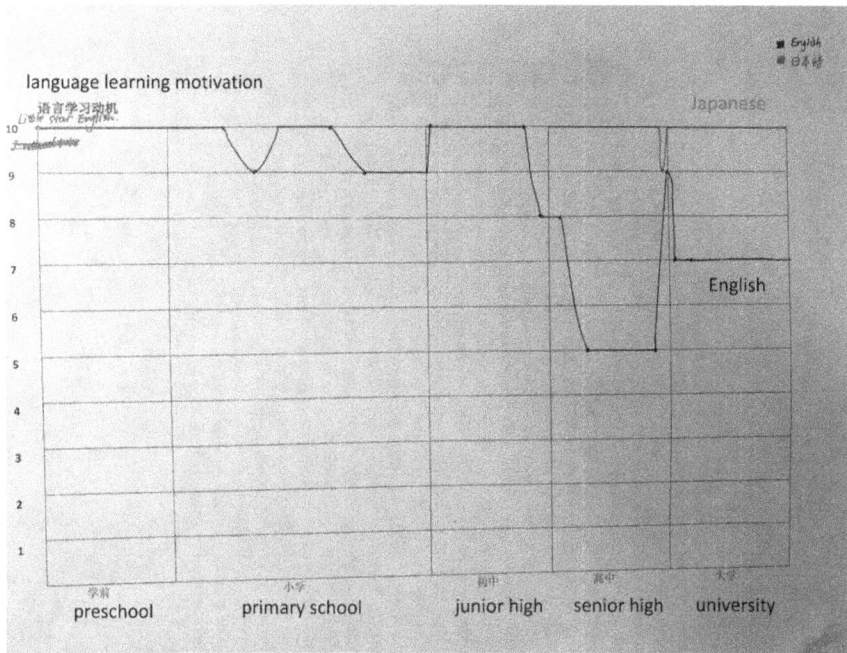

Figure 4.1 Xiaoming Motigraph

Reshaping Social Identity in Ethical Experience

Under the influence of social and educational discourses, Cheng Yuanyi used to hold an unfavorable attitude toward Japan in junior high school: "I received Communist education, grew up under the red flag and learned about the history of Japan's invasion and extremely loathed Japan";

12. I was among the first ones to join the Communist Youth League in my cohort and was a very patriotic person, very passionate about Marxism and Maoism. In junior high, I didn't touch Japanese at all. Nor Japanese products or anime. Back then there was an anti-Japan movement, and I was quite in favor of it.

He described himself as "quite anti-Japan" and stayed away from his peers who liked Japanese cultural products such as anime. Such anti-Japan sentiments led him to reject the possibility of learning the language that he closely associated with Japan, as learning Japanese was perceived to be in conflict with his existing national identity at that time. Therefore, he made the conscious choice not to

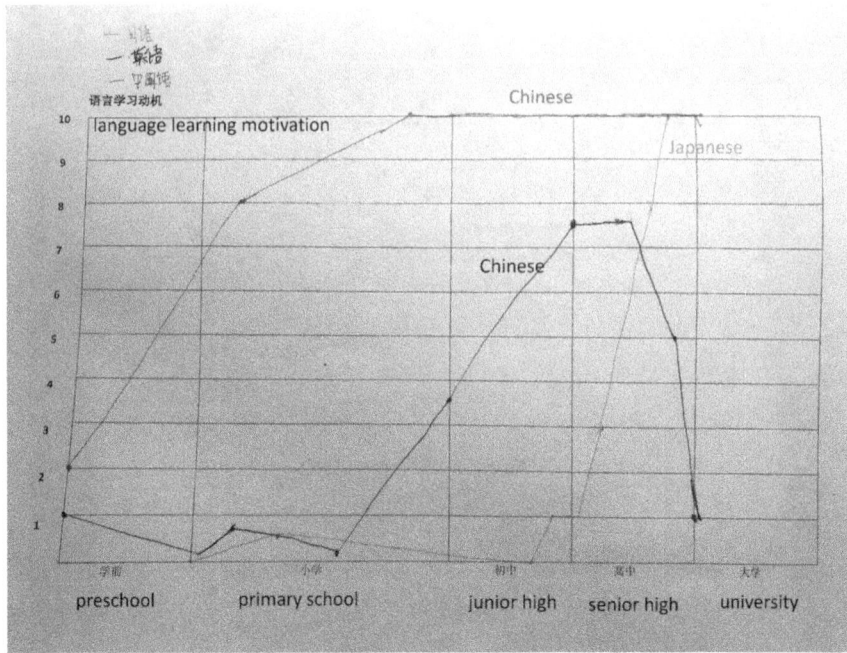

Figure 4.2 Cheng Yuanyi Motigraph

learn Japanese and was not motivated to learn Japanese at all. His motivation to learn Japanese was fairly low at that time (see Figure 4.2).

In his transition from junior high school to senior high school, however, Cheng Yuanyi began to engage in watching Japanese anime. The senior high school he went to was a new environment for him and he did not manage to make new friends, so he felt lonely, did not have much to do, and was recommended by an old friend to watch some Japanese anime. His engagement in watching Japanese anime not only provided him with company in times of social isolation, but also changed his attitudes toward Japanese culture and Japanese language:

13. Because of this (*Akame ga Kill!*[2]), I learned about Japanese people's way of thinking and their creative writing and found their way of thinking amazing… well, first of all, the plot was unpredictable but reasonable. Their value of right and wrong was also new to me. Before that, I had used to think, under the Chinese way of education, that things are either black or white, but the Japanese anime showed otherwise. Many people have their own reasons for doing things and fighting for their ideas even though in the process they may have to hurt others or break some rules.

I found that mind-opening. Also, I was touched more by Japanese shows than Chinese ones. Their emotions are expressed sincerely and accurately, especially with the Japanese language. I think that has to do with their national culture.

As can be seen in the above extract, Cheng Yuanyi learned from the anime a new moral perspective, which he considered to be different from the moral judgement taught at school in China. This "mind-opening" moral and emotional experience was not a single occurrence. Later in senior high, when he was not having a smooth time with his study life and dating life, he watched *Yoguga no Sora*[3] and *Sword Art Online*[4]:

14. First of all, it (*Yosuga no Sora*) gave me a new way of thinking; also, I was attracted by their sincere feelings. I think the value of that country is greatly different from that of the one we are in. That is a free and confident country and I was attracted ... Then I started to take the initiative to learn the language, including the fifty sounds and some simple phrases. I was in senior high and had coursework, so I couldn't learn it systematically, but I learned it on my own in my spare time. Then in the third year of senior high, I was under a lot of pressure at school and my relationship wasn't going smoothly and I watched another one. So my life has been influenced by anime to a great extent. That anime is called *Sword Art Online* and is really good ... one day I didn't go to school. I was quite stressed. I went to get a room in a hotel and stayed there on my own to watch all fifty episodes on TV in one day ...

He escaped from academic and interpersonal frustrations into the world of anime where he found the plot of *Yogura no Sora* to be "broadening my horizon" and "subverting traditional morals" and de-stressed himself by watching *Sword Art Online*. A shift can be seen in his view of and attitudes toward Japan through his intensive engagement with Japanese anime. As can be seen in extracts (13) and (14), he started to project his perception of the virtual world depicted in anime onto his view of Japan: he thought that the value judgement in Japan is different from that in China and that Japan is a free and confident country. Thus, he started to see or imagine Japan in a more positive light and such positive attitude was projected onto Japanese language. The attitudinal shift led him to start learning Japanese in his spare time, as he said in extract (14).

When his interest in Japanese was increasing in senior high, Cheng Yuanyi experienced dissatisfaction with his school life which negatively influenced his view of China and his sense of identity as a Chinese national and made him write in his diary that he wanted to go to Japan:

15. Cheng Yunayi: … I was not happy with the school system. I was not happy with classes. I was not happy that I didn't have freedom. Also, I was in the Student Union. I wasn't happy with how SU dealt with things. I wasn't happy with the teacher in charge. I was a cynic. I felt that the system of the country needed to be fixed to let more people have a better life. That couldn't be achieved so I would have to leave for a while…

Interviewer: So you wanted to go to Japan?

Cheng Yuanyi: I needed to find a way of living that I looked forward to…

In that situation, he had some unpleasant experience in China and was exposed to Japanese anime. With the negative comparisons between values of China and Japan in extracts (13)–(15), Japan became his target country to start a new life: "games and anime reflect a way of living"; "in order to have a better way of living in the future, I needed to go to Japan and stay away from Chinese people." The Japanese anime that he watched challenged his previous understanding of ethics and morality and provided him with new ethical and moral possibilities with which he was able to escape from his personal struggles and construct an imagined ideal world highly related to Japan. Meanwhile, different from the patriotic person described in extract (12), he started to distance himself from Chinese people and his sense of identity as a Chinese national became less salient.

To this point, the perceived tension caused by Japanese learning and his self-positioning as a patriotic Chinese national against Japan was resolved, as his perception of Japanese languaculture was transformed. A moral and ethical dimension was added to his perception of Japanese in addition to the aforementioned geopolitical dimension regarding China-Japan contentions. His motivation thus rocketed to ten out of ten and remained high, as is shown in Figure 4.2. After senior high school, he applied to major in Japanese learning at university and carried on with his Japanese learning: "that world was appealing to me and it is still guiding me now" was his response to why he was in the Japanese department. That response, along with his comment that "till now I still have immense interest in Japanese and this interest will never go away," points to his investment in Japanese learning as well as in his imagined identity in an imagined community.

Emergence of Humanistic Motivation

The three stories presented in this chapter suggest that learners' experiences of language engagement go beyond the L2 learning experience defined predominantly within the formal education setting (Dörnyei 2009, 2019, 2020). Xiaotang's experiences of both failures and successes in exams, both negative and positive teacher feedback and peer comparison, are instances of learner engagement in the immediate formal language learning environment. Xiaoming's and Cheng Yuanyi's stories show that language learning also takes place outside the classroom in a learner's day-to-day life and learner engagement with Japanese-mediated cultural products outside formal education can fuel motivation. In the case of this study, such informal language engagement is made possible largely by the salient presence of the Japanese language and its cultural products in China, in particular the popularity of Japanese anime and manga (Hashimoto 2018). The three participants' data also demonstrate the multi-facetedness and transformative potential of language engagement (Dörnyei 2019): their involvement in the academic, aesthetic, and ethical aspects of language engagement afforded their experiences of transformations in their self-confidence, self-understanding, and self-identity.

The self-transformations experienced in aspects of language engagement interact with language learning motivation through the mediation of learners' changing perceptions of themselves and their relations with language. The transformations of the three participants presented in this chapter were related to Japanese engagement in one way or another and thus to some extent changed their personalized perceptions of Japanese. The academic aspect of language engagement involves learning for academic purposes in formal education, which can pose challenges as well as provide transformative opportunities for learners. For instance, while engaged in formal Japanese learning, Xiaotang transformed her self-confidence not only in the academic domain but also in the global domain, which led her to realize that Japanese is not only a subject of study but also a means for her to be distinctive. The aesthetic experience includes artistically appreciating language in its own form or as part of culture and/or making use of its expressive function (Kramsch 2009; Ros i Solé 2016). The ethical language engagement involves learning about values and ethics presented in foreign-language-mediated cultural products. For learners like Xiaoming and Cheng Yuanyi, cultural products such as Japanese anime and literature provide them with a platform to find emotional and social support and engage with the language aesthetically and ethically. In the platform as a third space, they can shuttle between the perceived self and the presented other through engagement in their emotional, cognitive, and social experiences as multilingual subjects (Kramsch 2009); construct and re-construct their (imagined) identities (Norton & Pavlenko 2019); and experience learning motivation as part of their maturation and self-formation (Clarke & Henning 2013; Harvey 2017). Language engagement can be particularly transformative when learners are in a transitional stage where their views of their self and their social positioning are challenged. This was the case with all the three stories presented in this chapter: when they experienced self-transformations, Xiaotang was in her transition from secondary education to tertiary education and Xiaoming and Cheng Yuanyi were in their transition from junior high to senior high. Having had such transformative experiences, learners tend to see language learning as "a means… to transform themselves in multiple domains—intellectual, emotional and spiritual" (Clarke & Henning 2013: 86). It is worth pointing out that although I presented three stories each of which focuses on one dimension of language engagement, the different dimensions are not mutually exclusive but are in fact interconnected and overlapped with one another.

Through reflecting on language and language learning in their transformative experience, learners develop a humanistic orientation in their motivation that emerges from or is enriched by their language engagement. In other words, learners' language learning motivation is oriented toward the humanistic value of language, or more specifically the transformative potential of language engagement to boost self-confidence, enhance self-understanding, and socially position themselves. Learners' awareness of the transformative potential of language learning emerges from their language engagement and generates motivation for further continued conscious engagement, demonstrating the motivational role of transformative power as a means and as a goal (The Douglas Fir Group 2016). By focusing on what is meaningful to learners and their lives, humanistic motivation incorporates their social identity goals (Norton 2013; Wang et al. 2021), ideological becoming (Harvey 2017), ethical formation (Clarke & Hennig 2013), and much more in terms of their personal development. In the next section, I explore pedagogical implications regarding the role of personal reflections in encouraging humanistic motivation in language learning.

Encouraging Humanistic Motivation

It might seem, from the three stories presented in this chapter, that the emergence of a learner's humanistic motivation is based on their idiosyncratic life experience and that there is not much teachers can do about it. It is true that motivation cannot be engineered or forced, because such humanistic motivation is emergent, as is presented and discussed previously. However, a closer look at the three stories indicates that personal reflections are at the heart of learners' transformative experience and humanistic motivation (Leung & Scarino 2016; Muir 2020; Ros i Solé 2016), which teachers can utilize to encourage the emergence of humanistic motivation.

Xiaotang was aware of the positive impact of her self-reflection on her motivation throughout her university experience. When she reflected on her participation in the research in the last interview, she said: "if you just keep doing something, you might go in the wrong direction, but if you reflect, you will suddenly realize that I shouldn't do that and can change my direction in time. It helps." Her retrospective and introspective self-reflection was initiated and facilitated by her participation in this study (Lamb 2018), as she explicitly commented in the last interview:

16. In the past, I would not analyze in such details. Through this research, I needed to think carefully and retrospect carefully. Afterwards I would go back and reflect if I needed to regulate my learning and things like that.

For Xiaoming and Cheng Yuanyi, while their transformations presented in their stories happened in their early adolescent years, they still pointed to the role of the ongoing reflections in enhancing their self-understanding. Xiaoming commented that participation in the study "was a way to let me know myself" and Cheng Yuanyi also commented on his participation:

17. Sometimes something happened and I didn't pay much attention and thus didn't realize its influence on me, but when you asked, I would think about it and realize maybe that really (had influence). I would have an understanding of myself, including the influence of some things on me. I can't say it (my participation) has really made a difference (to me), but is there anything more delightful than understanding oneself?

Therefore, it seems that allowing learners some time and space for personal reflection and meaning making could help encourage humanistic motivation.

Teachers who are interested in including self-reflection in their teaching need to make it clear to learners that this is a non-judgmental and non-evaluative space for learners to be themselves. Learners need to know that they will not be judged or evaluated for how they feel and what they think to open up in their self-reflection. This would be extremely helpful for students who are in a transitional stage when they are likely to experience struggles in their personal life and/or academic progress, as is the case with the three participants in this chapter. Their motivational journeys and personal transformations were accompanied by both positive and negative emotions and feelings within and outside the classroom, such as frustration, disappointment, (un)happiness, loneliness, and feeling touched and pleased. While positive emotions make people better learners and increase motivation (Helgesen 2016), it is also important for teachers to normalize the presence of and acknowledge the potential of negative emotions experienced within the classroom and beyond (See also Chapter 1, this volume). By doing this, teachers may be able to help facilitate learners' transition in a way that also facilitates the emergence of humanistic motivation.

From the three participants' stories, it can be seen that personal reflections that give rise to humanistic motivation in language learning are not restricted to language learning activities. Rather, those reflections center around learners themselves, such as their life histories, feelings and emotions, competences, personalities, aspirations and identities, thus allowing them to synthesize a personal perspective. While students should be given the time and space to focus their reflection on themselves in their own ways, teachers could use the following set of questions as a starting point for learners' personal reflections:

1. What is my personal story with the language?
2. How has language learning influenced my personal growth and development?
3. How am I feeling now (as a person with multiple roles including a language learner)? Why am I feeling this way?

Questions 1) and 2) aim to elicit learners' retrospection on their language engagement histories and invite them to construct their own narratives or stories to make their life experience personally meaningful (Barkhuizen 2015; Kramsch 2009). Since language engagement is a potentially subversive and empowering experience (Ros i Solé 2016), the two questions would hopefully contribute to learners' realization of their past transformation(s) facilitated by language engagement and/or awareness of its transformative potential. Question 3) encourages learners to think about their current experience as a language learner and as a person with other roles and to explore their relationship with various aspects of language learning process (Dörnyei 2019, 2020). This can be also used as a point of reference and comparison for future reflections, hopefully contributing to their development of self-understanding.

Time commitment of personal reflections can be of concern especially to teachers in formal education settings, and the frequency of personal reflections is indeed one thing worth deliberating on. To illustrate, although Xiaotang found reflections to be helpful, she considered the weekly reflection assignment in her speaking module to be "too frequent" and "boring" and less frequent reflections (one in-depth interview every four or five months) to be "more meaningful." The takeaway message for teachers is that it is not the amount of time but the depth of thinking that matters in encouraging humanistic motivation among learners.

Conclusion

In the chapter, by analyzing the three learner stories, I have highlighted that humanistic motivation emerges from language learners' experience of transformation as learners associate language learning with understanding their own competences, desires, and identities. The findings not only echo the call for a more humanistic view of motivation, but also shed light on the motivational power of transformative language engagement. Looked at from a humanistic perspective, learners' motivation to learn a language is linked to their motivation to develop self-awareness and achieve personal growth. This chapter also provides implications for language teachers to help cultivate learners' humanistic motivation through engaging them in personal reflections.

Notes

1. *Natsume's Book of Friends* tells the journey of a teenager Takashi Natsume, who has the ability to see spirits and is isolated by his peers, to return the contracts in his grandmother's notebook to the spirits.
2. *Akame ga Kill!* tells a story of a young boy who joins an assassin group to fight against the corrupt empire.
3. In *Yosuga no Sora*, the male protagonist has a romantic relationship with his twin sister.
4. *Sword Art Online* tells the story of a teenage boy fighting to beat the game when he and other players are trapped in virtual reality simulation.

References

Barkhuizen, G. (2015), "Narrative Inquiry." In B. Paltridge & A. Phakiti (eds), *Research Methods in Applied Linguistics*, 169–85, London: Bloomsbury.

Benson, P. (2019), "Ways of Seeing: The Individual and the Social in Applied Linguistics Research Methodologies." *Language Teaching*, 52 (1): 60–70.

Cameron, L. & Low, G. (1999), "Metaphor." *Language Teaching*, 32: 77–96.

Clarke, M. & Hennig, B. (2013), "Motivation as Ethical Self-formation." *Educational Philosophy and Theory*, 45 (1): 77–90.

Darvin, R. & Norton, B. (2021), "Investment and Motivation in Language Learning: What Is the Difference?" *Language Teaching*. doi:10.1017/S0261444821000057

Dörnyei, Z. (2009), "The L2 Motivational Self System." In Z. Dörnyei & E. Ushioda (eds), *Motivation, Language Identity and the L2 Self*, 9–42, Bristol: Multilingual Matters.

Dörnyei, Z. (2019), "Towards a Better Understanding of the L2 Learning Experience, the Cinderella of the L2 Motivational Self System." *Studies in Second Language Learning and Teaching*, 9 (1): 19–30.

Dörnyei, Z. (2020), *Innovations and Challenges in Language Learning Motivation*. Oxon: Routledge.

The Douglas Fir Group. (2016), "A Transdisciplinary Framework for SLA in a Multilingual World." *Modern Language Journal*, 100: 19–47.

Duff, P. A. (2017), "Commentary: Motivation for Learning Languages Other than English in an English-Dominant World." *Modern Language Journal*, 101 (3): 597–607.

Hashimoto, K. (2018), "Cool Japan and Japanese Language: Why Does Japan Need 'Japan Fans'?" In K. Hashimoto (ed.), *Japanese Language and Soft Power in Asia*, 43–62, Singapore: Palgrave Macmillan.

Harvey, L. (2016), "'I am Italian in the World': A Mobile Student's Story of Language Learning and Ideological Becoming." *Language and Intercultural Communication*, 16 (3): 368–83.

Harvey, L. (2017), "Language Learning Motivation as Ideological Becoming." *System*, 65: 69–77.

Helgesen, M. (2016), "Happiness in ESL/EFL: Bringing Positive Psychology to the Classroom." In P. D. MacIntyre, T. Gregersen & S. Mercer (eds), *Positive Psychology in SLA*, 305–23, Bristol: Multilingual Matters.

Heller, M. (2010), "The Commodification of Language." *Annual Review of Anthropology*, 39: 101–14.

Henry, A. (2015), "The Dynamics of L3 Motivation: An Interview/observation Based Study." In Z. Dörnyei, P. D. MacIntyre & A. Henry (eds), *Motivational Dynamics in Language Learning*, 315–42, Bristol: Multilingual Matters.

Holborow, M. (2012), "What Is Neoliberalism? Discourse, Ideology and the Real World." In D. Block, J. Gray & M. Holborow (eds), *Neoliberalism and Applied Linguistics*, 14–32, London: Routledge.

Kramsch, C. (2009), *The Multilingual Subject: What Foreign Language Learners Say about Their Experience and Why It Matters*. Oxford: Oxford University Press.

Lamb, M. (2018). "When Motivation Research Motivates: Issues in Long-Term Empirical Investigations." *Innovation in Language Learning and Teaching*, 12 (4): 357–70.

Leaver, B. L., Davidson, D. E. & Campbell, C. eds. (2021), *Transformative Language Learning and Teaching*. Cambridge: Cambridge University Press.

Leung, C. & Scarino, A. (2016), "Reconceptualizing the Nature of Goals and Outcomes in Language/s Education." *Modern Language Journal*, 100 (S1): 81–95.

Muir, C. (2020), *Directed Motivational Currents and Language Education*. Bristol: Multilingual Matters.

Norton, B. (2013), *Identity and Language Learning: Extending the Conversation*. Bristol: Multilingual Matters.

Norton, B. & Pavlenko, A. (2019), "Imagined Communities, Identity, and English Language Learning in a Multilingual World." In X. Gao (ed.), *Second Handbook of English Language Teaching*, 703–18, Switzerland: Springer.

Pinner, R.S. & Sampson, R. J. (2021), "Humanizing TESOL Research through the Lens of Complexity Thinking." *TESOL Quarterly*, 55 (2): 633–42.

Ros I Solé, C. (2016), *The Personal World of the Language Learner*. London: Palgrave Macmillan.

Shaules, J. (2019), *Language, Culture, and the Embodied Mind: A Developmental Model of Linguaculture Learning*. Singapore: Springer.

Ushioda, E. (2009), "A Person-in-Context Relational View of Emergent Motivation Self and Identity." In Z. Dörnyei & E. Ushioda (eds), *Motivation, Language Identity and the L2 Self*, 215–28, Bristol: Multilingual Matters.

Ushioda, E. (2011), "Language Learning Motivation, Self and Identity: Current Theoretical Perspectives." *Computer Assisted Language Learning*, 24 (3): 199–210.

Ushioda, E. (2017), "The Impact of Global English on Motivation to Learn Other Languages: Toward an Ideal Multilingual Self." *Modern Language Journal*, 101 (3): 469–82.

Ushioda, E. (2020), *Language Learning Motivation: An Ethical Agenda for Research*. Oxford: Oxford University Press.

Wang, Z., McConachy, T. & Ushioda, E. (2021), "Negotiating Identity Tensions in Multilingual Learning in China: A Situated Perspective on Language Learning Motivation and Multilingual Identity." *The Language Learning Journal*, 49 (4): 420–32.

Wee, L. (2008), "Linguistic Instrumentalism in Singapore." In R. Rubdy and P. Tan (eds), *Language as Commodity: Global Structures, Local Marketplaces*, 31–43, London: Bloomsbury.

Developing Embodied Learning Activities to Teach English Causatives

David Wijaya

Introduction

Grammar teaching and learning in the second language (L2) classroom is often associated with the teacher dictating a set of prescriptive rules of target grammatical structures along with a list of exceptions to the rules (Tyler 2012). This practice is an application of the generative approach to language which views language as a structural system whose rules and properties are largely abstract and arbitrary. The generative approach also posits that there is an innate language acquisition device in the human mind that is responsible for language acquisition, whilst being disassociated from the rest of cognition (Chomsky 1965). This view of language learning suggests that language acquisition happens as a result of changes in the learner's internal mental state, and grammar teaching that incorporates explanations of abstract linguistic rules may help shape learners' underlying linguistic competence (White 2015; Whong et al. 2013).

Undoubtedly, some rules are quite straightforward and could therefore be relatively easy for teachers to introduce and for learners to learn. Consider, for instance, the rule for the English simple past tense which states that this tense, regularly expressed by the verb ending -ed, is used when we talk about completed past events. However, some other grammatical features have multiple, complex, and less straightforward rules such as English articles, prepositions, and modals. Further, even grammatical structures that seem to have straightforward rules such as the simple past tense have uses that seem to defy the rule. For instance, the notion of completed action in the past may be conveyed through the simple present tense to create a sense of immediacy (e.g., *I was on the bus to my school when someone suddenly **snatches** my phone from my pocket*), whereas the simple past tense form may be used to refer to a present fact to produce a special communicative effect (e.g., *I'm sorry, what **was** your name again?*) (Radden & Dirven 2007).

Whilst attempting to cover all the rules and exceptions relating to a given grammatical feature explicitly is likely to ensure exhaustive treatment of grammatical items, it also becomes more difficult to present a coherent picture of how rules are connected to each other. Consequently, teaching could become tedious and ineffective as learners are cognitively overloaded with this kind of learning task.

In contrast, there is currently increasing interest in embodied views of language and language learning that offer a deeper and potentially more productive way to learn L2 grammar (e.g., De Knop 2020; Giovanelli 2015; Suñer & Roche 2021). Central to embodied views of language learning is the idea that linguistic knowledge is intimately related to our bodily movements and perception, and thus learning a new language can be optimized by utilizing our bodies and perceptual senses. Such a view is particularly prominent within the field of Cognitive Linguistics (CL), which serves as the main theoretical inspiration in this chapter. Given its emphasis on embodied meaning, this chapter argues that CL analyses of linguistic meanings can be used to support embodied learning activities in the L2 classroom and help create the potential for deep learning. The chapter considers the utility of a CL-inspired embodied approach to teaching and learning L2 grammatical constructions and aims to show that such an approach is effective. Taking English periphrastic causative constructions as the target constructions, I shall explore how these constructions can be taught using embodied learning activities.

Cognitive Linguistics (CL) as an Embodied Approach to Language

CL posits that language mirrors our cognitive processes, our highly social nature, and our ordinary interaction and experience with the physical world, pointing to the idea of embodied meaning (Tyler 2012). For example, usage such as "*John is at the peak of his career*" and *Megan will rise to the top in that company* has both social and physical basis: "status is correlated with social power and (physical) power is UP" (Lakoff & Johnson 1980: 17). CL also holds that language is usage-based. This means that language is not innate or genetically endowed; rather, it is learnt through experience as it occurs in a context of use (Ortega et al. 2016; Tyler 2012). By emphasizing meaning and language in use, CL treats linguistic constructions as a range of grammatical choices that language speakers use to achieve communication goals in context (Giovanelli 2015; Wijaya & Hidarto 2018). These core characteristics present CL as an appealing descriptive pedagogical grammar (Giovanelli 2015) and arguably a deep approach to learning grammar as CL offers "more comprehensive, revealing, and descriptively adequate" semantic accounts that can inform L2 grammar instruction (Langacker 2008: 8). CL-grounded embodied instruction can also make grammar teaching and learning more engaging as learners are encouraged to use their bodies and eyes to construct meaning in the L2. As will be elaborated below, engagement with meaning is characteristic of a deep approach to learning (Smith & Colby 2007).

In what follows, I will first consider the concept of causation and provide an overview of English periphrastic causatives from a CL perspective. I will then discuss how CL can be a basis for developing a deep approach to learning grammar and how CL theories are compatible with the notion of embodied cognition. Following this discussion, I will propose a series of embodied learning activities which utilize bodily movements and visuals and which English teachers can use to promote a deeper understanding of the target constructions. Finally, I will present a brief quantitative report on an experimental study that suggests the potential effectiveness of an embodied approach to instructing causatives and thus lend weight to applications of a CL-inspired embodied approach to L2 grammar teaching and learning.

The Notion of Causation

As we go through our daily lives, we often directly and intentionally manipulate objects around us to bring about expected changes of state in the objects, such as shortening a skirt, opening a door. This act is often referred to as causation, a basic concept that we always apply to domains of activity in order to function successfully as humans in the socio-physical world (Lakoff & Johnson 1980). This concept is so fundamental that it is an integral part of the underlying structure of human language (Baron 1973). Causation is expressed in a wide range of constructions in many languages. In English, for example, we say, "The tailor shortened my black trousers," "I tore my black trousers," and "I had the tailor repair my black trousers." These sentences are all termed as "causative constructions." In English language teaching (ELT), the first two types of sentences, which are labelled as a morphological causative construction and a lexical causative construction, respectively, are usually taught as vocabulary items and instances of simple past tense. The third sentence is a syntactic periphrastic causative construction that consists of a causative verb (e.g., *make*, *have*, and *get*) that controls a complement clause (e.g., bare infinitive and *to*-infinitive), and is taught as a grammatical structure.

A periphrastic causative conveys the idea that a CAUSER does something to a CAUSEE to generate an EFFECT. This construction is arguably more complex than the other two types of causative construction as it involves knowledge of which causative verb to use, and how to construct the complement in order to convey what causation has actually occurred. This complexity poses great difficulty to even advanced second language (L2) learners (Gilquin 2010, 2016; Wijaya & Winstin 2021). For instance, how would we explain to our L2 students the differences among the following sentences?

1. My dad had me clean the bathroom.
2. My dad made me clean the bathroom.
3. My dad made me cry.
4. My dad got me to clean the bathroom.

First language (L1) speakers of English intuitively know that the sentences are different in meaning from each other but explaining what each sentence means and how it differs from the others to L2 learners of English could be challenging. Many materials developers and ELT practitioners in general are aware of this and have proposed definitions and rules of causative constructions. However, the definitions and rules commonly found in ELT resources are less than comprehensive and accurate, and are mostly concerned with the structural patterns, with very little attention given to what each causative verb means and when to use them (Gilquin 2010). For instance, in explaining how the three verbs are not identical in meaning, Azar and Hagen (2016) state that *make* is used if the causee has no option because of the causer's insistence, *have* is used if the causer asks the causee to do it, and *get* is used if the causer is able to persuade the causee. The meaning description provided for *make* might be helpful to understand sentence (1). However, it cannot be used to explain sentence (3), which is a more frequently used *make* construction (Gilquin 2010). The meaning descriptions for *have* and *get* are obscure and may lead learners to (wrongly) assume that to decide which of the two verbs to use, they only need to observe if the causer had to provide a good reason to cause the causee to perform an action, which may not always be the case. Azar and Hagen (2016) also assert that there is little or no meaning difference between the passive causatives *get* and *have*, disregarding the pragmatic aspects and lexical preferences of the two causative verbs. An equally important limitation lies in the way these constructions are represented: the sole use of language in communicating explanations. As will be shown and elaborated later, periphrastic causatives carry abstract conceptual meaning. Therefore, exclusive reliance on verbal descriptions or rules limits students' learning experience, and this will result in either simplistic or inadequate knowledge of the constructions in question.

CL Accounts of English Causative Constructions

As introduced earlier in the chapter, CL posits that the language we use reflects our cognitive processes and interaction with the socio-physical world. Cognitive linguists maintain that periphrastic causatives are a linguistic realization of a cognitive concept referred to as the action chain. This concept "reflects a transmission of energy from an entity (human being, animal, concrete, object, abstract concept, etc.) to one or several entities" (Gilquin 2010: 61). An action chain has a head, which is the source of energy. The head transmits the energy to another entity, which then transmits the energy to another entity until the energy reaches the tail, where the transmission of energy stops (Langacker 1991). Figure 5.1 illustrates the notion of action chain.

This can be exemplified through sentence (5). In this sentence, David is the head and acts as an agent that initiates the energy transfer. The energy is first transferred to a stone, which corresponds to the role of an instrument. The energy from the stone is then transferred to Goliath, who has the role of a patient and consumes the energy through his dying. This action chain, represented by the diagram in Figure 5.2, can be realized through other constructions such as sentences (6) and (7).

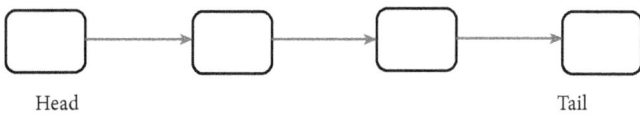

Figure 5.1 Action Chain (adapted from Langacker 1991: 283)

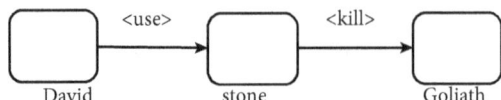

Figure 5.2 Linguistic Realization of an Action Chain (adapted from Gilquin 2010)

5. David killed Goliath with a stone.
6. David used a stone to kill Goliath.
7. David threw a stone at Goliath and Goliath died.

A periphrastic causative extends an action chain by adding another link and, in the case of sentence (5), the original source of energy could be included, as in (8). The periphrastic causative sentence is illustrated by Figure 5.3a. In (8), the head and the original source of energy is God, whereas David receives the energy. Additionally, as pointed out by Gilquin (2010), sentences like (8) can be construed as involving two different events, viz. "causing" and "killing," as illustrated by Figure 5.3b. The action chain in Figure 5.3b represents "a sequence of separate, but causally related events, as indicated by the imbricate boxes" (Gilquin 2010: 64). In the first event, the head, God, with its energy initiates the process of energy transfer that affects David, and in the second event, as a consequence of the first one, David kills Goliath (the jagged arrow signifies the consummation of energy by Goliath, that is the tail of the action chain). Gilquin (2010) also notes that causation can be conceptualized differently through a two-element action chain, where the transfer of energy only occurs between CAUSER and CAUSEE (see Figure 5.3c). In sentence (9), the "dying" component is construed as more prominent than it would otherwise be.

8. God caused David to kill Goliath.
9. David caused Goliath to die.

Further, cognitive linguists hold that constructions that are structurally different must also differ in their meanings and functions, a principle known as "Principle of No Synonymy" (Goldberg 1995), and thus should be considered individually (Gilquin 2010). This is certainly the case with periphrastic causatives that have been traditionally suggested as fundamentally synonymous in meaning as they arise from the same deep structures (Brame 1976). By following the Principle of No Synonymy, cognitive linguists are able to account for the structural and semantic aspects that differentiate the constructions from each other.

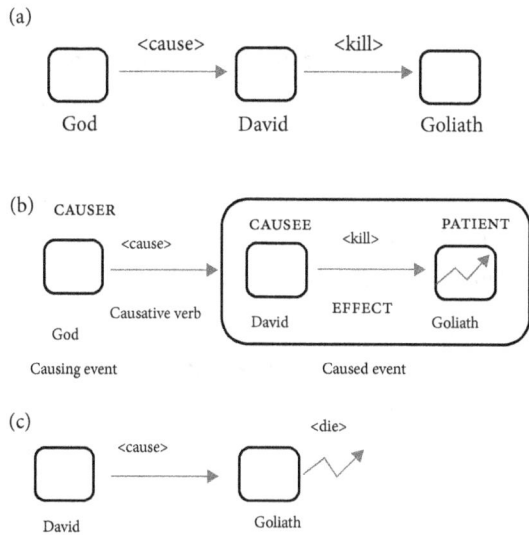

Figure 5.3 An Action Chain of Causativization (adapted from Gilquin 2010: 65)

Applying the natural semantic metalanguage approach to English periphrastic causatives, Wierzbicka (2006) argues that every verb in the constructions reflects the emphasis on preserving personal autonomy in interpersonal relationships that is a core characteristic of Anglo culture. That is, the choice of causative verbs depends on how a person's personal autonomy is treated and on how the power relationship between CAUSER and CAUSEE is conceived. Even in hierarchical relationships where causal events often occur (e.g., the one between a waiter and a customer, the one between a parent and a child, and the one between a boss and a subordinate), the CAUSEE's personal autonomy should not be neglected. In this kind of relationship, the CAUSEE acknowledges that they have to be willing and ready to take the CAUSER's instruction or directions, and the CAUSER, despite having authority over the CAUSEE, has to recognize the CAUSEE's personal autonomy. In other words, although the CAUSEE would not say, "I don't want to do it" to the CAUSER who has expressed their will, the CAUSEE cannot be expected to do whatever the CAUSER wants the CAUSEE to do. This kind of relationship is implied by causative *have*, as exemplified in sentence (10). On the other hand, in a situation where the CAUSER has no such power or authority over the CAUSEE, the CAUSER is aware of the possibility of the CAUSEE refusing to do the CAUSER's will. Therefore, the CAUSER needs to do something to influence the CAUSEE. If that is successful, the CAUSEE willingly carries out the CAUSER's will. This is what is implied by causative *get* and exemplified in sentence (11). In some situations, personal autonomy is abrogated by the CAUSER, resulting in the CAUSEE feeling under pressure and unwillingly perform something the CAUSER wants the CAUSEE to do. This sort of situation is captured by causative *make* and illustrated in sentence (12).

10. The boss had her secretary arrange her schedule for tomorrow.
11. I got my cousin to take me to the airport.
12. The robber made the boy give him his money.

Although revealing, these analyses are focused only on interpersonal causatives. Additionally, register is not considered in these analyses. That is, it is not mentioned whether a certain causative verb occurs more frequently in writing or in speech. Analyzing naturally produced language data, Gilquin (2010) agrees that causative *make* expresses coercion, as in sentence (12). However, she also found that it is mostly used to convey that something happens to the CAUSEE independent of its will. The CAUSEE can be either an animate or inanimate object, as illustrated in sentences (13) and (14).

Further, she found the causative *get* conveys difficulty and effort. This explains why sentence (11) is felicitous: the CAUSER (i.e., I) needs to make effort to persuade the CAUSEE to perform his will. Sentence (15) may serve as a clearer example where it is noticeable that the CAUSER expresses their effort and difficulty through the word *manage*. Sentence 17 also conveys the same meaning since doing homework requires effort. Causative *have*, on the other hand, often refers to professional service involving payment, as exemplified in sentences (16) and (18). She also found that causatives *get* and *have* (as in sentences 17 and 18) often occur with a past participle in informal speech and rarely in writing.

13. That movie made me cry.
14. Let's make it happen!
15. We managed to get him to share his cooking secret.
16. We had Barbara, who is an architect, build this lovely house.
17. I'll try to get my homework done tonight.
18. My mom always has her nails done at that nail salon.

The differences in syntax (i.e., complementation and passivization) also entail meaning and functional differences. Levshina, Geeraerts, and Speelman (2013) observe that the different complements "reflect different degrees of integration of the causing and caused events" (p. 829). A present participle indicates that the caused event is construed to remain for some time (or be in progress) after it is activated by the causing event. This complement only appears in *get* and *have* constructions such as (19) and (20). Also, it attracts verbs of movement such as *go* and *run* and verbs of position such as *stand* and *sit* (Gilquin 2010).

19. Let's get Uncle Roger going about how to cook proper Asian dishes.
20. Let's burn some firewood. Have a little fire going.

A *to*-infinitive suggests that the causing event and the caused event are spatiotemporally distinct. The *to* in the *to*-infinitive encodes a path-goal configuration and therefore is connected to the preposition *to* (Langacker 2002). To reach a goal, a doer has to tread through time and space, with some effort. Given this conceptualization, among the three causative verbs addressed in this chapter, the *to*-infinitive only occurs with causative *get*, whose conceptual meaning is associated with effort and difficulty and yields an indirect and less immediate causal relation (Verspoor 1996). Such spatiotemporal distinction is not assumed if the non-finite complement is a bare infinitive, and as a result, the causal relation is "immediate," "very direct," and construed as "spatially and temporally contiguous" with a focus on its resultant state (Verspoor 1996: 434). As such, this kind of causal relation only occurs with causatives *make* and *have*. For instance, we can imagine in sentence (13) that the crying immediately takes place after perhaps a saddening scene is viewed by the CAUSEE. On the other hand, in causatives with past participle, the CAUSEE is backgrounded and therefore not mentioned, similar to passive constructions (Levshina et al. 2013). For instance, in sentence (18), the CAUSEE is presumably a manicurist, but it is not mentioned because it is less important than the caused event itself (i.e., the nails done).

Translating Linguistic Theory into Pedagogical Practice: Embodied Cognition and Embodied Learning Activities

CL-Grounded Grammar Teaching as a Deep Approach to Learning Grammar

In this section, I aim to connect a CL-informed view of grammar with a deep approach to learning. Using the framework developed by Marton and Säljö (1976), Smith and Colby (2007) define a deep approach to learning as an approach that directs students' attention to meaning, helps them construct hypotheses about a given concept, and fosters their intrinsic interest in learning, thereby leading to deeper processing. This stands in contrast to a surface approach to learning in which students are simply instructed to identify and memorize "details" such as rules. As mentioned at the outset of this chapter, teaching grammar at surface levels (i.e., by having students memorize rules and practice using the target language through mechanical drills) has been the dominant practice in L2 classrooms (Tyler 2012). Although interest in applying a task-based approach is increasing, the presentation of grammatical structures still tends to revolve around rules and exceptions. CL, on the other hand, treats grammar as meaningful, central to language use, and therefore providing more comprehensive and revealing grammatical accounts (Langacker 2008). A CL approach equips students with analytical tools that can point students to the underlying meaning and function of a given grammatical construction in naturally occurring discourse (Tyler 2012). As such, it helps students construct and convey meaning as opportunity to use the target language arises.

As elaborated above, cognitive linguists maintain that language reflects general cognitive processes, and conceptual meaning has grounding in humans' bodily experience and interaction with their socio-physical world. Thus, CL theories have been considered as some of the first theories that support the notion of embodied cognition in cognitive science (Barsalou 2008). This notion holds that "our bodies" movements through and interactions with their immediate physical environment influence the ways in which our minds operate (Giovanelli 2015: 43). Most linguistic structures are not seen as arbitrary; rather, they are motivated by "recurring patterns of embodied experience (i.e., image schemas), which are often metaphorically extended" (Gibbs 2005: 12). If language is motivated, the use of a given linguistic construction can be explained meaningfully. We have seen above how periphrastic causative constructions can be accounted for, and why a certain periphrastic causative can mean a certain thing, which distinguishes it from the other periphrastic causatives. The question is then how do language teachers engage their students with these constructions? If we recognize the embodied nature of cognition, our instruction should employ embodied learning activities.

Embodied learning activities refer to activities that make use of speech, bodily movement, and physical visualization (Giovanelli 2015). These three features can serve as learning resources that can help students to make and express meaning in the classroom. Using the body for language learning has received empirical backing from research in neuroscience and cognitive science

(Macedonia & Mueller 2016; Macedonia 2019). As listed in Atkinson (2010), some important findings of research in those two fields include:

- The brain areas responsible for language get activated during sensorimotor experience (Bonda et al. 1994)
- Brain "motor regions" activate when we read action words that refer to our body parts (e.g., kicking, licking, and picking) (Hauk et al. 2004)
- A sub-set of neurons that are activated when we do a physical action is also activated when we perceive someone doing the same action, a phenomena referred to as "mirror neurons" (Gallese & Goldman 1998; Rizzolatti & Craighero 2004)
- Embodiment effects are present in memory (Glenberg 1997)
- Embodied experience with objects helps us understand them (Carlson & Kenny 2005)

The notion that the body can play an important role in learning would not be something new to many language teachers. Many teachers will have used role-plays and drama activities in their language classrooms. In those activities, they teach gestures that L2 speakers use to enhance communication and encourage their students to incorporate gestures into their L2 speech. Another way to use gesture in the classroom is to utilize a technique called total physical response (TPR) (Asher 1988). However, Littlemore (2009) points out that TPR has not been used to teach abstract grammatical concepts and is not a communicative approach. There needs to be a pedagogy that utilizes CL-informed gesture to learn abstract concepts and can be combined with a more communicative approach such as Task-based Language Teaching.

Such a pedagogy has been developed by Jean-Rémi Lapaire, a French cognitive linguist. He developed a kinesic approach to learning abstract grammatical concepts called *kinegrams* (Lapaire 2007). He argues that grammatical concepts contain perceptual and motoric equivalents that can give rise to meaningful imagistic-kinetic representations. The imagistic-kinetic representations of a certain grammatical concept can be expressed through metaphoric gestures referred to as *kinegrams*. Through this kinegrammatic approach, inherently abstract grammatical concepts are given concrete shape, making them "graspable" by learners. According to Giovanelli (2015), the kinegrammatic approach is an instance of what Holme (2012) refers to as "actual embodied experience" as kinegrams allow learners to experience conceptual meaning through active physical movement. Giovanelli (2015) adds that learners could also benefit from visualization strategies such as diagrams and pictures that externalize concepts. In this way, learners get "virtual embodied experiences," as opposed to "actual embodied experiences" (Giovanelli 2015: 54).

Creating Embodied Learning Activities to Teach English Causatives

The embodied learning activities for teaching and learning English causatives that I will present here optimally use the body and the eye. That is, following the embodied learning activities that Giovanelli (2015) proposes for teaching other grammatical concepts, they utilize learners' physical movement (actual embodied learning activities) and visual perception through diagrams and pictures (virtual embodied learning activities).

As the notion of action chain is a basic cognitive concept of causatives, in teaching periphrastic causatives, teachers should begin with it first. In fact, the virtual embodied learning activities proposed in this chapter will utilize the diagrams in Figures 5.3b and 5.3c. Given the embodied nature of the notion, any actual embodied learning activity that highlights the transfer of energy from one entity to another is appropriate for teaching the concept. In the classroom, the teacher could briefly explain to the students that human language has strong bases in how we perceive and experience the socio-physical world, and to better understand the meaning and function of a linguistic structure, we should first understand the physical concept underlying the structure. The teacher, then, could make use of readily available resources in the school to introduce the concept of action chain. For instance, the teacher could demonstrate a domino effect by putting a row of three books upright, with a gap separating each book. After pushing the first book with a finger, the subsequent book in line will be knocked over, hitting the last book and causing all the books to fall to the ground. The teacher then presents the diagram in Figure 5.1 and points out that the teacher is the head and the tail is the ground. The teacher introduces the concept of action chain and explains that the energy comes from the head, transferred to the first book and so on, and the ground as the tail consummates the energy. The teacher tells students that this concept is realized in causative constructions and shows them some sentences such as (5), (6), and (7), along with an accompanying picture of David and Goliath and explains how the concept underlies the sentences.

The teacher now informs the students that today they are going to learn one type of causative constructions called analytic causative constructions. Then, the teacher gives an example sentence as in (21), performs it by putting scrunched paper on her hand and blowing it, and asks the students to make scrunched paper and do the same thing. The teacher may discuss briefly the connection between sentence (21) and the concept of action chain. The teacher then tells the students that the construction X *make* Y V$_{inf}$ is an analytic causative construction and *make* is a causative verb. The teacher then points the students to the meaning underlying the *make* construction, emphasizing that this causative is used to represent an involuntary action (i.e., an action that happens independently of a doer's will). To help students better understand this meaning and to enable them to use the construction meaningfully, the students can be shown pictures and statements that can affect them, and they should make sentences using the *make* construction to respond to the pictures and statements after they are affected. Pictures such as joke memes can generate the sentence "The joke made me laugh," whereas pictures of news clippings can generate sentences such as "this news made me feel (sad)," depending on the content of the news. The teacher concludes this activity by restating the meaning of causative *make*.

21. I made the paper fly away.

Still using the diagram in Figure 5.3b, the teacher then explains to the students that the meaning of causative *make* can also be extended to the notion of "coercion" and that it is synonymous to "force." On a PowerPoint slide, the teacher shows sentence (12) with Figure 5.3b and an image depicting a robber with a knife and a boy that is handing over money (see Figure 5.4 below) to enhance explanation. Additional sentences with accompanying pictures could

Figure 5.4 A Kinegram of Someone Making Someone Else Do Something

be presented to reinforce this knowledge. In linking the notion of coercion to the notion of involuntary action, the teacher emphasizes that similar to sentence (21), the CAUSEE in sentence (12) performed an involuntary action. That is, the CAUSEE did not actually want to do it but did it anyways. The teacher could point to the CAUSER's frown as a clue that the CAUSER forces the CAUSEE to do it.

The teacher now introduces another causative verb, namely causative *have*. In introducing the conceptual meaning of *have*, the teacher explains that this verb often refers to professional service that deals with payment while showing sentences (16) and (18) with accompanying pictures and Figure 5.3b. An example of a kinegram as shown in Figure 5.5 could be used to offer a way for students to explore this meaning. Students' attention could be drawn to the hand pointing gesture, a gesture that one usually makes when ordering one's subordinate to do something. The teacher also highlights the relationship between the CAUSER and the CAUSEE, which makes ordering appropriate.

Finally, the teacher introduces causative *get* through sentences (11), (15), and (17) and their accompanying pictures. After explaining that this verb expresses difficulty and effort, the teacher shows Figure 5.6 that depicts a boy with his hands kept together and a girl. As can be seen in the speech bubbles, the boy is asking the girl to do something, and the girl agrees. The teacher also indicates the relationship between the boy and the girl (i.e., between friends). Students then are pointed toward the boy's hands and told that we often make this gesture when we make a request. Making a request is different from ordering someone in that the former requires more effort than the latter.

Figure 5.5 A Kinegram of Someone Having Someone Else Do Something

Figure 5.6 A Kinegram of Someone Getting Someone Else to Do Something

The teacher now raises students' awareness of the complement of causative *get* by asking them the structural difference between the constructions [X *make* Y do Z], [X *have* Y do Z], and [X *get* Y to do Z]. The teacher explains that the *to*-infinitive indicates that the caused event in causative *get* is perceived as occurring less immediately due to the effort and difficulty experienced by the CAUSER, whereas the bare infinitive in causatives *make* and *have* represents a caused event that takes place immediately. To help students understand these meanings, the teacher could ask two students to come up and perform role plays that represent the three constructions, and students are asked if the CAUSER is making effort to cause the CAUSEE to perform their will. Expressions that express persuasion (e.g., *I wanted to know if you could do this*) could be included in the dialogue for [X *get* Y to do Z], whereas expressions that convey coercion (e.g., Do it or I will ...) and directive (e.g., please do this) could be included in the dialogues for [X *make* Y do Z] and [X *have* Y do Z], respectively. Role plays like this could get students engaged more fully in the learning process and reinforce the conceptual meanings of the causative verbs.

The teacher informs the students that in informal speech, *have* and *get* constructions are often used in the passive voice with past participle. To teach the passivized causatives *get* and *have*, the teacher could show Figure 5.7 and tell students that in these passive causatives the focus is given to the caused event (as indicated by the thick outline) and the CAUSEE is not mentioned because it is

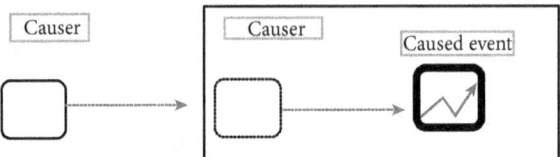

Figure 5.7 A Diagram of the Passivized Causative Construction (adapted from Gilquin 2010)

not important (as indicated by the small dashes). The teacher also points out that in passive causative *get* the subject is very often the CAUSEE him- or herself and shows sentence (17) as an example. To strengthen students' knowledge about this, the teacher could show some visual realizations of these constructions. For instance, a picture of a food delivery guy handing over a meal box to a lady could be used to generate the sentence "*The lady had the meal delivered*," and a picture of a boy struggling to do his assignment and another picture of the same boy looking happy with his homework done could be used to generate the sentence "*He got his homework done*."

These embodied learning activities can be combined with pedagogic tasks to further enhance learning and to encourage them to construct meaning. The teacher could begin with [X *make* Y V_{inf}] and [X *have* Y V_{inf}]. Have students think about house chores that they have to do and categorize the chores into two lists: house chores that they do obediently and house chores that they feel forced to do. Then, have them create sentences from the lists using constructions [X *make* Y V_{inf}] and [X *have* Y V_{inf}]. For students to practice using [X *get* Y to do Z] and comparing it with [X *have* Y V_{inf}], create a conversation about twin sisters who are arranging their upcoming birthday party. In the conversation, the twins discuss who they will ask for a favor (e.g., *Let's ask Andy to take our photos*) and who they will hire (e.g., *Let's pay Anita to redesign our old birthday dresses*) to help them throw the party. Based on the conversation, have students create sentences using [X *get* Y to do Z] and [X *have* Y V_{inf}] constructions. For instance, "*The twins will get Andy to take their photos*" and "*They will have Anita redesign their old birthday dresses*." For passivized constructions [X *get* Z done] and [X *have* Z done], have students think of and list some jobs that they have done by themselves in order to save money (e.g., cutting their own hair) and some other jobs that they pay professional people to do because they cannot do them themselves (e.g., fixing water pipes). Then, have them write sentences based on the lists using constructions [X *get* Z done] and [X *have* Z done].

Exploring the Effect of Embodied Learning Activities on Learning Causatives

Like any other instructional approaches, embodied approaches to language teaching and learning also deserve to be subject to empirical scrutiny. From a theoretical perspective, research on the effect of embodied learning activities on the learning of particular grammatical constructions is still scarce, and therefore such research would add to the body of literature on the effectiveness of embodied approaches. From a practical point of view, findings from research could help with teacher buy-in and encourage teachers to reconsider their view of language and how languages are learned. Therefore, in this section, I will present a summary of an experimental study that I conducted to explore the utility of embodied learning activities in instructing the target constructions to Indonesian EFL learners.

As mentioned above, periphrastic causatives pose immense challenge to English L2 learners due to their semantic and syntactic complexities. Wijaya and Winstin's (2021) study on Indonesian EFL learners' knowledge and use of causative constructions showed that learners had difficulty in using causatives *have* and *get* and in producing the complements. Learners also generally struggled to demonstrate sufficient explicit knowledge of the constructions that could have helped them choose the felicitous causative verbs and produce the correct complement. It also suggested that EFL learners might benefit from CL-grounded grammar instruction on these causatives. This became the basis of a collaboration with a separate colleague to design such grammar instruction for high-school students at a private school in Jakarta, Indonesia, and test its effectiveness (Novita & Wijaya 2018).

The research question was primarily concerned with the effect of CL-grounded explicit instruction on Indonesian EFL learners' performance on their production of causative constructions as measured by an immediate post-test and a delayed post-test. Participants were thirty-one twelfth grade high school students aged 16 to 18. As an instructional intervention, we provided them with a teacher-fronted explanation presented on PowerPoint slides and pedagogical tasks spread over 4 × 45 minutes. The PowerPoint slides consisted of cartoon illustrations that represent the diagrams and kinegrams shown above, brief statements of the meanings, and example sentences. The explanation of each causative was followed by a comprehension-based and a production-based tasks. The pre-test was conducted a day prior to the treatment, the immediate post-test was administered immediately after the treatment, and the delayed post-test was

Table 5.1 Descriptive Statistics

	Mean	Std. deviation	N
Pre-test score	12.612	3.508	31
Post-test score	14.871	4.849	31
Delayed post-test score	15.838	3.152	31

given a week after the treatment. The tests consisted of several tasks (i.e., a fill-in task, a free production task, and a judgment task); however, in the interest of space, only the results of the fill-in task in which participants had to complete twelve sentences with the correct causative verb and the correct complement will be presented. All the sentences in the tests were adapted from the Corpus of Contemporary American to ensure that the causative constructions were naturally produced by English L1 speakers.

Results showed that participants experienced gains on the immediate post-test and delayed post-test (see Table 5.1). A one-way repeated measures ANOVA run on the pre-test, post-test, and delayed post-test indicated that there was a significant difference among the three tests, $F(2, 60) = 10.471, p =.000$, partial $\eta^2 =.259$, a medium effect size. Post-hoc tests using Bonferroni's correction revealed that there was a significant difference between the pre-test and the immediate post-test ($p =.030$), and between the pre-test and the delayed post-test ($p =.000$). No significant difference was observed between the immediate post-test and the delayed post-test ($p =.456$).

These findings suggested that the visual presentation of the embodied effectively helped learners process new information regarding causative constructions. The pedagogic tasks further helped them intuitively grasp the target constructions. To increase leverage for optimal embodied learning experience, teachers could combine the virtual presentation with activities that emphasize learner movement and investigate its potential by means of a pre-test and a post-test. Teachers could then explore students' perception toward this embodied approach to learning grammar through a questionnaire on their learning experience.

Conclusion

The chapter has argued that CL analyses of embodied linguistic meanings could be developed into embodied learning activities that would encourage learners to make and engage with meanings through embodied experience, making CL-grounded embodied learning activities a deep approach to learning. Such activities have the potential to make grammar teaching and learning more meaningful, engaging, and rewarding as they can effectively help learners acquire the target linguistic constructions. While this chapter focuses on causative constructions, applied cognitive linguists have analyzed many other English grammatical constructions, offering semantic accounts that ELT professionals would find insightful (see Tyler et al. 2010). Further, these insightful accounts could be delivered to students in the form of embodied learning activities. A main challenge is to create embodied learning activities that fully retain the underlying meanings and functions identified by the theoretical models and are practicable in the L2 classroom. One way to overcome this challenge is to develop an understanding of the target meanings, identify gestures, bodily movements, and visuals that best represent the target grammatical concepts, turn them into learning activities, and test them out in the classroom. This chapter has explored such a procedure and thus represents a progressive approach markedly different from those which rely on verbal memorization of abstract linguistic rules.

To be sure, our view of language and language learning guides our pedagogical practices. Given the increasing evidence that language reflects humans' experience of their socio-physical surroundings and that bodily engagement is useful for learning, particularly language learning, grammar pedagogy should strive toward a more embodied view that is conducive to deeper, more meaningful and intuitive forms of learning.

References

Atkinson, D. (2010), "Extended, Embodied Cognition and Second Language Acquisition." *Applied Linguistics*, 31 (5): 599–622.
Asher, J. (1988), *Learning Another Language through Actions: A Teacher's Guide*. Los Gatos, CA: Sky Oaks.
Azar, B. S. & Hagen, S. A. (2016), *Understanding and Using English Grammar*, 5th edn. New York: Pearson Longman.
Baron, N. S. (1974), "The Structure of English Causatives." *Lingua*, 33: 299–342.
Barsalou, L. (2008), "Grounded Cognition." *Annual Review of Psychology*, 59: 617–45.
Bonda, E., Petrides, M., Frey, S. & Evans, A. (1994). "Frontal Cortex Involvement in Organized Sequences of Hand Movements: Evidence from a Positron Emission Topography Study." *Society for Neurosciences Abstracts*, 20 (1): 353.
Brame, M. K. (1976), *Conjectures and Refutations in Syntax and Semantics*. Amsterdam: North-Holland.

Carlson, L. & Kenny, R. (2005), "Constraints on Spatial Language Comprehension: Function and Geometry." In D. Pecher & R. Zwaan (eds), *Grounding Cognition*, 35–64, New York: Cambridge University Press.

Chomsky, N. (1965), *Aspects of the Theory of Syntax*. Cambridge, MA: The MIT Press.

De Knop, S. (2020), "From Construction Grammar to Embodied Construction Practice." *Constructions and Frames*, 12 (1): 121–48.

Gallese, V. & Goldman, A. (1998), "Mirror Neurons and the Simulation Theory of Mind Reading." *Trends in Cognitive Science*, 2 (12): 493–501.

Gibbs, R. (2005), *Embodiment and Cognitive Science*. New York: Cambridge University Press.

Gilquin, G. (2010), *Corpus, Cognition and Causative Constructions*. Amsterdam and Philadelphia: John Benjamins.

Gilquin, G. (2016), "Input-dependent L2 Acquisition: Causative Constructions in English as a Foreign and Second Language." In S. De Knop & G. Gilquin (eds), *Applied Construction Grammar*, 115–48, Berlin and New York: De Gruyter Mouton.

Giovanelli, M. (2015), *Teaching Grammar, Structure and Meaning. Exploring Theory and Practice for Post-16 English Language Teachers*. New York, NY: Routledge.

Glenberg, A. (1997), "What Memory Is for." *Behavioral and Brain Sciences*, 20: 1–55.

Goldberg, A. E. (1995), *Constructions. A Construction Grammar Approach to Argument Structure*. Chicago, IL: University of Chicago Press.

Hauk, O., Johnsrude, I. & Pulvermüller, F. (2004), "Somatotopic Representation of Action Words in Human Motor and Premotor Cortex." *Neuron*, 41: 301–7.

Holme, R. (2012), "Cognitive Linguistics and the Second Language Classroom." *TESOL Quarterly*, 46 (1): 6–29.

Lakoff, G. & Johnson, M. (1980), *Metaphors We Live By*. Chicago, IL: University of Chicago Press.

Langacker, R. W. (1991), *Foundations of Cognitive Grammar*, Vol. II: *Descriptive Application*. Stanford, CA: Stanford University Press.

Langacker, R. W. (2002), *Concept, Image, and Symbol. The Cognitive Basis of Grammar*, 2nd edn. Berlin: Mouton de Gruyter.

Langacker, R. W. (2008), "The Relevance of Cognitive Grammar for Language Pedagogy." In S. De Knop and T. De Rycker (eds), *Cognitive Approaches to Pedagogical Grammar: A Volume in Honour of René Dirven*, 7–36, New York: Mouton de Gruyter.

Lapaire, J. (2007), "The Meaning of Meaningless Grams—or Emptiness Revisited." In W. Oleksy & P. Stalmaszczyk (eds), *Cognitive Approaches to Language and Linguistic Data*, 241–58, Frankfurt: Peter Lang.

Levshina, N., Geeraerts, D. & Speelman, D. (2013), "Mapping Constructional Spaces: A Contrastive Analysis of English and Dutch Analytic Causatives." *Linguistics*, 51 (4): 825–54.

Littlemore, J. (2009), *Applying Cognitive Linguistics to Second Language Learning and Teaching*. Houndsmills, UK: Palgrave.

Littlemore, J. (2010), *Applying Cognitive Linguistics to Second Language Learning and Teaching*. Houndsmills, UK: Palgrave.

Macedonia, M. & Mueller, K. (2016), "Exploring the Neural Representation of Novel Words Learned through Enactment in a Word Recognition Task." *Frontiers in Psychology*, 7: 953.

Macedonia, M., Repetto, C., Ischebeck, A. & Mueller, K. (2019), "Depth of Encoding through Observed Gestures in Foreign Language Word Learning." *Frontiers in Psychology*, 10: 33.

Marton, F. & Säljö, R. (1976), "On Qualitative Differences in Learning: Outcome as a Function of Learners' Conception of Task." *British Journal of Educational Psychology*, 46: 115–27.

Novita, S. & Wijaya, D. (2018, April), Applying Construction Grammar to Teaching English Periphrastic Causative Constructions [Paper presentation]. Konferensi Linguistik Tahunan Atma Jaya Keenam Belas Tingkat Internasional 2018, Jakarta, Indonesia.

Ortega, L., Tyler, A. E., Park, H. I., & Uno, M. (eds). (2016), *The Usage-Based Study of Language Learning and Multilingualism*. Georgetown University Press.

Radden, G. & Dirven, R. (2007), *Cognitive English Grammar*. Amsterdam: John Benjamins.

Rizzolatti, G. & Craighero, L. (2004), "The Mirror-neuron System." *Annual Review of Neuroscience*, 27: 169–92.

Suñer, F. & Roche, J. (2021), "Embodiment in Concept-Based L2 Grammar Teaching: The Case of German Light Verb Constructions." *International Review of Applied Linguistics in Language Teaching*, 80 (3): 421–47. doi: http://doi.org/10.1515/iral-2018-0362.

Tracy, W. S. & Colby, S. A. (2007), "Teaching for Deep Learning." *The Clearing House: A Journal of Educational Strategies, Issues and Ideas*, 80 (5): 205–10.

Tyler, A. (2012), *Cognitive Linguistics and Second Language Learning: Theoretical Basics and Experimental Evidence*. New York, NY: Routledge.

Tyler, A., Huang, L. & Jan, H. (eds). (2018), *What Is Applied Cognitive Linguistics?: Answers from Current SLA Research*. Berlin and New York: Mouton de Gruyter.

Tyler, A., Mueller, C. M. & Ho, V. (2010), "Applying Cognitive Linguistics to Instructed L2 Learning: The English Modals." *AILA Review*, 23 (1): 30–49.

Verspoor, M. (1996), "The Story of -ing: A Subjective Perspective." In M. Pütz & R. Dirven (eds), *The Construal of Space in Language and Thought*, 417–54, Berlin: Mouton de Gruyter.

White, L. (2015), "Linguistic Theory, Universal Grammar, and Second Language Acquisition." In B. VanPatten & J. Williams (eds), *Theories in Second Language Acquisition*, 34–53, New York, NY: Routledge.

Whong, M., Gil, K. H. & Marsden, H. (eds). (2013), *Universal Grammar and the Second Language Classroom*. New York, NY: Springer.

Wierzbicka, A. (2006), *English: Meaning and Culture.* New York, NY: Oxford University Press.

Wijaya, D. & Ong, G. (2018), "Applying Cognitive Linguistics to Teaching English Prepositions in the EFL Classroom." *Indonesian Journal of Applied Linguistics*, 8 (1): 1–10.

Wijaya, D. & Winstin, E. (2021), "Investigating Indonesian EFL Learners' Knowledge and Use of English Causative Constructions." *International Review of Applied Linguistics in Language Teaching.* Ahead of print. doi: https://doi.org/10.1515/iral-2021-0031

6

Encouraging Deep Learning through an Interactive, Intercultural Approach to Shakespeare

Duncan Lees

QUEEN KATHERINE:

O, good my lord, no Latin:
I am not such a truant since my coming,
As not to know the language I have lived in:
A strange tongue makes my cause more strange, suspicious:
Pray, speak in English:

(*Henry VIII*, 3.1, 45–9)

Introduction

For the Spanish-born Queen Katherine, wife of England's King Henry VIII, language matters. Visited by two cardinals, who press her on her refusal to accede to the king's wish that their marriage be annulled, Shakespeare presents Katherine as acutely aware of her vulnerability as a foreign woman in the English court. When one cardinal addresses her in Latin, she asks him to speak in English instead. Life in England, she says, has made her perfectly able to use its common tongue: "I am not such a truant since my coming, / As not to know the language I have lived in" (*Henry VIII*, 3.1.46–7). More importantly, she fears that using a "[s]trange tongue" positions her as an outsider, making her situation "more strange," and even "suspicious" (48). Here, "strange" suggests not only unfamiliarity, but also another of the word's senses in Early Modern

English: the idea of something being "foreign, alien, from abroad" (Crystal & Crystal 2002: 425). While today "strange" does not have quite the same connotations, Shakespeare's language itself has come to be associated with a certain foreignness. Despite the relative closeness of the English of Shakespeare's time and that of today, even those who speak English as a first language often perceive Shakespeare as archaic and alien—technically the same language, but experientially foreign (Blank 2014). This perception, coupled with Shakespeare's high cultural status, can make his language a source of anxiety and bafflement for students in Anglophone countries—especially those whose cultural and linguistic backgrounds mean they already have a complex relationship with English (Espinosa 2016). For learners of English as a Foreign Language (EFL) the challenge can seem even greater, and the rewards even less clear. With dominant modes of foreign language education emphasizing instrumental goals related to communicative efficiency and employability (Ros-i-Solé 2016), studying centuries-old dramatic literature might seem impractical and counterproductive. If Shakespeare's English is strange for those who supposedly live in that language, why inflict it on students for whom English is already foreign?

But is it necessarily a bad thing for languages—or anything else—to be strange? In Shakespeare's time, in addition to conveying foreignness or distance, the word "strange" had a host of other meanings that, by the Jacobean period, were used for a range of creative and cultural purposes (Davies 2021). Indeed, David and Ben Crystal's *Shakespeare's Words* lists no fewer than nine different senses of "strange," including some with positive connotations: "rare, singular, exceptional" and "special, particular, very great" (2002: 424–5). This chapter contends that, in the context of foreign language education, it is also not a bad thing for languages to be, or be made, strange. Whether in the contemporary sense of being unfamiliar, or the early modern senses of being both foreign and special, this chapter argues that if Shakespeare's language is "strange," then this can actually help to encourage deeper learning in the English language classroom. It does so by outlining a pedagogy that draws on what are variously called active, creative, or rehearsal room approaches to Shakespeare (Banks 2014; Gibson 1998; RSC 2013; Stredder 2009), and combining these with an intercultural perspective on language teaching and learning (Liddicoat & Scarino 2013; McConachy 2018).

After introducing Shakespeare's language in context and the theoretical underpinnings of the chapter's pedagogical inspirations, practical examples are given from my own classes with learners of English at universities in China and the UK. These examples demonstrate the fundamentally social and embodied nature of this approach, as students experience the excitement of Shakespeare's dramatic language by collaboratively playing with, interpreting, and enacting speeches from another of Shakespeare's histories, *King John*. Such engagement is also inherently intercultural, as processes of (de)familiarization and mediation encourage learners to reflect more deeply on their linguistic and cultural assumptions and identities. Consequently, it can be used to foster a form of deep learning that goes beyond the instrumental acquisition of linguistic and cultural "facts" that are to be deployed in narrowly defined communicative contexts, and that is instead concerned with a more holistic, transformative engagement with meaning-making in all its complexity. Rather than being remote or abstract, Shakespeare's "strange" language thus becomes a vehicle through which English learners can acknowledge their emotions and inner lives, and reflect on their understandings of themselves and others.

Shakespeare's Language in Context

The idea that Shakespeare's language not only merits special attention but also requires specialist knowledge to be fully understood has a long history. From Abbott's 1869 *A Shakespearian Grammar* to more recent examples (e.g., Blake 2002; Crystal 2008; Crystal 2016; Crystal & Crystal 2002; Johnson 2014; Kermode 2000; Magnusson with Schalkwyk 2019), numerous books have offered everything from general explorations of Shakespeare's language, to guides specifically covering grammar, pronunciation, and vocabulary. However, Culpeper & Archer (2020: 191) have argued that much of this writing exhibits something of a "split personality," addressing linguistic and literary perspectives, but in practice often privileging one over the other. In historical terms, the basic biographical outlines of Shakespeare's life—he was born in 1564 and died in 1616—position him as a user of what is now called Early Modern English (EME). However, when people today refer to Shakespeare's language they are typically referring to the language found in his plays and poems. If, as Culpeper and Archer argue, adequately addressing the linguistic and the literary is a challenge for scholars, it also seems a formidable barrier to using Shakespeare in EFL contexts. At its most instrumental, mainstream EFL privileges practical English, of the sort that is supposedly encountered—and is therefore *useful*—in everyday situations. Defining the "useful" and the "everyday" can actually be very contentious, given the drastically different socioeconomic and cultural situations of the world's EFL learners. However, it is true that few learners will actively *need* to be able to write speeches or poems in EME in their educational and working lives. Fewer still will need to know what to say when confronted by witches (*Macbeth*) or fairies (*A Midsummer Night's Dream*), let alone when announcing that they have baked their enemy's sons into a pie (*Titus Andronicus*). This fact is reflected in a question raised whenever I begin Shakespeare sessions with my MA TESOL students: "What's the point of teaching learners such out-of-date, impractical language?"

However understandable such reservations are, they make assumptions about both Shakespeare's language and EFL teaching that merit further examination. Certainly, the idea that Shakespeare's language is outdated—and therefore more difficult and less practical than today's English—needs to be explored. In strictly historical terms, and certainly when compared to Old and Middle English, EME is technically not *that* different from the English of today. In light of this, Crystal and Crystal (2002) argue that there are many passages in Shakespeare in which the vocabulary is almost identical to that of today's English, and even more where unfamiliar terms are easily understandable in context. Just such a stretch can be found in one of the excerpts from *King John* that is used later in this chapter (see Example 2):

> I am not mad: this hair I tear is mine:
> My name is Constance: I was Geoffrey's wife:
> Young Arthur is my son, and he is lost: (*KJ* 3.3.46–8)

There is nothing difficult here in terms of syntax or vocabulary, and nothing "strange" in the sense of being foreign or unfamiliar. The final "lost" may not operate as literally as the words in the rest of the extract, but the fact that Constance is talking about her son possibly being dead—rather than just having lost his way—becomes clear in the context of the scene. In any case, this sense of "lost" is still current in English, and would be a perfectly reasonable thing to teach EFL learners of an appropriate level. An example like this demonstrates Crystal and Crystal's contention that there is plenty in Shakespeare that is no more difficult than, nor much different to, English as it is used today.

However, while there might be good pedagogical arguments for presenting, and perhaps even surprising, learners with stretches of Shakespeare that seem easier and more familiar than they might be anticipating, it is necessary to acknowledge that their experiences will not always be so seamless. Indeed, while it was easy to cherry-pick the above example from the extracts chosen for this chapter, there is much within them—and within Shakespeare as a whole—that seems more obviously difficult, and more strange. Certainly, many of the things that Murphy et al. (2020) found that students, including EFL learners, identify as difficult in Shakespeare—including archaisms, contractions, and complicated lexis—occur in this chapter's extracts. The line before the short stretch above, for example, reads "Thou art not holy to belie me so" (KJ 3.3.45), using EME forms of both you (thou) and are (art). The speech then continues with EME contractions ("'tis" for it is), modals ("shalt" for shall) and items of vocabulary that are highly culturally specific ("thou shalt be canonized, cardinal"), or archaic ("clouts" for cloths or rags). If anything, the other extracts I have chosen contain even more obvious examples of the difficult and the strange, including complicated and archaic vocabulary, deliberately unsettling imagery, and words that lexically or orthographically do not look like English at all ("adieu" and "[A]ssurèd" in Example 1). As their ideas stretch across multiple lines, the syntax also becomes more complex and even convoluted.

Therefore, although Crystal and Crystal (2002: xii) contend that there are "very few passages in Shakespeare where the combination of alien grammar and vocabulary makes the text comparable to it being in a foreign language," this may be true in only a technical, rather than an experiential, sense (Blank 2014, 2018). This undoubtedly adds another dimension to the reception of Shakespeare by EFL learners, such as the participant in one of my workshops at a Chinese university who commented that "Shakespeare's language is a foreign language in foreign language."

Faced with such a situation, the most obvious response might be simply to avoid using Shakespeare with EFL learners. And yet the student quoted above made their comment in the course of discussing how much they enjoyed tackling Shakespeare in English—which included enjoying the challenge this posed, and the satisfaction they felt at being able to rise to this challenge. Similarly, Murphy et al. (2020) do not conclude that students' experiences of difficulty mean that Shakespeare has no place in EFL teaching. Instead, they recommend a "mixed pedagogical approach" to teaching Shakespeare, which incorporates corpus-based elements alongside more common "textual, contextual and performance aspects" (2020: 22). Crucially, they stress that the use of corpus-based activities in the classroom is predicated on the "active involvement of learners, treating language in a contextualized fashion and focussing on the language itself" (2020: 2). It is this "active involvement of learners" that this chapter will focus on, as a way of making a virtue out of having EFL learners engage with language that can seem difficult, and strange. However, the emphasis here will not be on corpus methods, but on what Murphy et al. refer to as "performance" aspects that harness and explore affective, embodied, and imaginative engagements with Shakespeare's language. Specifically, this chapter draws on a tradition of what are known as active, creative, or rehearsal room approaches (Banks 2014; Gibson 1998; RSC 2013; Stredder 2009), which the following section introduces.

Overview of Active Shakespeare Pedagogy

As Banks (2014) and Olive (2015) have pointed out, "active" techniques for Shakespeare involving performance elements were advocated as far back as the first two decades of the twentieth century. However, the pedagogy now known broadly as "active" approaches to Shakespeare is most commonly associated with Rex Gibson (1998), whose *Shakespeare and Schools* project had a huge impact on the teaching of Shakespeare within British education (Winston 2015). Gibson's influence can be seen in a number of guides for teachers that have proved popular in the UK, especially Stredder's *The North Face of Shakespeare* (2009), *The RSC Shakespeare Toolkit for Teachers* (2013), and Banks's *Creative Shakespeare* (2014), which outlines Shakespeare's Globe's version of active methods. Given the extent of his influence, it is useful to quote Gibson's original definition:

> Active methods comprise a wide range of expressive, creative and physical activities. They recognise that Shakespeare wrote his plays for performance, and that his scripts are completed by enactment of some kind. The dramatic context demands classroom practices that are the antithesis of methods in which students sit passively, without intellectual or emotional engagement.
>
> (1998: xii)

Despite some variation in individual and institutional practices, and alternative names such as "rehearsal room" or "creative" approaches, all the aforementioned texts echo Gibson's belief in the importance of enacting—rather than just reading—the plays. This does not, however, mean that the aim is always to produce performances that will be viewed by an audience beyond the classroom. Instead, various "expressive, creative and physical activities" (Gibson 1998: xii) are advocated to help students engage with and understand Shakespeare as they play out, and play with, his texts. Finally, and most contentiously, all present this approach as an improvement on a generalized vision of deskbound, teacher-centered, literary critical teaching of Shakespeare, which is seen as reinforcing the idea that Shakespeare is "as indifferent and unscaleable" as an icy mountain peak (Stredder 2009: 3).

These shared principles translate into practices that emphasize the teaching of Shakespeare as a collaborative, playful, physical endeavor. Tables and chairs are often pushed back, signalling the transformation of the classroom into a rehearsal room (Banks 2014; RSC 2013), a stage, or even a "theatrical laboratory" (Stredder 2009: 8). Accordingly, students and teachers become more like actors and directors, albeit with an emphasis on learner-centered collaborative exploration. This sees the focus shift from the teacher-director, to the student-actors as "co-owners" and "doers" (Stredder 2009: 11). The teacher thus becomes a knowledgeable "enabler and fellow explorer" (RSC 2013: 9), allowing learners to ask questions and actively create meanings. Typically this is done through activities that put the text "on its feet" to be explored using playful techniques, which borrow from the professional rehearsal room. As well as reimagining the classroom and the roles within it, this approach also implies a different attitude to Shakespeare. Gibson (1998: 7) insisted that Shakespeare's plays should be presented to learners as "scripts," not "texts," because while the latter "implies authority, reverence, certainty," the former "suggests a provisionality and incompleteness that anticipates and requires imaginative, dramatic enactment for completion." For the most influential proponents of this tradition, such an approach restores the dramatic element to the study of plays that were written to be performed, in ways that more textual and/or historical approaches arguably cannot. These methods are "active," therefore, not only physically, but because they give students agency over the text, as they respond to Shakespeare emotionally, intellectually, and imaginatively.

The techniques associated with this tradition have in many cases been developed through years of artistic and educational practice, but Winston (2015) has set out a theoretical rationale for the RSC's "rehearsal room" approach, which is broadly applicable to the tradition as a whole. He organizes this around five areas of learning—*learning through playing, through experience, through the body, through beauty* and *learning together*—which will now be briefly elucidated with reference to this chapter's focus on language education:

- *Learning through playing:* Winston (2015: 76) notes that play is often dismissed as "pleasurable and therefore not difficult or challenging," and as "not serious and therefore not to be taken seriously." He contrasts this with how scholars such as Johan Huizinga and Richard Schechner have emphasized play's importance as a fundamental aspect of life, which can be deeply serious and meaningful. Significantly, Winston gives particular attention to Cook's (2000) work on language play, which argues that, far from being frivolous, play is central to how we learn, use, and create meaning through language. Cook contends that for language teaching to engage with the full range of uses to which we put language, it needs to include far more "nonsense, fiction, and ritual, and many more instances of language use for aggression, intimacy, and creative thought" (2000: 193). Shakespeare's work clearly fits into Cook's expanded conception of language use and learning, and Winston (2015) adds that it exemplifies the three interlocking levels—formal, semantic, and pragmatic—at which Cook suggests language play works. Thus, as well their formal play of rhythm and rhyme, Shakespeare's texts work at the semantic level, offering the pleasure of stories and "novel, strange or opaque uses of language," and the pragmatic level, whereby communal language play "create[s] solidarity as well as competitiveness, and build[s] a feeling of congregation as well as intimate interaction" (Winston 2015: 77). Shakespeare's dramatic language is thus a vehicle through which students can learn through playing, whether they are learning it in a first or a foreign language (Cheng & Winston 2011).

- *Learning together:* As a prerequisite for, and a consequence of, this playful approach, the RSC's educational work revolves around the theatrically inspired idea of the "ensemble" or "company." While Winston (2015: 87) notes that the RSC's model of "ensemble" has sometimes rested on a utopian intention "to embody a particular conception of the good society," the need for a trusting, collaborative atmosphere is common to active approaches to Shakespeare in general. In this model, hierarchies are flattened, and teachers and students come together in a spirit of constructive, collective endeavor (Stredder 2009). This develops "soft" social skills, and even more importantly establishes a space in which individual learners can be "challenged and inspired to move beyond [their] comfort zone" (Winston 2015: 90). This can include tackling the supposed difficulty and strangeness of Shakespeare's language in a spirit of collective exploration, not competitive assessment.

- *Learning through the body:* Active approaches achieve a trusting, cooperative atmosphere in part through a different conception of the physical in education. Open spaces are favored, with tables and chairs absent or pushed aside, and circles take precedence over rows or squares. Movement is far easier within these more open spaces and is integral to the learning taking place within them, as Winston stresses the educational importance of embodiment, and asserts that physical activities can be used to analyze Shakespearean texts. Specifically, he references the philosophy of Mark Johnson (2008), who, he writes, "rejects the idea of a disembodied mind and situates bodily experience and higher propositional thinking along the same continuum rather than seeing them as fundamentally different" (Winston 2015: 84). In drama, as in life, meaning-making is an intellectual *and* physical endeavor, which is felt with and expressed through our bodies—something that drama can bring to language learning (Piazzoli 2018).

- *Learning through experience:* Experience is hugely important within this pedagogical tradition, in ways that often recall the ideas of John Dewey (e.g., 1916, 1938). Neelands and O'Hanlon (2011: 240), for example, propose that engaging with Shakespeare's works should be a "double entitlement"—both cultural and curricular—that opens possibilities for Shakespeare to be "a source of pleasure" for learners, and "a reference point for understanding the complexities of their own and other lives." Such possibilities, they stress, should be "life-long and life-wide," as school should be about more than narrow instrumental aims related to assessment and employability (ibid.). Here, "experience" refers not merely to learners being taught about or discussing situations that commonly occur in everyday life (e.g., in the world of work), but to the "genuine situation of experience" (Dewey 1916: 167) they can encounter in meaningful educational interactions. Such experiences occur through activities that allow learners to actively engage in tasks that matter—aesthetically, emotionally, intellectually—and that they can bring to a satisfying conclusion through their own acts of experimentation and interpretation.

- *Learning through beauty:* Following Dewey's (1916) distinction between everyday experiences and those that are singular and significant, Winston (2015: 81) argues that "[w]hat turns *any* experience into *an* experience—into something memorable, intrinsically worthwhile, satisfying and rewarding in itself—is its aesthetic quality." In *Beauty and Education*, Winston had already written that "[t]o engage with Shakespeare's dramatic poetry is to experience the expressive power of language at its most intense and beautiful" (2010: 102), but this is not simply through learners coming into contact with something beautiful and/or sublime in a Kantian sense. In active approaches, the aesthetic and formal qualities of Shakespeare are not merely noticed, but dynamically experienced through physical, playful engagement in a cooperative atmosphere, which lessens the hold of self-consciousness and individual preoccupations, marking the experience out from run-of-the-mill everyday life.

Encompassing learning through playing, experience, beauty, and the body, as well as learning together, Winston's (2015) theoretical rationale thus resonates strongly with deep learning as conceived in this chapter, as something concerned with students' emotions, inner lives, and transformative potential.

This pedagogical approach has, however, attracted various criticisms (Olive 2015), including some that specifically target its playful, physical nature (McLuskie 2009). Some of these critiques are essentially only relevant to academic Shakespeare studies, rather than Shakespeare in EFL contexts, but two reservations expressed by Murphy et al. (2020) are important to address here. The first is that what they call "performance" methods are extremely time-consuming. This can certainly be true, and, as a result, extracurricular or occasional active Shakespeare sessions can be a good option in highly time-pressured and test-oriented learning contexts (Coles 2009). A second issue raised by Murphy et al. (2020) is that performance-oriented approaches neglect the texts themselves. McLuskie (2009: 131) makes a similar point about active approaches in schools, claiming that they can "produce exciting educational experiences" but ones that are only tangentially related to Shakespeare, and may be insufficiently rigorous for use at more advanced levels. It is true that a few techniques associated with active methods deal only indirectly with text, but Gibson (1998), Banks (2014), and Stredder (2009) all stress the fundamental importance of learners engaging with Shakespeare's language. The performative elements of active approaches are there to facilitate this engagement, and, certainly, all the activities shared below involve exploring and interpreting the language of Shakespeare's texts—albeit through physical, expressive means, rather than more conventional analysis. On that note, it is important to consider what goals such analysis might have. Murphy et al. (2020) stress that the play-text, in all its contextual, historical, and literary complexity, should be the primary object of analysis (in their case of the stylistic kind). However, language educators are under no such obligation. They do need to understand the language, literary devices, and context of extracts they are using, but a sustained literary and/or historical analysis of an entire play-text need not be the goal. Indeed, as is argued below, isolated extracts from Shakespeare can serve as "authentic" materials for language education, providing opportunities for learners to engage emotionally, physically, and imaginatively with beautiful, dramatic, strange language (Cheng & Winston 2011). The next section outlines how this can be done in ways that incorporate an intercultural perspective on language teaching and learning.

Language Teaching and Learning from an Intercultural Perspective

The connection between language and culture has attracted considerable debate in language education (Liddicoat & Scarino 2013; Kramsch 1993). Byram and Fleming (1998) have noted that although a cultural dimension was integral to the post-war development of audio-lingual and audio-visual methods in Western Europe and the United States, in practice this often meant teaching languages as systems, and then separately providing information about countries where they were spoken. Today, such a separation appears less and less tenable. A view of the connections between languages, cultures, and nation-states as fixed and discrete looks increasingly divorced from reality, and there is growing awareness of the sociocultural dimensions of language use and learning (Risager 2007). An intercultural perspective on language education attempts to address these complex interrelationships by making them a focus of how languages are learned and taught (Liddicoat & Scarino 2013). This does not mean abandoning what might be seen as the traditional foundations of language education: grammar and vocabulary are still taught, but with a more explicit focus on how sociocultural assumptions influence how we use language to make meaning (McConachy 2018). Accordingly, instead of merely being informed about other cultures, learners' interpretive skills and reflexivity are harnessed and developed, as they are encouraged to (re)consider the influences of their understandings of language(s) and culture(s) (Liddicoat & Scarino 2013). In this way, language education with an intercultural orientation "focuses on languages and cultures as sites of interactive engagement in the act of meaning-making and implies a transformational engagement of the learner in the act of learning" (Liddicoat & Scarino 2013: 49). Consequently, intercultural language education can be recognized as fostering a form of deep learning, which goes beyond the acquisition of knowledge, and helps learners to consider more deeply the processes involved in meaning-making, and question their understandings of language(s), culture(s), and themselves.

Moreover, the ways in which this intercultural perspective can be applied to language teaching, as proposed by Liddicoat and Scarino (2013), share much with Winston's (2015) aforementioned rationale for teaching Shakespeare. Both pedagogies place the learner at the center, both stress the importance of taking a whole-person view of the learner, and both see learning as "not an abstract, but rather an embodied process" (Liddicoat & Scarino 2013: 51). Indeed,

Liddicoat and Scarino's five principles for teaching and learning languages from an intercultural perspective—*active construction, making connections, social interaction, reflection,* and *responsibility*—converge in multiple ways with the general principles of active approaches to Shakespeare:

- *Active construction*: This principle refers to how learners make sense of languages and cultures they are encountering, through "purposeful, active engagement in interpreting and creating meaning in interaction with others," in a process of "continuous development as thinking, feeling, changing intercultural beings" (Liddicoat & Scarino 2013: 57). This echoes Winston's (2015) emphasis on learning through experience, whereby, rather than simply receiving information, learners actively make meaning through their own exploration of texts and situations.
- *Making connections*: Liddicoat and Scarino (2013: 57) point out that learners do not learn (about) languages and cultures in isolation. They therefore need "to connect the new to what is already known," both *intraculturally*, considering their own linguistic and cultural positionings, and *interculturally*, engaging beyond them. Again, this resonates with Winston's (2015) discussion of learning through experience, in which active meaning-making incorporates, but goes beyond, what learners already know.
- *Social interaction*: This principle recognizes that "learning is a fundamentally interactive act and that interaction with others is the fundamental purpose of language use" (Liddicoat & Scarino 2013: 57). Intercultural language education needs to offer opportunities for using and exploring language, and for negotiating understandings, in interaction with others, echoing Winston's (2015) emphasis on learning together.
- *Reflection*: Being centered on active interpretation, reflection is a key principle for intercultural language education. Liddicoat and Scarino (2013) emphasize that this reflection has both cognitive and affective dimensions. Encountering "other" people, languages or cultures can trigger emotional responses—positive and negative—that learners must recognize, before reflecting upon why they have reacted in a particular way. Emotional responses are also integral to learning through play in Winston's (2015) rationale, as well as to how educational encounters become significant experiences, distinct from the unreflective character of everyday life.
- *Responsibility*: Just as a moral dimension is identifiable in active approaches to Shakespeare that view the company or ensemble as modelling a way of being in society, intercultural language education is seen as helping

to model an ethical way of "being in diversity" (Liddicoat 2013). In keeping with its learner-centered principles, this places a responsibility on learners to develop and act with intercultural sensitivity and understanding well beyond the classroom.

These five principles are put into practice through a series of interconnected processes: *noticing, comparing, reflecting,* and *interacting* (Liddicoat & Scarino 2013). Elements of these will be apparent in the exercises illustrated below, but a key point to reiterate here is the role that interpretation plays in this view of intercultural language education, and of communication more widely (Crutchfield & Schewe 2017). Drawing on the work of Wittgenstein (1953), Liddicoat and Scarino (2013: 48) argue that learning and communication are language games that fundamentally rely on interpretation, and in which "language is integrated with action in order to achieve local aims." The same word(s) can be used to do very different things by different people in different contexts—something that is crucial for language learners to be alert to, but that is not always adequately addressed by the narrowly prescriptive linguistic formulae found in certain types of EFL teaching and materials. The emphasis on making, interpreting, and negotiating meaning as being grounded in the social world finds another expression in McConachy's (2018) application of an intercultural perspective to the exploration of pragmatics in foreign language education. He stresses that a key part of a learner's development of an intercultural perspective on language use is their "ability to view language use as a form of social action and reflect on the ways in which meanings and impressions are constructed and negotiated among speakers" (2018: 57).

One method McConachy proposes for achieving this is an activity he calls contextual analysis, which involves learners collaboratively analysing constructed conversational dialogues, considering the speakers' linguistic choices, potential sociocultural influences on these choices, and the consequences of these choices in their interactional context. As such, this activity exemplifies Liddicoat and Scarino's (2013) practices for intercultural learning—noticing, comparing, reflecting, and interacting—and their five principles for teaching and learning languages from an intercultural perspective. Consequently, it also exemplifies how intercultural language education can involve a form of deep learning that accommodates identities and understandings beyond the classroom, as learners actively engage in rich, multi-layered processes of meaning-making. In work on the uses of performance-based approaches in intercultural education, this learner-centered and deeply interpretive perspective is further enhanced through an emphasis on active physical and affective engagement (Braüer 2002; Crutchfield & Schewe 2017; Fleming 1998).

However, as the constructed dialogues of Shakespeare's dramas are very different from, for example, those of McConachy's (2018) contextual analysis activities, it is important to address how Shakespeare is suited to intercultural language education. As Liddicoat and Scarino (2013: 95) point out, the authenticity of resources is not simply a question of whether they are "real" examples of everyday, contemporary language use—which Shakespeare certainly is not—but depends on "a dynamic interaction between the resources, their use, and the learning that they are designed to produce." Consequently, active approaches to Shakespeare for intercultural language education harness and respond to particular qualities of Shakespeare's texts in interactional, intercultural ways. So, while Shakespeare's works are fictional and were composed at a historical distance, the integration of language and local action is fundamental to their use in active approaches. As Kao and O'Neill (1998: 4) have written in their influential work on process drama and second language learning:

> Drama does things with words. It introduces language as an essential and authentic method of communication. Drama sustains interactions between students within the target language, creating a world of social roles and relations in which the learner is an active participant.

Thus, although Shakespeare's dramatic texts involve heightened situations that might be assumed to be historically and culturally remote, through processes of embodied enactment and interpretation learners explore many of the same elements they would in an activity such as contextual analysis. Specifically, the activities illustrated below involve active exploration of linguistic choices (of Shakespeare and the characters/speakers), potential sociocultural influences on these choices (in terms of both the dramatic context within the play, and the context in which it was written), and the consequences of these choices (for the characters, performers, and spectators).

Furthermore, the beauty and strangeness of Shakespeare's language itself offers possibilities for teaching English from an intercultural perspective. For Pulverness (2014), a certain estrangement is inevitable when encountering and learning (about) other languages and cultures. As a consequence, he advocates the use of literary texts as an effective way of working through this, by exploring the sense of estrangement in relation to the "foreign" and challenging taken-for-granted assumptions about the "familiar." Drawing on *ostranenie* (Остранение), the notion of *defamiliarization* developed by Russian formalist critics in the early twentieth century, Pulverness points out that literature can render the familiar strange, so that we see things and our relationships to them in a new light. In intercultural terms, such literature can help learners to decenter their own perspectives when encountering a new text (or language or culture), as they explore and reflect upon the constructedness of both the "foreign" and the "familiar" (Liddicoat & Scarino 2013). For this purpose, Pulverness (2014: 133) recommends literary works that either directly represent contemporary "experiences of cultural estrangement"— i.e., fiction that focuses on the stories of immigrants and minority groups—or genres such as fantasy and science fiction, which in some respects mimic these experiences. However, Shakespeare can also be highly effective in facilitating this kind of intercultural decentring. The fact that learners today—wherever they were born and whatever language(s) they speak—are engaging, in Shakespeare, with something from another time and another cultural milieu itself vividly illustrates that languages and cultures are dynamic and changing, rather than fixed and stable. But, just as importantly, experiencing the dramatic intensity of Shakespeare's words through active approaches' unconventional methods can give heightened and unfamiliar situations a new immediacy and power, and help us see in a new light our assumptions about how we perceive and communicate in the world (Cheng & Winston 2011; Fleming 1998).

Examples of Interactional, Intercultural Activities: *King John*

This chapter's final section demonstrates the interactional, intercultural approach outlined above, using extracts from Shakespeare's *King John*. Written at the end of the sixteenth century, about historical events that took place in England two centuries before that, *King John*'s story is likely to seem obscure to most learners. This in itself provides an element of surprise, as the vivid language and situations found in these extracts invite activities that bring this seemingly distant time and place powerfully to life. *King John*'s shifting critical fortunes—it was one of Shakespeare's most popular plays in the nineteenth century and is now one of the least well-known (Cohen 2018)—can also be a useful reminder that even something as supposedly timeless as Shakespeare is still subject to socioculturally contingent processes of interpretation. The examples below are based on sessions I have conducted with English majors at several Chinese universities, and MA TESOL students in the UK. As such they particularly suit tertiary English learners but can easily be adapted for other groups. Useful synopses of the play can be found online, as can the trailer for the RSC's 2019 production, which showcases interpretive choices (including cross-gender casting and modern dress) that can spark debate.[1] However, the aim of these exercises is not to teach the play as a whole. Instead, the extracts provide opportunities for English learners to explore and play with complex and exciting dramatic language (Cheng & Winston 2011). As such, these examples work as standalone activities through which learners collaboratively build, and build upon, their own interpretations of the language and dramatic situations (Fleming 1998). Each extract, therefore, is preceded by only brief general notes, and in most cases it should not be necessary to give learners much more of an introduction to the context than is contained in these—the exercises themselves involve discovering more about the characters and their predicaments. These initial notes are followed by outlines of activities that can be used individually or combined with others. Fuller descriptions of the techniques employed can be found in the guides to active approaches discussed earlier (Banks 2014; Gibson 1998; RSC 2013; Stredder 2009). While the activities have been chosen for these specific extracts, they can also work well with other scenes from Shakespeare and non-Shakespearean dramas.

Example 1: "The sun's o'ercast with blood: fair day, adieu!"

BLANCHE

> The sun's o'ercast with blood: fair day, adieu!
> Which is the side that I must go withal?
> I am with both, each army hath a hand,
> And in their rage, I having hold of both,
> They whirl asunder and dismember me.
> Husband, I cannot pray that thou mayst win:-
> Uncle, I needs must pray that thou mayst lose:-
> Father, I may not wish the fortune thine:-
> Grandam, I will not wish thy wishes thrive:
> Whoever wins, on that side shall I lose:
> Assurèd loss before the match be played.
>
> (*KJ*, 3.1.259–69)

General notes: In this extract, Blanche voices despair at her predicament, as her wedding day erupts into war between England (under her uncle, King John) and France (under King Philip, whose son Blanche has just reluctantly married). As with the following examples, each learner should get a handout with the extract in a large (16–18 point) font, but no additional dialogue or notes that could distract them.

Initial readthrough: Learners read out the extract in pairs/small groups, circling anything that seems strange or unexpected—either in the context of somebody's wedding day, or in terms of the words themselves. The former will likely include negative, even violent vocabulary, which will help illustrate how Blanche feels; the latter, some unfamiliar words that can be used to challenge essentialist conceptions of "English." These could include archaisms (withal, mayst, etc.) and apparently non-English words (e.g., adieu, which rhymed with "you" in EME), demonstrating that languages are dynamic and porous, not fixed and discrete. ("Assurèd" may look "foreign," but the accent is connected to stress—see below.)

Iambic pentameter: Running through this extract, like much of Shakespeare, is iambic pentameter, in which each line has ten syllables, with the even syllables stressed: "I **am**/ with **both**/ each **ar**/my **hath**/ a **hand**/." Learners can physicalize this rhythm by standing in a circle and marching on the spot (lifting one foot on an unstressed syllable and placing it down on a stressed syllable), or by alternately clapping softly or loudly for unstressed and stressed syllables. Made up sentences (e.g. I **need**/ a **cup**/ of **cof**/fee **right**/ away) can be thought up by the teacher and learners. After starting exaggeratedly, learners can begin using the iambic pentameter more lightly, to read the lines more fluidly. When learners query "o'ercast," tell them it is a contraction and see if they can guess which word it shortens (overcast) and why (the two syllables of "o'ercast" fit the rhythm, while the three of "overcast" do not). "Assurèd" may also make more sense to them now—the accent indicates that its "-ed" ending is pronounced /ɪd/, not /d/, to maintain the iambic pentameter. Some learners may notice that the lines beginning "Husband" / "Uncle" / "Father" / "Grandam" all open with a stressed and then an unstressed syllable (a trochee). In discussion, some may feel that this marks a turning point in how Blanche is talking, and to whom, which can feed into the next exercise.

Embodied readthrough: Learners read the speech in a circle, either chorally or individually, in turns. After one or two readthroughs, they hold their scripts in one hand, using the other to point at themselves every time Blanche refers to herself (I, me). As the reading continues, ask who else is being referred to, and ask volunteers to stand in for the other characters who will be pointed at when mentioned. Help clarify the two sides: England (Blanche's uncle, King John, and grandmother (grandam)) versus France (Blanche's husband and father(in-law)). Divide the group into two, and have one learner read out Blanche's part, moving quickly between England and France as appropriate. This will visually illustrate Blanche's dilemma, and dramatize the delivery, as the breathing of the learner playing Blanche alters with their movement. In groups comfortable with physical contact, each army can literally "ha[ve] a hand," forcing the learner-as-Blanche to struggle free as they try to address the different characters (while another student holds up their script for them). If time allows, this can become a short performance, with learners deciding how lines are allocated (individually, chorally?) and delivered (spoken, chanted, sung?), and what movement and physical arrangements are used. (Note the aim is *not* to perform the speech as it would typically be done on stage.)

Example 2: "Thou art not holy to belie me so"

CONSTANCE

> Thou art not holy to belie me so:
> I am not mad: this hair I tear is mine:
> My name is Constance: I was Geoffrey's wife:
> Young Arthur is my son, and he is lost:
> I am not mad: I would to heaven I were!
> For then, tis like I should forget myself:
> O, if I could, what grief should I forget!
> Preach some philosophy to make me mad,
> And thou shalt be canonized, cardinal;
> For, being not mad, but sensible of grief,
> My reasonable part produces reason
> How I may be delivered of these woes,
> And teaches me to kill or hang myself:
> If I were mad, I should forget my son,
> Or madly think a babe of clouts were he:
> I am not mad: too well, too well I feel
> The different plague of each calamity.

(*KJ* 3.3.45–61)

General notes: In this extract, Constance, the widow of King John's brother, fears for the life of her son, Arthur, who is seen as a rival for the throne. Here she is responding to a cardinal who accuses her of uttering madness. The first seven lines of this extract provide a relatively simple contrast to Example 1, so for some groups it could even be cut to just this first section.

Reading in a circle: In a circle, with scripts in their left hands, each person reads one word (later one line) to the person on their right, touching their shoulder and making eye contact (if appropriate). This emphasizes the urgency of what Constance is conveying, as learners collaboratively produce the entire speech. It also helps the teacher to overhear anything that is causing difficulties so that it can be sensitively addressed between readthroughs, rather than identified as anyone's "mistake." The starting point and direction can be changed if necessary. After several readthroughs, ask what words learners have heard repeated (both "mad" and "grief" are prominent) and how they think Constance is using them.

Tackling unfamiliar words: In the circle, or in pairs/smaller groups, learners identify unfamiliar words, and see what interpretations they can come up with based on context, and their existing linguistic resources. Some words will need to be explained (e.g., "babe of clouts" (ragdoll), "canonized"), but learners will hopefully work out "thou" (you), "art" (are), "shalt" (shall) and "tis" (it is), helping them make more sense of this and other Shakespearean texts. (The aim with all of these example activities is for learners to explore and play with the language first, with explanations and definitions coming later as necessary, in order to avoid them becoming dictionary driven exercises.)

Punctuation shift/walking the punctuation: Learners spread out, reading the speech at low volume while walking around the room, turning ninety degrees when they reach a comma, and one-hundred-and-eighty degrees for all other punctuation marks. At some points they will have full- or multi-line utterances before turning, and at others just a single "O." Doing this, learners physically follow the internal logic of Constance's speech, helping them interpret her arguments about madness and grief, and understand her emotions. (Learners should be told that the punctuation in modern editions is not Shakespeare's, but has been mediated by scribes, printers, and successive generations of editors. However, with a well-chosen speech—including real life political addresses—this can be a very productive activity.)

Example 3: "No, I defy all counsel, all redress"

CONSTANCE

> No, I defy all counsel, all redress,
> But that which ends all counsel, true redress,
> Death, death; O amiable lovely death:
> Thou odoriferous stench: sound rottenness:
> Arise forth from the couch of lasting night,
> Thou hate and terror to prosperity,
> And I will kiss thy detestable bones,
> And put my eyeballs in thy vaulty brows,
> And ring these fingers with thy household worms,
> And stop this gap of breath with fulsome dust,
> And be a carrion monster like thyself:
> Come, grin on me, and I will think thou smil'st
> And buss thee as thy wife: misery's love,
> O, come to me!

(*KJ* 3.3.23–36)

General notes: This extract, in which Constance refuses to be mollified over Arthur's fate, is actually what prompts the cardinal to call her mad in Example 2. The two can be used together or independently, but if presented in this reverse order, this extract's strange, gruesome juxtapositions can really surprise learners who have been examining the logic of the extract above. In the following activities, learners are encouraged to enjoy playing with the sound and feel of strange and unfamiliar words, and to reflect on how the sense and meaning made through language depend on much more than what the words literally mean.

Initial readthrough: For these exercises it is crucial that learners speak and hear the words—whether in a circle or pairs/small groups—rather than reading silently. This will help them hear certain repetitions (e.g., "death," "redress"), and certain things that stand out as vivid or surprising ("kiss," "monster," "worms," etc.). Learners can then call out other words that seem to match these, building up a fuller picture of the extract. You can also ask if they can work out, from the context, which word is an archaism for "kiss" ("buss").

Exploring polarities: After a couple of readthroughs, learners will likely have noticed some odd juxtapositions of words, sometimes in a single oxymoron (e.g., "amiable lovely death"). These apparent contradictions can be explored by learners giving a thumbs up/thumbs down when they hear clearly positive/negative words. This will help them understand why Constance, in her grief, appears to be embracing the thought of death, and as a pattern emerges, learners may also be able to work out the gist of some of the more unfamiliar terms (realising, for example, that "sound" before "rottenness" is likely to be positive in this context). From here, and especially if there are any disagreements over what learners identify as positive or negative, a discussion can be developed about the importance of context, and interpersonal and intercultural factors, in interpreting meaning.

Imaging/playing with delivery: Individually or in small groups, learners take a short stretch of the speech, and pick one word from each line that they think is the most striking, either in meaning or in sound. They then need to say their chosen words in an appropriately exaggerated way and devise bold physical gestures to match. When ready, learners share their words and gestures as a "highlight reel" with the group. From here, learners can move to reading the whole speech, while playing with the sounds of the words in various ways (e.g., by exaggerating the vowels or consonants) and noticing what stands out when they do this. As this is drama, and both Shakespeare and Constance are trying to make an impact, learners should be encouraged to make their delivery and movements as big as possible, really hitting the vivid line-ending words and using the series of lines that begin with "And" to keep building the drama. The two "O" sounds can be especially enjoyable to work with. Learners can experiment with different ways of passing the sound to one another, playing with and comparing the pragmatic consequences of different lengths, pitches, and intonations in English and other languages they speak. As with Example 1, this could easily be built by the learners into a collaborative, non-naturalistic performance piece. Alternatively, learners could respond with a piece of creative writing that plays with the sounds of different words and/or makes a different kind of sense through the juxtaposition of apparently contradictory words and images.

Conclusion

The monologues above were chosen deliberately to demonstrate how even a single speaker's words can be turned into active, collaborative explorations of intercultural meaning-making. Of course, stretches of dialogue or short scenes can also work extremely well, and the use of techniques such as "Five Point Chase," "One-Word Dialogues," and "Scene Studies" (RSC 2013: 293–7) opens up further possibilities for exploring intercultural interactions. However, whether an extract features the words of one speaker or several, this chapter has tried to illustrate how the strangeness of Shakespeare's dramatic language—its unfamiliarity and difference, but also its rare beauty and power—can be used to facilitate interactional, intercultural learning in EFL contexts. Rather than teaching linguistic and cultural "facts" designed to be useful in narrowly defined communicative contexts, this approach seeks a deeper learning that engages the emotions and the intellect, and helps learners reflect on, and develop their understandings of other people, cultures, and languages—and themselves. This deeper learning can be achieved through combining active approaches (Banks 2014; Gibson 1998; RSC 2013; Stredder 2009), which teach Shakespeare as a collaborative, playful, physical endeavor, with principles, and practices for intercultural language education (Liddicoat & Scarino 2013), through which learners actively engage in multi-layered processes of interpreting and negotiating meaning in interaction. Together, these approaches place the learner at the center of powerful educational experiences, which stimulate affective, physical, and intellectual responses, and address learners' identities within, and beyond, the classroom. In the extract from Shakespeare's *Henry VIII* which opened this chapter, Queen Katherine fears that a "strange tongue" will make her seem more alien, and her cause less sympathetic. As a result she wants to communicate in English instead, a language she has come to know intimately having "lived in" it. In Katherine's precarious situation this is understandable, but we do not have to take the same attitude when it comes to language education. An interactional, intercultural approach to Shakespeare can remind us that, just as the languages we already live in can be made strange—both unfamiliar and wondrous—we can also find excitement and recognition as we start to live in and through languages that might seem "foreign" to us, but may not remain so.

Note

1 See https://www.shakespeare.org.uk/explore-shakespeare/shakespedia/shakespeares-plays/king-john/ for written and video synopses of *King John*, and https://www.rsc.org.uk/king-john/trailer for the RSC trailer.

References

Banks, F. (2014), *Creative Shakespeare*. London: Bloomsbury Arden Shakespeare.
Blake, N. F. (2002), *A Grammar of Shakespeare's Language*. Basingstoke: Palgrave.

Blank, P. (2014), "Introducing 'Intrelinguistics': Shakespeare and Early/Modern English." In M. Saenger (ed.), *Interlinguicity, Internationality and Shakespeare*, 138–55, Montreal: McGill Queen's University Press.

Blank, P. (2018), *Shakesplish: How We Read Shakespeare's Language*. Stanford: Stanford University Press.

Braüer, G. (2002), *Body and Language: Intercultural Learning through Drama*. Westport: Ablex.

Byram, M. (1997), *Teaching and Assessing Intercultural Communicative Competence*. Clevedon: Multilingual Matters.

Byram, M. & Fleming, M. (1998), "Introduction." In M. Byram & M. Fleming (eds), *Language Learning in Intercultural Perspective: Approaches through Drama and Ethnography*, 1–10, Cambridge: Cambridge University Press.

Cheng, A. Y. M. & Winston, J. (2011), "Shakespeare as a Second Language: Playfulness, Power and Pedagogy in the ESL Classroom." *Research in Drama Education*, 16 (4): 541–56.

Cohen, R. A. (2018), *Shakesfear and How to Cure It*. London: Bloomsbury Arden Shakespeare.

Coles, J. (2009), "Testing Shakespeare to the Limit: Teaching Macbeth in a Year 9 Classroom." *English in Education*, 43 (1): 32–49.

Cook, G. (2000), *Language Play, Language Learning*. Oxford: Oxford University Press.

Crutchfield, J. & Schewe, M. (2017), *Going Performative in Intercultural Education*. Bristol: Multilingual Matters.

Crystal, D. (2008), *Think on My Words: Exploring Shakespeare's Language*. Cambridge: Cambridge University Press.

Crystal, D. (2016), *The Oxford Dictionary of Original Shakespearean Pronunciation*. Oxford: Oxford University Press.

Crystal, D. & Crystal, B. (2002), *Shakespeare's Words: A Glossary and Language Companion*. London: Penguin.

Culpeper, J. & Archer, D. (2020), "Shakespeare's Language: Styles and Meanings via the Computer." *Language and Literature*, 29 (3): 191–202.

Davies, C. (2021), *Strangeness in Jacobean Drama*. Abingdon: Routledge.

Dewey, J. (1916), *Democracy and Education*. New York: Macmillan.

Dewey, J. (1938), *Education and Experience*. New York: Macmillan.

Espinosa, R. (2016), "Stranger Shakespeare." *Shakespeare Quarterly*, 67 (1): 51–67.

Fleming, M. (1998), "Cultural Awareness and Dramatic Art Forms." In M. Byram & M. Fleming (eds), *Language Learning in Intercultural Perspective: Approaches through Drama and Ethnography*, 147–57, Cambridge: Cambridge University Press.

Fletcher, J. & Shakespeare, W. (2012), "The Life of King Henry the Eighth." In J. Bate & E. Rasmussen (eds), *The RSC Shakespeare: King John and Henry VIII*, 163–2, Basingstoke: Macmillan.

Gibson, R. (1998), *Teaching Shakespeare*. Cambridge: Cambridge University Press.

Johnson, K. (2014), *Shakespeare's English: A Practical Linguistic Guide*. Abingdon: Routledge.

Johnson, M. (2008), *The Meaning of the Body: Aesthetics of Human Understanding*. Chicago: University of Chicago Press.

Kao, S. & O'Neill, C. (1998), *Words into Worlds: Learning a Second Language through Process Drama*. Stamford: Ablex.

Kermode, F. (2000), *Shakespeare's Language*. London: Allen Lane.

Kramsch, C. (1993), *Context and Culture in Language Teaching*. Oxford: Oxford University Press.

Liddicoat, A. J. & Scarino, A. (2013), *Intercultural Language Teaching and Learning*. Chichester: Wiley-Blackwell.

Magnusson, L. with Schalkwyk, D. (2019), *The Cambridge Companion to Shakespeare's Language*. Cambridge: Cambridge University Press.

McConachy, T. (2018), *Developing Intercultural Perspectives on Language Use: Exploring Pragmatics and Culture in Foreign Language Learning*. Bristol: Multilingual Matters.

McLuskie, K. (2009), "Dancing and Thinking: Teaching 'Shakespeare' in the Twenty-First Century." In G. B. Shand (ed.), *Teaching Shakespeare: Passing It On*, 121–40, Chichester: Wiley-Blackwell.

Murphy, S., Culpeper, J., Gillings, M. and Pace-Sigge, M. (2020), "What Do Students Find Difficult when They Read Shakespeare? Problems and Solutions." *Language and Literature*, 29 (3): 302–26.

Neelands, J. and O'Hanlon, J. (2011), "There Is Some Soul of Good: An Action-Centred Approach to Teaching Shakespeare in Schools." *Shakespeare Survey*, 64: 240–50.

Olive, S. (2015), *Shakespeare Valued*. Bristol: Intellect.

Piazzoli, E. (2018), *Embodying Language in Action: The Artistry of Process Drama in Second Language Education*. Cham: Palgrave Macmillan.

Pulverness, A. (2014), "Material for Cultural Awareness." In B. Tomlinson (ed.), *Developing Materials for Language Teaching*, 132–44, London: Bloomsbury.

Risager, K. (2007), *Language and Culture Pedagogy: From a National to a Transnational Paradigm*. Clevedon: Multilingual Matters.

Ros-i-Solé, C. (2016), *The Personal World of the Language Learner*. London: Palgrave Macmillan.

Royal Shakespeare Company (2013), *The RSC Shakespeare Toolkit for Teachers*. London: Methuen.

Shakespeare, W. (2012), *The Life and Death of King John*. In J. Bate & E. Rasmussen (eds), *The RSC Shakespeare: King John and Henry VIII*, 23–104, Basingstoke: Macmillan.

Stredder, J. (2009), *The North Face of Shakespeare*. Cambridge: Cambridge University Press.

Winston, J. (2010), *Beauty and Education*. Abingdon: Routledge.

Winston, J. (2015), *Transforming the Teaching of Shakespeare with the Royal Shakespeare Company*. London: Bloomsbury Arden Shakespeare.

Wittgenstein, L. (1953), *Philosophische Untersuchungen*. Chichester: Blackwell.

Reader Response, Aesthetics, and Deep Learning in the German Language-Culture Classroom

Chantelle Warner

Introduction

Drawing from a range of theoretical and empirical perspectives, scholars in second language and culture teaching have, with increasing insistence, emphasized the importance of meaningful experiences for deep learning (e.g., Dubreil & Thorne 2017). Within the context of these discussions, the predominance of "transactional" language use that has been a hallmark of proficiency-oriented and communicative language teaching for the past few decades (e.g., NCSSFL and ACTFL 2017, Council of Europe 2001) has been subject to ever-increasing criticism (e.g., Byrnes et al. 2010; see also Allen & Paesani 2010: 121–2; Warner & Dupuy 2018). "Transactional" is here typically understood in something like Brown and Yule's (1983) sense of language in the service of information exchange, and it contrasts and complements the other primary function, the interactional, i.e., language use for the maintenance and negotiation of social relationships. The intrinsically social nature of language has been emphasized within frameworks of language education that propose alternatives to the primacy of transactional, typically oral language use as the goal and measure of learning. These include most notably those informed by sociocultural theory, with its roots in the theories of Lev Vygotsky (e.g., Lantolf & Thorne 2006; Levine 2020), and social semiotics as inspired by the linguistic models of M.A.K. Halliday (e.g., Byrnes 2007). Both theories foreground socialization and semioticization in language use and learning. As one of the primary semiotic (read: meaning making) systems through which humans make sense of the world and their roles and relationships with others within it, these approaches argue, language mediates our experiences, ideas, and relationships in profound ways. Coincidentally, something like this complexity is captured by the notion of "transaction" as conceptualized by a scholar working in literary studies rather than linguistics; for Louise Rosenblatt "transactional reading" involves a unique, potentially aesthetic experience in which the reader and text continuously act and are acted upon by each other.

This chapter takes this tension between "transactional" language use and "transactional reading" as a point of departure for theorizing the importance of aesthetic dimensions of language and literacy learning that are often neglected (it is argued) in predominant models based in communicative, sociocultural, and social semiotic frameworks. Such attention to aesthetics has already been implied within contemporary design approaches to second language literacy, which emphasize the "creative human processes" (Kern 2015: 2; see also Allen 2018) involved in making meaning from the material, social, and individual semiotic resources available. Drawing from Rosenblatt's theories of reader response and working with a case study from an intermediate German language-culture class at a US university, I propose that centering transactional reading and aesthetic response as part of an approach to second language literacy can enable language educators to realize the pedagogical desideratum of going beyond "transactional" (read: propositional) meanings by connecting other functions of language deliberately with affect and ethics. This is envisioned as part of an approach to second language-culture education that sees learners as not only potential social actors who can "do things with words," but as reflective *languagers* (Phipps & Gonzales 2004) who are attentive to how different ways of making meaning afford them alternative ways of being in the world. And reading and writing of literary texts is a vital part of kind of transformative learning.

In the sections that follow, I begin by outlining the aspects of Rosenblatt's reader response model that are most important for this discussion of transactional reading in the language-culture classroom and draw connections between these theories and relevant discussions within the fields of applied linguistics and language education. I then use the case of a student, Klara, and her responses to a cluster of texts she read as part of a unit in an intermediate German language-culture course in order to illustrate how aesthetic reading can impact learner wellbeing in unexpected and transformational ways. A central focus of this discussion will be a creative writing composition written by Klara, through which she explored how her story and experiences intersected with the narratives she had read in class. Finally, I will conclude with some suggestions for how transactional literacy can be a part of educators' pedagogical practices in language and culture teaching.

Toward a Transactional Theory for the Language-Culture Classroom: Rosenblatt's Reader Response in Dialogue with Contemporary Second Language and Literacy Studies

Within fields of applied linguistics, literacy studies, and language education, Louise Rosenblatt is most often cited for her distinction between "efferent" and "aesthetic" reading—a pair of concepts which too often get shorthanded as reading for information and reading for pleasure. Within literary studies—the discipline in which she led her career—Rosenblatt has (until relatively recently) been overlooked almost completely. In a contribution to a 2007 volume of *College English* focusing on Rosenblatt and the "Ethical Turn in Literary Studies," Elizabeth Flynn suggested that this might be because Rosenblatt committed a dual faux-pas—she was both interested in pedagogy and she was a woman at a time when literary theory was almost the exclusive domain of men. Over the last decade—in part in connection with emerging interest in ethics and affect— her work has been the object of renewed interest. For example, the 2019 theme for the annual convention of the Modern Language Association (the largest professional organization for scholars of language and literature in North America), "Beyond Text and Transaction," deliberately played off of one of her core concepts, "the textual transaction."

Rosenblatt's interest in pedagogy was an extension of her literary theory, at the center of which was a critique of tendencies to treat the text first and foremost as an object. This, she argued, can lead to impoverished efferent modes of reading literary texts; to read literature qua literature requires instead an aesthetic transaction. By working out why they respond to a literary work in the way that they do, Rosenblatt argued, readers can clarify their values and share in the values of others. Allowing space for aesthetic response in our approach to literary texts can thus be the basis for ethical activity—which she, fueled by anti-authoritarian sentiments rooted in the post-Second World War time period, associated with democratic education (comp. Vytniorgu 2018).

In cursory citations of efferent and aesthetic reading, it often gets overlooked that Rosenblatt's theories of literary reading are deeply ecological—in ways that resonate with sociocultural and social semiotic models within applied linguistics (e.g., Byrnes et al. 2006; Levine 2020; van Lier 2004; comp. Leander et al. 2017) and in ways that might augment models of second language literacy. Leo van Lier, whose book *The Ecology and Semiotics of Language Learning* has been seminal in discussions of ecological approaches to language teaching and learning, described the self in an ecological understanding of language as "not just a detached observer taking in the world through the window of the mind, but [...] an ongoing project of establishing one's place in the world" (2004: 115). In a comparable observation, Rosenblatt argued that language should not be seen as "a self-contained, ungrounded, ready-made code of signifier and signifieds, but as embodied in transactions between individuals and their social and natural context" (1986: 123). Within these contexts, we are constantly engaged in "choosing activity"; in the event of reading, the reader consciously or unconsciously chooses a stance, a "selective attitude," "bringing certain aspects into the center of attention and pushing others into the fringes." (Rosenblatt 1988: 5). Rosenblatt conceptualized this push and pull of attention along a dynamic continuum of efferent and aesthetic, depending on whether attention is more focused on what is to be done when the reading ends (efferent) or whether the reader welcomes into awareness the sensations, images, feelings, and ideas evoked through reading (aesthetic). When transposed into pedagogical practice, the former might prioritize reading for information or for the names, dates, and plot highlights that characterize literary study guides and Wikipedia articles; only through aesthetic reading can more transformative learning take place.

Reader response theories in general and those of Rosenblatt more specifically are sometimes cast as a sort of solipsism or hyper-personalization that feels at odds with contemporary theories of interculturality and literacy, where the social and cultural nature of meaning making is emphasized (e.g., Kern 2000; Kramsch 1993; Liddicoat & Scarino 2013).[1] Contemporary multiliteracies theories, which have had a significant influence on North American language-culture teaching over the last two decades (e.g., Allen & Paesani 2010; Paesani et al. 2015), offer a framework for reconceptualizing the connections between personal aesthetic response and sociocultural practices of meaning making as *design*. This notion, originally proposed by the New London Group (1996) and inspired heavily by M.A.K. Halliday's social semiotics, treats language and other modes of communication as dynamic resources, *Available Designs*, for meaning making. These undergo constant changes through acts of *Designing* as language users attempt to achieve their own purposes in new contexts. *Designing* leads to the emergence of *the Redesigned*, new meanings through which the world and the meaning maker alike are transformed (New London Group 1996: 73-6). *Design* is intended to foreground the creative, generative potential of language, while also providing a framework for conceptualizing the recurrent, conventionalized ways in which many available designs are taken up in practice.

Rosenblatt's model of transactional reading is not incompatible with this notion of design, although it also diverges in scope and focus in some key ways. For Rosenblatt one's individual, personal response should be the beginning, not the entirety of the transactional process and she is critical of extreme forms of subjectivism; deep aesthetic reading needs to be conscienceful and responsible, maintaining an attentiveness to the intentions of the author of a text. We assume, after all, that a thinking, feeling being (or beings) selected the symbols before us. She emphasizes, however, that the reader's relationship (at least in the act of reading) is not with the author, but the text and that it is thus fundamentally a semiotic relationship. The printed "text stirs up elements of the linguistic/experiential reservoir" (Rosenblatt 1988: 5), what she describes as an inner capital of "funded assumptions, attitudes, and expectations about the world—and about language" (Rosenblatt 1988: 3). And part of being a responsible reader is developing a sensitivity to the textual cues of intersubjectivity points, or what we might describe as the *designs* of the text that evoke different responses (compare Council of Europe 2018).

Rosenblatt described this kind of aesthetic reading experience as "a reciprocal, mutually defining relationship in which the elements or parts are aspects or phases of a total situation or event" (Rosenblatt 1986: 122–3). Aesthetic reading is thus not just pleasure reading nor is some kind of solipsistic response in which readers impose their meaning on a text, rather it is a complex process of evocation and response, in which we as readers

> … respond to the very story or poem that we are evoking during the transaction with the text. In order to shape the work, we draw on our reservoir of past experience with people and the world, our past inner linkage of words and things, our past encounters with spoken or written texts. We listen to the sound of words in the inner ear; we lend our sensations, our emotions, our sense of being alive, to the new experience which, we feel, corresponds to the text. We participate in the story, we identify with characters, we share their conflicts and their feelings. At the same time there is a stream of responses being generated. There may be a sense of pleasure in our own creative activity, an awareness of pleasant or awkward sound and movement in the words, a feeling of approval or disapproval of the characters and their behavior. We may be aware of a contrast between the assumptions or expectations about life that we brought to the reading and the attitudes, moral codes, social situations we are living through in the world created in transaction with the text (1982: 270).

This "interanimating" (Rosenblatt 1978: 53) relationship between the text and the reader is what inspired her to choose the term "transaction" instead of "interaction," which she felt suggests that these are two discrete entities. Also for this reason, she cautioned against imposing the interpretations of *professional readers*, such as critics and scholars, or pushing students to move too quickly to an abstracted *reading*, which can cut short the "sensed, felt, thought nature of evocation" (p. 135). The initial encounter with the text is vital for Rosenblatt, because, unlike the critic or scholar, the readers' "primary subject matter is the web of feelings, sensations, images, ideas" woven between them and the text (1978: 137; see also Flynn 2007: 65).

Rosenblatt's commitment to the centrality of the lived experience of reading anticipates the more recent critiques of design approaches from within literacy studies (e.g., Leander & Boldt 2013; Pahl & Rowsell 2020), as well as poststructuralist theories of affect within applied linguists (e.g., Kong 2019; Prior 2019). While noting the value of multiliteracies frameworks for expanding the scope of literacy and language education, Kevin Leander and Gail Boldt's (2013) critical re-reading of the New London Group's (1996) influential manifesto takes issue with the hyper-rationality often implied in the design metaphor on the basis that literacy-related activity is often not projected toward some textual end point or clearly defined purpose but "as living its life in the ongoing present, forming relations and connections across signs, objects, and bodies in often unexpected ways" (p. 26). Leander and Boldt argue further that literacy activity "is saturated with affect and emotion; that it creates and is fed by an ongoing series of affective intensities that are different from the rational control of meanings and forms" (p. 26). Literary studies scholar, Christian Ehret, draws on non-representational theory to suggest that literacy events have major and minor keys; whereas the former relates to "the structural tendency that organizes itself according to predetermined definitions of value," (Manning 2016: 1; cited in Ehret: 567) such as designs, the latter "produces transformations that are primarily felt" (p. 571). Ehret's overarching argument is that we as scholars and educators of language and literacy must work to attend to both. This idea of keying is a potentially helpful heuristic for both recognizing that much of what constitutes a literacy event is emergent and undirected, there is also a push and pull between these feelings and affects and the structures of value shaped by our social histories of reading, including those of the classroom.

Rosenblatt's transactional readers are responsive in the moment, but they are also self-aware and reflective, which is where the potential for ethical learning enters. By helping individual readers to work out why they evoked a literary work the way they did and spurring them to talk to others about their experiences with the same text it is not only reader response, but readerly responsibility that is fostered through the kinds of awareness at play in aesthetic reading and this (for Rosenblatt) is the ethical potential of literature, because it enables us to (at least provisionally) participate in the needs, aspirations, and affective dispositions of other personalities—those of the characters in the text and those of other readers—and to potentially develop a deeper awareness of our own.

Rosenblatt's discussion of the democratic potential of aesthetic reading anticipates some aspects of the critical pedagogical frameworks and social justice orientations found within contemporary educational discourse, but also reflects the concerns and biases of the historical moment within which she wrote. Noting its subversive potential, Suzanne Keen leans heavily on Rosenblatt's transactional theory to develop her model of narrative empathy, arguing that "intersectional axes of identity" play an important role in reader response (2013: 53)—although she also notes that Rosenblatt's commitment to individual readings does not prevent her from often postulating readers who are seemingly without race or class, and we might also add that their genders are diverse only within a binary (Keen 2013: 59). This is at least in part a symptom of her time; Rosenblatt's provocation that readers need not be "ideal" or "educated" and they certainly do not need to be male literary critics was a provocation in itself.

Despite these blind spots, Rosenblatt remained devoted to an idea of cultural plurality, which she believed could be fostered through aesthetically oriented education. Literature was for her a way for "aiding us to understand ourselves and others, for widening our horizons to include temperaments and cultures different from our own, for helping us to clarify our conflicts in values, for illuminating our world" (1982: 276). Thus, although Rosenblatt, as an English literature scholar in an English dominant country, does not directly address the particularities of second language and culture learning, aspects of her model of transactional reading are readily adaptable for the transcultural space of the second language-culture classroom and even resonate with theories of interculturality, such as those of Claire Kramsch. In her early work, Kramsch proposed the notion of third place, a place that preserves diversity—"of styles, purposes, and interests" (1993: 247)—as an alternative to models on intercultural competence, where differences are often treated as something to be overcome. The reflexivity enabled through the insider/outsider status of the language learner, Kramsch argued, allows for a mode of participation that is different from the sort of foreign visitor status often evoked within language pedagogy that prioritizes appropriateness. In Kramsch's more recent work, the notion of third place is extended into the concept of symbolic competence, which is discourse-based, historically grounded, aesthetically sensitive, and that takes into account the actual, the imagined, and the virtual worlds in which we live (Kramsch 2011: 354). Symbolic competence much more clearly directs the reflective potential of the third place toward capacities related to "embodied experiences, emotional resonances, and moral imaginings" (2006: 251) and for this reason, Kramsch argues that symbolic competence "ought to be nourished by a literary imagination at all levels of the language curriculum" (2006: 251). This echoes Rosenblatt's claims that personal response can serve as a matrix for analyzing the social cultural influences on a reader, and furthermore suggests that aesthetic experiences such as those evoked during transactional literacy events can contribute toward the development of a person's sense of themselves as what Kramsch (2009) describes as a *multilingual subject,* which entails the capacity to think, feel, and act across multiple languages and semiotic systems.

In the section that comes next, Klara's case study from an intermediate/advanced level German language-culture class provides an example of how transactional reading can play out in an instructed language class in unexpected ways. Whereas many of the contemporary studies of affect and literacy are based on ethnographic data, often from outside of the classroom, I will rely on Klara's course work, my notes, and impressions from teaching the course, and an email exchange we had after the course had ended. Because my concern is how educators and curriculum developers can make space for aesthetic response in the context of language teaching, although this data lacks some of the empirical richness of a truly ethnographic study, it also provides an opportunity to reflect on how we can recognize both the major and minor keys of literacy activity (Ehret 2018) in the flow of pedagogical practice. This is a point I will then return to in the final section, which concludes with implications for teacher-scholars of second language literacy.

Klara's Story: A Case of Creative Fiction as Reader Response from the German Classroom

At the time of this case study, Klara was an undergraduate student in a fifth-semester German as a second language classroom taught at a large public university in the US American Southwest. The course was typically described as intermediate/advanced, because it included both students who had come directly from the basic language sequence, i.e., the first two years of instruction or who had tested in from high school and students who had spent the summer before in an intensive study abroad program, as Klara had done. Although there was a range of proficiency levels and experiences represented in the class, the students were overwhelmingly majoring or minoring in German at this point. Klara at this point had declared German as a minor and stated in a student survey at the start of the semester that she hoped to someday study medicine in Germany.

The multiliteracies-inspired curriculum of the course was structured around three topics, which were each linked to a particular genre family (see Table 7.1). The readings for each unit related to the theme, but also were selected as models of the genre or aspects thereof. For example, the second unit—where the lesson at the center of this study was situated—included examples of narratives in multiple modalities and in a variety of forms including poetry, prose, film, and recorded testimony. The primary assessments were three literacy-based tasks completed across multiple drafts: a descriptive text, a narrative, and an argumentative essay. The readings from the corresponding unit served as models for designing each of these compositions, but the connection to the theme was more implicit. This was intentional in order to allow enough openness in the tasks for students to have some freedom in what they wrote, while also providing them with enough reflection on the kinds of available designs that might be relevant, e.g., past tense verbs, causal adverbs, and temporal expressions in a narrative. Additionally, students were asked to write a more informal response to each text read or viewed for the class in a journal, which was assessed based on completion every two weeks. Students were sometimes given suggested writing prompts for these journals, but they were envisioned as a space where to respond more freely to the readings, while also giving the instructors a chance to dialogue a little with each student's thoughts—since this was otherwise not easily afforded by the large size of the class (twenty-two students).

While the stated objectives of the course were organized around specific available designs, i.e., those related to the three genre families associated with each unit, both my co-teacher and I had extensive discussions throughout the semester about how to also make space for student responses to the texts. Rather than foregrounding the historical context or dominant readings, as is often done in second language-culture textbooks (see Gramling & Warner 2011; Warner 2014), we tried to promote an iterative process of reading, where discussions of the students' first responses and evocations were guided toward questions that allowed the students to revisit the text with new forms of self-awareness. For example, in the second unit, which will be the focus of this case study, students were provided with a digital version of the text that included hyperlinked explications and intertextual references related to some of the cultural allusions in the text but were encouraged to consult these only when so moved during the first reading. In class, as questions about the context and how we might interpret the narrators' actions within that cultural-historical moment arose, students

Table 7.1 Curriculum overview

THEMATIC FOCUS	FEATURED GENRE FAMILIES
The Individual in Society *(Das Individuum in der Gesellschaft)*	Description/Portrayal/Vignette
Stories from German History *(Geschichten aus der deutschen Geschichte)*	Narrative
Gaming and Game Culture *(Gaming und Spielkulturen)*	Position paper/Opinion piece

were asked to return to the annotations to see what possible answers they could find. In this way, text and context alike were left more open to reader response.

The second unit included four thematic sub-modules, each representing a different moment of twentieth or twenty-first century German history: post-war Germany, the student movements, contemporary German society, and the Berlin Wall and everyday life in East Germany. The intended learning objective for each of these sub-modules was not for the students to master the particular historical contexts—although the texts, media, and supplemental materials offered them a sense of key events, figures, and discourses; rather all of the mini modules were connected by a set of questions related to the ways in which personal narratives can stand in for broader experiences. Students' core assessment for this unit was then a personal recount, which they were told could be fictional or non-fictional.

The case I will focus on comes from the last of these mini modules. The primary readings included the poem "Naturschutzgebiet" (1982; Nature Preserve) by Sarah Kirsch, which is a first-person description of the space surrounding the Berlin Wall, an excerpt from the novel *Helden wie wir* (1995; Heroes Like Us) by Thomas Brussig, which is a parody memoir about growing up and being socialized into East German society and specifically into the youth group *Die junge Pioniere* (the Young Pioneers), and two autobiographical vignettes from the collection *Meine freie deutsche Jugend* (2003; My Free German Youth) by Claudia Rusch, which depict her experiences as the child of political dissidents in East Germany. The latter three texts all partake in a cultural phenomenon during the 1990s and early 2000s that is often described as *Ostalgie*, a portmanteau of the German words for "east" (Ost) and "nostalgia" (Nostalgie). A defining feature of literary works associated with *Ostalgie* is the focus on making sense of what it meant to grow up in East Germany and humor is often evoked to express the related feelings of ambivalence that this conjured up for many authors. Kirsch's poem stood out a little from the other readings, both because of the poetic form and the position of the narrating perspective contemporary with the time of the Berlin Wall and the existence of the German Democratic Republic; but it shares with the other texts an ambivalent rather than explicitly critical stance on the institutions and actions of the East. In addition, students watched scenes from a German-Polish documentary, *Mauerhase* (2010; lit. "Wall Rabbit," released as *Rabbit à la Berlin*), which tells the story of the Berlin Wall from the point of view of the wild rabbits inhabiting the zone between the two walls separating East and West Berlin.

Student responses to the personal recounts from East Germany were mixed. While some enjoyed the opportunity to learn about a time in German history that they felt they knew little about, others felt frustrated by the *insiderliness* of the narratives, which included a large number of cultural references that are very specific to kids and teens in the 1980s in East Germany. Several reported that they felt excluded by this way of writing. It was clear in the class discussions of the poem "Naturschutzgebiet" that most of the class had also never considered the East German state as anything other than an authoritarian regime and at least a couple had believed that the Berlin Wall was built by the Soviet Union to imprison the residents in the German Democratic Republic. In many instances, students' feelings of dissonance with this set of readings echoed some of the tensions Kramsch and Byram (2008) describe in connection with another group of US-based students of German language and culture who similarly struggled to make sense of narrators who did not actively oppose but held more contradictory or unequivocal views about East German social practices and politics (see p. 27).

One of the students, Klara,[2] who was generally quite outspoken, made clear both during in-class discussions and in a reading journal entry completed following this unit that she did not like this mini module. She wrote that she found Brussig's and Rusch's stories "silly and boring." She preferred "romantic" stories. I was thus surprised to find that although almost all of the other students had chosen to tell a story from their own lives for the final composition in the narrative unit,[3] Klara submitted a narrative that related directly to the readings about East Germany. Klara's story, titled "Ich laufe…" (I run…), opened with the following:

> Ich laufe gerade, so schnell, aber es ist nicht schnell genug. Wo sollte meine Geschichte beginnen? Ich war ein Kind, ich war? Nein, das ist nicht meine Geschichte. Es war der 14. August 1961 und ich war in das Haus meines Freundes.

> *I am running now, so fast, but is it not fast enough. Where should my story begin? I was a child, I was? No, that is not my story. It was the August 14th, 1961 and I was in the house of my friend.*

In the next few lines, it becomes clear that the young, male narrator was visiting a friend in East Germany, when the wall went up and he was stuck there. He approached an "officer" and asked for assistance but was turned away.

> Ich hatte kein Pass, keine Mutter, kein vater, und keine Schwester. Ich war ein Kind hinder dem eisernen Vorhang.
>
> *I had no passport, no mother, no father, and no sister. I was behind the iron curtain.*

The narrator then describes how he was accepted into the home of his friend but missed his family. He attends school there, where she is learning Russian and has to attend Monday through Saturday—details about everyday life in East Germany that Klara had encountered in the readings. The narrator then sunk deeper and deeper into depression, as life became a boring cycle, "Schule, junge Pioneers … und dann?" (school, Young Pioneers … and then?). Finally, in an act of desperation, he decides to jump.

> Es war der 13. August 1964, ich bin nun 15 Jahre alt. Ich stand, ich wartete, ich dachte über meine Mutter und meinen Vater und meine Schwester, ich hatte für nichts zu leben. Ich lief. Jetzt laufe ich gerade, Ich springe über die erste Wand. Ich sehe die zweite Wand. Ich springe und ich höre einen Schuss und ich kann meine Beine fühlen nicht. Ich vermisse meine Eltern und meine Schwester. Ich habe für nichts zu leben.
>
> *It was the 13. August 1964, I am now 15 years old. I stood, I waited, I thought about my mother and my father and my sister, I had nothing to love for. I ran. Now I am running. I jump over the first wall. I see the second wall. I jump and I hear a shot and I cannot feel my legs. I miss my parents and my sister. I have nothing to live for.*

Klara's composition was striking to me at the time in a few ways. First, it bears nothing that, based on the metalanguage related to genres and the available designs that are associated with personal recounts we had used to articulate the learning objectives of this unit, Klara had clearly fulfilled the assignment and had shown substantial mastery over the lexico-grammatical forms related to narratives, which had been the focus of this part of the course. She also demonstrated cultural-historical knowledge in her description of school and recognition that the narrator would have to jump not once but twice to cross the Berlin Wall (which was in actuality two walls with a strip of land down the middle). Knowing Klara's frustration with the *Ostalgie* literature on the basis that it felt too unserious, I also found it intriguing that she had chosen to write a tragedy, and one that allowed her to incorporate her expanding repertoire of linguistic and cultural knowledge into a likely more familiar narrative of the Berlin Wall as a mechanism for imprisonment constructed by a malevolent state. The premise of Klara's story, that a teenager who is a citizen of West Germany would be held captive by the Berlin Wall was historically implausible, but seemed to create an opportunity for Klara to make sense of her aesthetic responses to the readings from the class. In this way, the creative writing provided an opportunity for transactional literacy as part of a series of interconnected aesthetic events.

A little more than a year after the course had ended, I re-encountered Klara's composition, when sorting through various learning artifacts from this course as part of a research study. Although Klara had not been a student in my class again, we had stayed in touch enough for me to know that she moved back to the city an hour away from our campus to live with her family. I reached out to ask if she remembered writing this story and why she had chosen to write what she did. She responded in an email, in which she affirmed that she remembered this assignment quite clearly and went on to share the following:

> This time in my life was particularly hard, my mom had cancer and that put a kind of depressing overtone to a lot of my writing ... I re-read the one you sent, and I have half a mind to correct it, lol.
>
> German helped me get out of my depression [...]
>
> I had really not known anything about the Berlin Wall, but thinking about that period of time, I had wondered what I would do if I was separated from my family for good instead of me just being a city away from them; not knowing how they were doing, not knowing if I'd ever see them again. And I think that's what prompted the story. If I was young and I wanted it that badly for that many years, would I try to do it; no matter what the costs?

This was a dimension of Klara's experiences with the readings that I had not been privy to during the class. Despite giving an impression of being outspoken and forthcoming, Klara had not shared anything of what was happening with her family life with me or in class. But this had also been a part of her aesthetic experience of the readings from the class including the *Ostalgie* texts. The narratives seemed to create an affective space of imagination within which she was able to experience feelings that were both familiar and defamiliarized. As she described it, writing the story enabled for Klara something like what Ehret describes as a *relational transformation*, a break "where the major's tendency is broken through a minor gesture" (2018: 571). In this case, a clash in narrative discourses related to the experience of living in East Germany perhaps contributed to this rupture. At the time of the course, the effects of this transactional experience were only minimally indexed through Klara's expressions of dislike and then through the act of creative writing in response to the readings.

Conclusion

Klara, like many students in the class, experienced an initial frustration with the *Ostalgie* texts, because they included many illusions that were opaque to her as someone who grew up in a different time and place and because they did not fit the more familiar tragic narratives of East Germany during the time of the Berlin Wall. Comprehension and historicist models for teaching literature in the language-culture classroom might compel us to address these complaints by helping the learners to understand how an ideal (i.e., native speaking) reader might have made sense of these works. For example, we might try to supply pertinent information about the cultural context of *Ostalgie* upfront and maybe talk about the reception of these works in German-speaking spaces. There is nothing inherently wrong with this approach; however, with Rosenblatt's help, we might think about what stances and positionalities we are affording learners as we decide how best to bring in these contexts and perspectives.

A learner might gain new knowledge about the historical context of East Germany, if we focus on explicating aspects of everyday life in the text, which they might find unfamiliar or confounding. But in privileging a more efferent stance over an aesthetic one, what might get lost is the ways in which *Ostalgie* is somewhat exclusionary and subversive by design, exactly because it offers an alternative insiderliness those who likewise counted the days until they could graduate from the *Junge Pioniere* or who celebrated important milestones with difficult to acquire Western treats from the *KaDeWe* in West Berlin, which stands in contrast to the normalizing effects of reunification. We must ask ourselves whether, in our attempts to help learners more readily comprehend the text and overcome those aspects of the text that make them feel excluded, do we destine them to miss out on the fun, the thrill, and yes the frustrations that come from entering into spaces that were not built to fit them? By framing interpretation as a predetermined place learners need to get to with the right information often results in a third reading stance, which Cheryl Hogue Smith (2012) in her expansion of Rosenblatt's theories has identified as *deferent* reading. Deferent reading focuses on meaning *finding* rather than meaning *making*, and thus takes the form of a kind of a didactic game of hide and seek. Deferent reading does often include affective or emotive responses, Hogue Smith notes; however, these are less aesthetic and more accurately anesthetic, in that reading becomes an emotionally numbing process. The emphasis is on performing an accepted reading on not on the students' experience. This also shuts of space for the kinds of meaningful *symbolic struggles* (Warner & Richardson 2017) that can contribute to the development of symbolic competence, by enabling learners to explore in thinking and feelings the difficulties and discomforts they may face when they try to position themselves within multilayered social spaces, such as those that emerge when fields of cultural production collide with educational spaces and historical moments collide with contemporaneous cultural practices and affect worlds.

In Klara's case—and as is often the case when we ask students to engage with literary texts with texts in a literary way—creating space for aesthetic response revealed something happening that was in excess of my pedagogical models and learning objectives, but which was intimately connected to literacy as lived experience. For Klara the experience of reading and creatively writing in response to the cluster of literary texts seemed to allow her to not only engage in some oppositional practice (Kramsch & Nolden 1994) vis-a-vis the symbolic meanings of the *Ostalgie* texts but also to weave in very personal, emotional experiences pertinent to her life in that moment by exploiting affect worlds and ethical values that were not her own. The ability to respond in creative writing, rather than being pushed to rationalize her responses immediately using the structural logic of a literary analysis, also allowed her to explore the colliding affect worlds of text and life before having to talk about them, for as Prior notes, "thinking or talking about emotions is not the same as having them" (2019: 519).

Reflecting back, even without the knowledge of Klara's mother's illness, I wish I had asked questions that would have helped me to discover whether she had wholesale rejected the feelings of ambivalence expressed by the narrators in the texts we read, in favor of a more comfortable and familiar affect world in which East Germany is oppressive and dark. Following Rosenblatt's arguments about ethics and the democratic potential of reading again, this could have allowed me to not only validate Klara's response to the readings, but to use that as more of an opportunity to consider what it might mean to experience life, history, and language quite differently. At the same time, only by leaving room for an aesthetic experience and for the expression thereof within the context of the class could I begin to ask these questions, that is only by moments of "difference, surprise, and unfolding that follow along paths that are not rational or linear or obviously critical or political" (Leander & Boldt 2013: 22, 44) and that therefore potentially depart from our curricular designs. In the tension between these two, transactional literacy offers language-culture educators the potential for fostering in students not only *critical thinking* but what we might describe as *critical feeling*, the capacity to revel in an experience and then reflect on why it evokes in us the feelings and responses that it does and the different feelings and responses it may evoke in others as part of an aesthetic dialogue.

For scholars and practitioners of language and culture teaching, transactional literacy poses two main questions for us to continue to consider:

1. *How do we make space for aesthetic response within the other constraints and obligations of our classrooms and curricula?* Here we can think of Ehret's discussion of major and minor keys. If the learning objectives, for example those related to narrative designs in the focal case from the German classroom, correspond to the major keys, how do we make sure that these are both salient and not in danger of silencing those minor keys? Some possible answers are suggested from this case study, such as providing opportunities for students to have and then to reflect on their responses at various stages and through both spoken activities (e.g., in-class discussion, digital social reading) and written activities (e.g., journaling, creative writing) and validating these responses by treating them as part of a constellation of possible effects and experiences. Prevalent and professional interpretations are a part of this constellation, but if these are presented as corrective, this encourages a deferent rather than an aesthetic reading stance. This involves openness in how learning activities are structured, which leads into the second question.
2. *How do we as educators respond when opportunities for transactional literacy arise unexpectedly, in the flow of activity, and in some moments in ways that are not directly commensurable with the learning objectives of the course?* Klara's story suggests that this requires above all a willingness to listen. Had my co-teacher and I scolded or corrected the students' feelings of discomfort with the East German narratives, we likely would have reduced their contributions to deferent readings. By weaving their responses

together with the exploration of the cultural and historical context, we were able to encourage different kinds of relationships to the different values, perceptions, feelings, and experiences those growing up in East Germany may have had. Klara's short story shows how difficult this can be; she in effect tries to consolidate some of the new information she has gleaned into a more familiar narrative. But had I not asked her about the decision to write this story, I would have missed that this was also evoked through the incommensurability of the satirical, laconic affect worlds of the literary texts and her feelings at the time. I might have been inclined to focus only on what she got wrong, i.e., the implausibility of the initial premise, and my own feelings about American tendencies to turn stories from East Germany into tragedies. To respond to aesthetic experiences in the flow of pedagogical activities, educators will need to develop practices of listening and to tune into their own aesthetic responses, both to the assigned readings and to the students' contributions, so that we can be open to complexity of transactional literacy. We must also begin to articulate connections between transactional reading and more competence-oriented goals of our curricula, such as those represented by the new CEFR descriptors related to literary reading, while recognizing that we cannot conflate aesthetic response with "reading for leisure" or "analysis of creative text" (compare Council of Europe 2018). At the same time, we must also be okay with not always knowing what our students are feeling in relation to a text. Klara shared these personal details with me in an act of trust, but students cannot be obligated to divulge intimate details of their lives that are part of the experience of their reading. This makes it all the more important that educators also keep an openness to the personal and impersonal forces that produce literacy events, even when we cannot always know them ourselves.

In conclusion, taking aesthetic response seriously as a part of language-culture learning and in a way that acknowledges learners as whole humans does not require that we abandon completely the attention to available designs or communicative functions that often shape our curricula and learning objectives, but it does ask that we infuse the activities that help our learners to realize these forms of learning with space for movement, for learners and ourselves to be moved through thoughts, feelings, and relations that are shared and unshared, and for meaning making to be as much in the moment-to-moment experiences of living in relation to texts as in the destination.

Notes

1. This conceptual tension is put clearly into practice in the most recent addenda to the Common European Framework, published in a companion volume in 2018. The new descriptors include a scale for "reading as a leisure activity" (2018: 65), a scale for "expressing a personal response to creative texts (including literature)" (2018: 206–7), and one for "analysis and criticism of creative text (including literature)" (2018: 208). The latter two scales are focused on the communicative expression of reader responses and do provide possible guidelines for how to connect transactional literacy to other kinds of proficiency-oriented competencies; however, there is an implicit assumption that these activities are distinct from "pleasure," which is the primary form of aesthetic response acknowledged in the first scale. As is often the case in scholarship on affect in second language teaching and learning, only positive emotions are treated as desirable or productive.
2. The name Klara is a pseudonym.
3. One other student wrote a work of fiction, but this was set in an unspecified time and place and did not seem to directly respond to the content of any of the readings.

References

Allen, H. W. (2018), "Redefining Writing in the Foreign Language Curriculum: Toward a Design Approach." *Foreign Language Annals*, 51: 513–32.

Allen, H. W. & Paesani, K. (2010), "Exploring the Feasibility of a Pedagogy of Multiliteracies in Introductory Foreign Language Courses." *L2 Journal*, 2 (1): 119–42.

Brown, G. & Yule, G. (1983), *Discourse Analysis*. Cambridge: Cambridge University Press.

Byrnes, H. (ed.). (2007), *Advanced Language Learning: The Contribution of Halliday and Vygotsky*. London: Bloomsbury.

Byrnes, H., Crane, C., Maxim, H. & Sprang, K. (2006), "Taking Text to Task: Issues and Choices in Curriculum Construction." *International Journal of Applied Linguistics*, 152: 85–109.

Byrnes, H., Maxim, H. H., & Norris, J. M. (2010), "Realizing Advanced Foreign Language Writing Development in Collegiate Education: Curricular Design, Pedagogy, Assessment." *The Modern Language Journal*, 94 (S1).

Council of Europe (2001), *Common European Framework of Reference for Languages: Learning, Teaching, Assessment*. Cambridge: Cambridge University Press.

Council of Europe (2018), *Common European Framework of Reference for Languages: Learning, Teaching, Assessment. Companion Volume with New Descriptors*. Strasbourg: Council of Europe.

Dewaele, J.-M. (2005), "Investigating the Psychological and Emotional Dimensions in Instructed Language Learning: Obstacles and Possibilities." *The Modern Language Journal*, 89 (3): 367–80.

Dubreil, S., & Thorne, S. L. (2017), "Social Pedagogies and Entwining Language with the World." In S. Dubreil & S. L. Thorne (eds), *Engaging the World: Social Pedagogies and Language Learning*, 1–11, Boston (MA): Cengage.

Ehret, C. (2018), "Propositions from Affect Theory for Feeling Literacy through the Event." In D. E. Alvermann, N. J. Unrau, M. Sailors & R. B. Ruddell (eds), *Theoretical Models and Processes of Literacy*, 563–81, New York: Routledge.

Flynn, E. (2007), "Louise Rosenblatt and the Ethical Turn in Literary Theory." *College English*, 70 (1): 52–69.

Gramling, G. & Warner, C. (2011), "Toward a Contact Pragmatics of Literature: Habitus, Text, and the Advanced L2 Classroom." In G. Levine & A. Phipps (eds), *Critical and Intercultural Theory and Language Pedagogy, AAUSC Issues in Language Program Direction*, 57–75, Boston, MA: Heinle.

Keen, S. (2013), "Empathy in Reading: Considerations of Gender and Ethnicity." *Anglistik: International Journal of English Studies*, 24 (2): 49–65.

Kern, R. (2000), *Literacy and Language Teaching*. Oxford: Oxford University Press.

Kern, R. (2015), *Language, Literacy and Technology*. Cambridge: Cambridge University Press.

Kirsch, S. (1982), "Naturschutzgebiet." In *Erdreich. Gedichte*, Stuttgart: DVA.

Kong, K. (2019), "Embracing an Integrative Approach toward Emotion in Language Teaching and Learning." *Modern Language Journal*, 103 (2): 539–44.

Kramsch, C. (1993), *Context and Culture in Language Teaching*. Oxford: Oxford University Press.

Kramsch, C. (2006), "From Communicative Competence to Symbolic Competence." *Modern Language Journal*, 90 (2): 249–52.

Kramsch, C. (2009), *The Multilingual Subject*. Oxford: Oxford University Press.

Kramsch, C. (2011), "The Symbolic Dimensions of the Intercultural." *Language Teaching*, 44 (3): 354–67.

Kramsch, C. & Nolden, T. (1994), "Foreign Language Literacy as (Op)positional Practice." In Roche, J. & Salumets, T. (eds), *Germanics under Construction: Intercultural and Interdisciplinary Prospects*, 61–76, Munich: iudicium.

Kramsch, C. & Whiteside, A. (2008), "Language Ecology in Multilingual Settings. Towards a Theory of Symbolic Competence." *Applied Linguistics*, 29: 645–72.

Lantolf, J. & Thorne, S. (2006), *Sociocultural Theory and the Genesis of Second Language Development*. Oxford: Oxford University Press.

Leander, K., Aziz, S., Botzakis, S., Ehret, C., Landry, D. & Rowsell, J. (2017), "Readings and Experiences of Multimodality." *Literacy Research: Theory, Method, Practice*, XX (X): 1–22.

Leander, K. & Boldt, G. (2013), "Rereading 'A Pedagogy of Multiliteracies': Bodies, Texts, And Emergence." *Journal of Literacy Research*, 45 (1): 22–46.

Levine, G. (2020), "A Human Ecological Language Pedagogy." *Modern Language Journal (Monograph Issue)*, 104 (S1): 1–130.
Liddicoat, A. & Scarino, A. (2013), *Intercultural Language Teaching and Learning*. Oxford: Wiley-Blackwell.
Manning, E. (2016), *The Minor Gesture*. Durham, NC: Duke University Press.
NCSSFL and ACTFL (2017), NCSSFL-ACTFL Can-do statements. [https://www.actfl.org/publications/guidelines-and-manuals/ncssfl-actfl-can-do-statements].
New London Group (1996), "A Pedagogy of Multiliteracies: Designing Social Futures." *Harvard Educational Review*, 66 (1): 60–92.
Paesani, K., Allen, H. W. & Dupuy, B. (2015), *A Multiliteracies Framework for Collegiate Foreign Language Teaching*. Upper Saddle River (NJ): Pearson Education.
Pahl, K. & Rowsell, J. (2020), *Living Literacies: Literacy for Social Change*. Cambridge, MA: MIT Press.
Phipps, A. & Gonzales, M. (2004), *Modern Languages: Learning and Teaching in an Intercultural Field*. London: Sage.
Prior, M. (2019). "Elephants in the Room: An 'Affective Turn,' or Just Feeling Our Way?" *Modern Language Journal*, 103 (2): 516–27.
Rosenblatt, L. M. (1938/1976), *Literature as Exploration*. New York: Noble & Noble.
Rosenblatt, L. M. (1978/1994), *The Reader, the Text, the Poem: The Transactional Theory of the Literary Work*. Carbondale (IL): Southern Illinois University Press.
Rosenblatt, L. M. (1982), "The Literary Transaction: Evocation and Response." *Theory into Practice*, 21 (4): 268–77.
Rosenblatt, L. M. (1986), "The Aesthetic Transaction." *Journal of Aesthetic Education*, 20: 122–7.
Rosenblatt, L. M. (1988), *Writing and Reading: The Transactional Theory*. Center for the Study of Reading. Champaign (IL): University of Illinois at Urbana-Champaign.
Rosenblatt, L. M. (1994), "The Transactional Theory of Reading and Writing." In R. B. Ruddell, M. R. Ruddell & H. Singer (eds), *Theoretical Models and Processes of Reading*, 1057–92, Newark (DE): International Reading Association.
Smith, C. H. (2012), "Interrogating Texts: From Deferent to Efferent and Aesthetic Reading Practices." *Journal of Basic Writing*, 31 (1): 59–79.
van Lier, L. (2004), *The Ecology and Semiotics of Language Learning: A Sociocultural Perspective*. Boston: Kluwer Academic.
Vytniorgu, R. (2018), "An Ethical Ideal? Louise Rosenblatt and Democracy—A Personalist Reconsideration." *Humanities*, 7 (29): 1–13.
Warner, C. (2014), "Mapping New Classrooms in Literacy-Oriented Foreign Language Teaching and Learning: The Role of the Reading Experience." In K. Arens, J. Swaffar & P. Urlaub (eds), *Transforming the Foreign Language Curriculum in Higher Education: New Perspectives from the United States*, 157–76, Heidelberg/New York: Springer.

Warner, C. & Dupuy, B. (2018), "Moving toward Multiliteracies in Foreign Language Teaching: Past and Present Perspectives… and beyond." *Foreign Language Annals*, 51 (1): 116–28.

Warner, C. & Richardson, D. (2017), "Beyond Participation: Symbolic Struggles with (in) Digital Social Media in the L2 Classroom." In S. Dubreil & S. Thorne (eds), *Engaging the World: Social Pedagogies and Language Learning*, 199–226, Boston (MA): Cengage.

8

Exploring Pragmatic Resistance and Moral Emotions in Foreign Language Learning

Troy McConachy

Introduction

In recent years, research on the learning of second language pragmatics has placed increased emphasis on the learner's subjective experience of coming to understand and use a second language (Eslami et al. 2014; Ishihara 2010, 2017, 2019a, b; Ishihara & Tarone 2009; McConachy 2018). In contrast to research approaches that aim to compare how learners' pragmatic performance compares to "native speakers" of the second language, this line of research aims to shed light on how language learners themselves interpret and evaluate issues of language use, context, and interpersonal relations within a multilingual and intercultural frame (McConachy & Liddicoat 2022). An important theoretical premise in much of this work is that the learning of a pragmatics deeply engages the whole person as a social and moral being. Many of the pragmatic features and speech acts that tend to receive attention in instructional contexts, such as greetings, requests, apologies, compliments, offers, are not only central to the construction and maintenance of interpersonal relations but are also central to the enactment of individual and social identities and speakers' embodied sense of socially and morally appropriate behavior (Garcés-Conejos Blitvich & Kádár 2021; McConachy 2018). Pragmatic decisions such as which request form to use, how to respond to a compliment, whether/how to greet strangers or not, and whether/how to express disagreement, etc. are fundamentally dependent on (unconscious) assumptions about dimensions of social relationships such as distance, hierarchy, power, or gender, attitudes such as respect, and broader values such as equality or fairness. This means that the experience of learning the pragmatics of an additional language can present a challenge to learners' sense of socially and morally desirable linguistic behavior within different roles, relationships, and contexts, as well as their own sense of comfort as a language user (Ishihara 2019a; Ishihara & Porcellato 2022; McConachy 2018).

In the literature, the notion of "pragmatic resistance" has come to refer to instances in which language learners seek to strategically depart from L2 pragmatic norms due to the perception that the norms are incongruent with elements of their own subjectivity, including cultural identities or deep-rooted assumptions about the social world and sense of right behavior (e.g., Gomez-Laich 2016; Ishihara 2009, 2017, 2019a; Ishihara & Tarone 2009; McConachy 2018; Siegal 1996). Whilst much work tends to look at pragmatic resistance in terms of learners' rational decision making and agency vis-à-vis their own language use, this chapter will focus more on the emotional side of pragmatic resistance, specifically the aversive emotional reactions that feed into learners' pragmatic decision making. As I will discuss in this chapter, the emotional side of pragmatic resistance is important not only because it relates to learner agency but because it has the potential to lead to negative evaluations of linguistic and cultural difference and can be difficult for learners to manage. I will argue that pragmatic decision making—including the decision to strategically depart from target language norms—is not a purely rational process but is rather an embodied process anchored in learners' felt sense of right and wrong social behavior and thus triggers complex evaluative processes with cognitive, emotional, and somatic dimensions. I draw on research at the intersections of pragmatics and moral psychology which offers insights into the role of moral emotions in the evaluation of behavior and suggest ways that teachers could engage their learners in exploration of moral emotions as a part of learning pragmatics.

The Phenomenon of Pragmatic Resistance

Research on pragmatic resistance has helped to foreground the fact that the learning of a second language is not simply a process of simply remembering linguistic rules, acquiring new cognitive representations, and forming new linguistic habits; it is a complex process that engages the learners' felt sense of being a legitimate social actor as well as deep-rooted assumptions about social relationships and notions of appropriate language use in context. It has shown that language learners can experience aversion to following a wide range of pragmatic features in an L2, including personal pronouns (Liddicoat 2006), politeness routines (Ishihara 2010), honorifics (McConachy & Fujino 2022; Siegal 1996), conversational routines (Davis 2007), request realization sequences (Eslami et al. 2014), refusals (Al-Issa 2003), and others. As such pragmatic aspects are closely linked to conceptualization of the interpersonal realm and the enactment of social practices by which individuals and groups maintain relations, cross-linguistic pragmatic differences can be felt as highly consequential for learners' sense of self and positioning vis-à-vis others.

One notable trend in the literature is that pragmatic resistance tends to be positioned as an agentive act—and sometimes an act of protest—in the face of pragmatic norms that the individual deems to be personally undesirable or even problematic. From a behavioral perspective, pragmatic resistance can take various forms, such as acts of omission (not carrying out expected pragmatic behaviors) or through following L1 pragmatic norms or hybrid alternatives. For example, the Jordanian learners of English in Ali-Issa's (2003) study seemed to perceive that the common pragmatic strategies for refusing an invitation, request, or offer of help in English would not normally allow for the same elaborate expression of deference toward the other, vagueness of reason for refusal, or incorporation of religious references that they felt were important to them in Arabic. This is indicative of the range of studies into pragmatic resistance in the sense that resistance stems from the perception of a mismatch between the sense of symbolic self that learners wish to convey and the target language resources perceived to be available (Kramsch 2011).

Ishihara (2019a) suggests that "[t]hrough pragmatic resistance, learners exercise agency and negotiate their culturally hybrid subjectivity in the uniquely crafted *third space* (Bhabha 1994), a metaphoric place for 'a discursive subject position' culturally diverse speakers construct in interaction" (p. 623). In other words, pragmatic resistance occurs in a zone of tension between the normative structures and understandings of the social world that underpin L2 pragmatic norms and the learners' own sense of agency to make self-directed linguistic decisions. The literature, thus, tends to be sympathetic to the idea that it is legitimate for learners to flout pragmatic norms if they feel that these norms are out of sync with the image of themselves that they wish to maintain and the identity positions they wish to carve out in relation to those in their social sphere. In this sense, pragmatic resistance tends to be regarded as a relatively normal and common (yet relatively under-researched) phenomenon that arises out of the need for the learner to sustain a sense of being oneself within different languages.

It should be noted that scholars who argue for the importance of learners' agency in determining their own pragmatic decisions generally do not advocate ignorance of L2 pragmatic norms. In fact, awareness of pragmatic norms is seen as an important element in making informed decisions (House 2008; Ishihara 2019b; Koutlaki & Eslami 2018; Liddicoat & McConachy 2019; McConachy 2018; van Compernolle & Williams 2013). Ishihara (2019a) is careful to distinguish pragmatic resistance from negative pragmatic transfer in that the former implies intentionality on behalf of the learner to consciously choose how one interacts and thus requires awareness of the interactional options. van Compernolle (2016) argues that learners' agency as a language user is shaped partly by their awareness of "recognizable patterns of meaning and language within a given community" (p. 63) and learners' own intent to create a particular kind of meaning. In this sense, agency is enhanced when learners have a clearer understanding of the meaning potential of pragmatic forms in a range of contexts. This is not a matter of internalizing overly simplistic pragmatic rules of thumb but is rather linked to learners' ability to reflect on different dimensions of interpersonal relations such as formality and distance. From an intercultural perspective, Liddicoat and McConachy (2019) argue that agency is dependent not on learners' awareness of L2 pragmatic norms in a narrow sense but on their capacity for interpreting the meaning-making potential of linguistic forms from multiple cultural perspectives and for recognizing how different assumptions about social relationships can lead to different perceptions of linguistic in/appropriateness. In this sense, they underscore the importance of learners' having reflexive awareness of their own assumptions and the ability to recognize different interpretations as potentially valid. Whilst the authors above are coming from different theoretical perspectives, they all emphasize the role of conscious understanding of pragmatic norms and learners' ability to think about how they want to position themselves.

Given the emphasis in the existing literature on analytical processes and seemingly rational consideration of preferable courses of action, what tends to be less explicitly theorized is the role of emotion in how learners perceive and react to pragmatic differences. This is an important topic beginning to attract attention in interdisciplinary work at the interface of pragmatics and moral psychology (e.g., Spencer-Oatey & Xing 2019; Spencer-Oatey & Kádár 2021). Before delving into such theoretical territory, it is first of all useful to look at a number of examples of pragmatic resistance in order to foreground different aspects of learners' embodied engagement with difference.

Illustrative Examples of Pragmatic Resistance

As an accessible entry point for exploring the phenomenon of pragmatic resistance, I will present two examples of pragmatic resistance from Anglo-background learners of Japanese, one of which comes from my own experience as a learner and user of L2 Japanese.

Pragmatic Resistance to Pronouns: The Case of "Watashi"

This reflection relates to my experience of resistance to the first-person pronoun—*watashi* (I) in Japanese. Although this is a versatile pronoun which is commonly used by both men and women, its predominant use as a neutral pronoun in professional contexts makes it the pronoun least capable of indexing a distinctly masculine identity. Interestingly, when I first began my language learning journey just before my teens, I did not think anything special about *watashi*—I saw it simply as the way to say "I" in Japanese. At a time when I still mainly saw languages as codes, these were just roughly interchangeable parts for expressing the same thing. It was not until I was majoring in Japanese at university in Australia and using it as a language of communication with Japanese friends in my hometown that I realized I struggled to refer to myself with this word. I was much more comfortable with the two other first-person pronouns commonly used by men; namely, *ore* and *boku*. The former is the most casual or perhaps "rough" way to say "I," while the latter is somewhere in between *ore* and *watashi*. Clearly, this was not a grammatical issue.

From a phenomenological perspective, the resistance I experienced to *watashi* is hard to explain, as it was not something I understood conceptually at that point. It was, rather, that the act of referring to myself with this "word" when I wanted to express an idea, preference, or stance made me feel awkward and squirmy. This word seemed to bring into being a persona which was detached from my usual way of "feeling myself" inside language. It felt colorless and stiff, even effeminate. It robbed from me my ability to present myself as the laid-back Aussie surfer that I thought I was (at that time). To refer to myself as *watashi* would be taking myself too seriously and to not be "cool." This would be out of sync with the "vibe" amongst my Japanese surfer friends whom I was interacting with on an almost daily basis and who had become my primary reference point for understanding the reality of Japanese language beyond what they tell you in the textbook. Even after several years of living in Japan and understanding that *watashi* was the normal way to refer to oneself in professional contexts, I had real trouble using it. Even though I knew that "ore" was completely inappropriate in a professional context, I would let it slip out during the first few years in Japan. In fact, often I knew I was doing it.

My own avoidance of *watashi* was certainly conscious and deliberate at particular points, though this was almost always accompanied by a sense of guilt for choosing a pronoun (i.e., *boku* or *ore*) whilst knowing that this risked upsetting my Japanese interlocutors, who were frequently my superiors. It is also potentially true that, my unconventional use of pronouns, combined with my status as a "foreigner," contributed to the construction of a hybrid subjectivity and distinct subject position (Ishihara 2019b). After all, my interlocutors may not have always expected my language use to be "nativelike." I also realize that my resistance to *watashi* occurred at an emotional level—in fact, as a form of aversion with aesthetic and somatic features—long before I started to rationalize that it might be due to specific aspects of my own identity, more specifically, attachments to a self-concept and notions of masculinity rooted in Aussie surf culture. What this means, essentially, is that my decision making was not really based on a sense of agency derived from conscious, rational understanding. It was primarily based on an embodied aversive reaction based on my, admittedly partial, understanding of the nuances of the Japanese pronoun system at that time. It was not until I had taken on my first role as an instructor working within the university system that I gradually managed to use *watashi* without a sense of awkwardness, as I had probably internalized a better understanding of Japanese role relations and the indexical potential of pronouns by then, and had been away from Australia for six years.

Pragmatic Resistance to Japanese Honorifics: The Example of "Tim"

I now turn to a second example which similarly relates to the learning of Japanese by another Anglo background learner, as reported in Ishihara & Tarone (2009). This example involves "Tim" an Anglo-American learner who had been learning Japanese for three years in total and had lived in Japan for eighteen months. Ishihara and Tarone (2009) report that although Tim had initially reported being very motivated to speak like a Japanese person and had been immersed in Japanese cultural practices such as martial arts, he later experienced resistance to the Japanese politeness system, particularly honorifics (*keigo*). Referring to initial encounters with Japanese politeness, he commented in an email to the researchers that:

> I didn't know how to use it, and then I would get upset, because we would go out with my friends, and we would bump into like their older friends, and they had to speak keigo to them, and they were kind of treated like little children and I was like, this is, you know, this isn't proper. And I didn't learn.
>
> (p. 4)

As can be seen here, Tim reports aversion to Japanese *keigo* not only in relation to his own language use but more generally in relation to the language use of others as well. He seems to be uncomfortable with the idea that relatively minor age differences should necessitate the choice of distinct language forms to indicate relative position in a vertical hierarchy. What is interesting in the first quote is that he experiences pragmatic norms as a moral issue—"this isn't proper"—and that he personally becomes upset at observing others interacting in their native language. Below, Tim's resistance is expressed from the viewpoint of his own language use, where he associates linguistic distinctions with the erection of communicative and relational barriers.

> In using *keigo*, I feel that I am placing a wall between whoever I am addressing, and myself. This wall causes me to feel uncomfortable when speaking and I become unable to fully express myself... in Japanese the level of language difference is so great that it can cause someone not to be heard.
>
> (p. 4)

Tim communicates a sense of discomfort and powerlessness, seemingly wanting for communication to take place on a more horizontal plain where each interactant has equal footing. Tim's pragmatic resistance, thus, is associated with a denial of the validity of L2 pragmatic norms and a moral objection to (perceived) overemphasis on linguistically marked hierarchical distinctions. His reactions seem to be predicated on egalitarian assumptions about social relationships that lead to negative judgments of Japanese politeness practices.

Pragmatic Judgments and Morality within an Embodied Perspective

Although space limitations prevent detailed presentation of more examples, those above help illuminate the fact that the experience of learning pragmatics can present a challenge not only to learners' rational, conceptual understanding of self, and others but more fundamentally to their felt sense of being a social actor and intuitive judgments about in/appropriate behavior. As Kramsch (2009) has highlighted in her work, "language elicits subjective responses in the speakers themselves: emotions, memories, fantasies, projections, identifications. Because it is not only a code but also a meaning-making system, language constructs the historical sedimentation of meanings that we call 'selves'" (p. 2). Thus, the process by which learners decide how they want to interact in the L2 and whether or not—or to what extent—they wish to follow particular L2 pragmatic norms is fundamentally an embodied one. This is to say that it evokes not only rational processes of sense-making but also aesthetic sensibilities, bodily responses, and emotionally driven judgments about right and wrong.

Even aspects of language that might seem relatively simple from a grammatical perspective such as personal pronouns or verb endings used to index politeness can become entangled with deep-rooted emotional attachments to the symbolic expression of the self. Importantly, this attachment to the familiar has consequences for how language learners perceive and evaluate pragmatic and broader cultural differences. It is for this reason that McConachy and Liddicoat (2022) argue for recognition that pragmatics learning "involves dealing with the adaptive demands of needing to carry out social acts through language in ways which may conflict with one's existing identity or assumptions about social relationships, and thus it involves learning to manage potentially ethnocentric judgments towards new pragmatic behaviours and people" (p. 10).

Recently, research at the intersections of pragmatics and moral psychology has contributed to understanding of the relationship between perceptions of linguistic behavior and moral evaluations (e.g., Culpeper 2014; Kádár & Haugh 2013; McConachy 2018, 2019, 2021; Spencer-Oatey & Xing 2019; Spencer-Oatey & Kádár 2021). Moral psychologists Turner and Stets (2006) explain that "morality ultimately revolves around evaluative codes that specify what is right or wrong, good or bad, acceptable or unacceptable" (p. 544). Further, they suggest that "any cultural code is moral *to the extent* that it carries evaluative elements that specify what is good-bad, right-wrong, and proper-improper" (p. 546, italics in original). Pragmatics researchers have similarly highlighted the fact that individuals tend to evaluate the communicative behavior and perceived characteristics of themselves and other people in terms of valenced categories such as polite/impolite, sincere/insincere, modest/immodest. Further, when asked to justify their evaluations as such, individuals will tend to appeal to notions with moral overtones such as "proper behavior," "politeness," "fairness," "dignity," "care," "respect", particularly when it is perceived that pragmatic norms have been violated (e.g., Kádár 2020; Sharifian & Tayebi 2017; Spencer-Oatey & Kádár 2021).

In their work on pragmatics and moral evaluations, Spencer-Oatey and Kádár (2021) have drawn attention to the fact that although evaluations of the appropriateness of language use can involve a conscious, rational component, they frequently take the form of snap judgments that stem from emotional reactions triggered by the experience of difference. They thus draw attention to the utility of dual process models of cognition to explain how evaluations occur. In the field of moral psychology, dual process accounts of cognition have developed to highlight the respective roles played by intuitive forms of cognition, which are closely linked with emotional and somatic experience, and more rational forms of cognition in moral judgments (e.g., Haidt 2012; Kahneman 2011). For example, Haidt's social intuitionist model of cognition invokes the metaphor of an elephant and a rider to characterize the relationship between intuitive (elephant) and rational (rider) forms of cognition and the role they play in moral judgments. Haidt argues that moral judgments are most frequently informed by moral intuitions and the experience of emotion rather than rational thought processes.

Whilst there is not necessarily universal agreement about the precise theoretical understanding of notions such as "emotion" or "feeling," one key feature of emotions is that they represent an internal appraisal of a situation. That is, emotions are a kind of evaluative reaction, often accompanied by physiological responses, to an event or circumstances in the immediate environment and to the individual's own thought processes (Myers 2004). In this sense, Haidt (2012) argues that emotions are not independent of cognition but central to it. He suggests that although the rider (rational mind) has the illusion of being in control, its actual role is to defend and justify the movements of the elephant (intuitions). This is in line with Kahneman's (2011) view of cognition which emphasizes a distinction between intuitive, automatic forms of cognition (System 1) and more conscious, rational forms of cognition (System 2). In essence, the rational mind attempts to make sense of experiences and reactions filtered through the body and affect.

Dual process models of cognition as described above provide theoretical support for the idea that evaluations of L2 pragmatic behaviors, particularly those that involve aversive reactions on behalf of the learner, are closely associated with intuitive judgments driven by the experience of emotion (Spencer-Oatey & Kádár 2021). This is not to deny that judgments are also subject to rationalization but rather to point out that more recognition is needed of emotional drivers of judgment in the learning of L2 pragmatics. It is my contention that much pragmatic decision making, and many instances of pragmatic resistance, are tied up with individuals' intuitive, moralized reactions to difference and the need to "defend" one's existing ways of thinking and feeling. As I explain below, this is closely linked to the experience of moral emotions.

The Role of Moral Emotions

Moral emotions are a particular sub-class of emotions which are considered to be a driving force in the assessment of social situations and evaluation of one's own and others' social conduct (Haidt 2003). Although they are ultimately experienced by the individual, moral emotions are thought to be intimately intertwined with the moral standards advocated within society and, as such, help individuals recognize when behaviors deviate from these standards or ideals (Haidt 2003). It is for this reason that moral emotions may play a key role in the assessment of L2 pragmatic behaviors, particularly when one's self-concept or assumptions about social relationships and normative social behavior are challenged (see Culpeper et al. 2014).

Moral psychologists have identified four main types of moral emotions (see (Haidt 2003)):

- Other-praising emotions: Positive feelings experienced when another person appears to enact or uphold moral standards (e.g., Gratitude, elevation).
- Other-suffering emotions: Feelings that occur when a person/victim is in a situation which violates moral standards (Sympathy).
- Other-condemning emotions: Negative feelings in relation to others who violate moral standards (e.g., Contempt, anger, disgust).
- Self-conscious emotions: Negative feelings about the self due to violating moral standards (e.g., Shame, embarrassment, guilt).

Of particular relevance to the phenomenon of pragmatic resistance is the category of "other-condemning emotions," particularly the emotion of disgust. Although it is suggested that the original function of disgust in humans was to avoid disease, it is now often activated in response to actions which are perceived to be associated with harm, unfairness, and disloyalty (Chapman 2018). In this sense, depending on the language and culture, there are many aspects of language use which could trigger the moral emotion of disgust, such as forms of person reference that are perceived to position one person as inferior to another (e.g., personal pronouns, honorifics), lack of expected display of humility (e.g., through orientation to compliment responses), lack of expected display of gratitude (e.g., omission of thanking forms), egregious forms of verbal aggression (e.g., harsh criticism), and more.

It can be noted in Tim's example above that he experienced Japanese politeness practices he witnessed as a moral violation—they were not simply different but "wrong." It can also be seen that it was this felt reaction that made him not want to learn. This is in line with research in moral psychology which suggests that different other-condemning emotions tend to lead to different behavioral responses. Specifically, it is thought that whereas anger results in approach behaviors, disgust and contempt tend to result in avoidance (Ford et al. 2018; Hutcherson & Gross 2011). Therefore, the emotion of disgust is closely linked to psychological resistance and serves to generate avoidance motivation.

In my own case of pragmatic resistance introduced above, although I did not experience Japanese personal pronouns as morally problematic in a general sense, (in hindsight) I probably did experience a mild disgust reaction to the pronoun *watashi* when I was personally in a context where I was expected to use it to refer to myself. It seemed to have a feminine character that I did not want to express, and this was something that surfaced through felt experience rather than conscious understanding initially. The Japanese pronoun system became quite an inconvenience, and I admit that I did wonder why it needed to be so complex. In essence, my perceptions were ethnocentric. Not only were they grounded in my sense of lived experience and own subjectivity, they were (again, in hindsight) based on relatively limited understanding of the complexity of the Japanese pronoun system and the capacity for each pronoun to index a wide range of meanings. In line with the literature, it is true that I exercised my agency as a language user, but this was inevitably within the framework of relatively limited understanding and was constrained by the tendency to impose understandings of language and gender from my own experiences as an English speaker growing up in a masculine surfing sub-culture in Australia. A further aspect to mention is that this agency was not necessarily accompanied by a sense of emotional ease or clarity. Negotiating my own use of Japanese pronouns with awareness that I was deviating from pragmatic norms and cultural expectations plagued me with a sense of guilt. After all, it was I—the new foreigner in the workplace—that was making linguistic decisions that could make others uncomfortable. It is in this area that research on moral emotions can again be useful.

As can be seen listed above, emotions such as shame and guilt are regarded as the "self-conscious emotions" that help regulate moral behavior. Although the literature on pragmatic resistance tends to emphasize positive aspects of learner agency and decision making, it is unlikely that the experience of knowingly going against pragmatic norms is without some degree of emotional ambivalence or sense of guilt or shame. Particularly in contexts where there is a need to establish oneself as a legitimate social actor in a new cultural environment, pragmatic decisions can be hugely consequential not only for expressing one's own subjectivity but also for showing respect for local ways of doing things and building interpersonal connections (McConachy & Fujino 2022). If learners are motivated to establish meaningful social connections through the medium of an L2 yet experience aversion to particular communicative practices essential for establishing these connections, they are likely to experience conflicting motivational pulls, as well as guilt or shame due to not meeting expectations. In dealing with these emotions, individuals can either accept the burden of these emotions themselves, or they can displace them onto others. As with the experience of disgust, what this means is that if individuals experience a sense of shame or guilt due to struggling to interact in the way that they want, it can also generate the defensive tendency to denigrate the language or speakers of the language. Thus, attempts to avoid experiencing self-conscious emotions take the form of "attribution, expectation states, repression, displacement, or projection that transmute the initial arousal of an emotion like shame into anger, fear, disgust, and hatred" (Turner & Stets 2006: 544). Thus, individuals seek to normalize their own reactions as being connected to the natural order of things and to distance the other as unusual or problematic.

Although existing work on pragmatic resistance tends to downplay the possible role of ethnocentrism in how language learners perceive and react to L2 pragmatic aspects they find problematic, it is important to acknowledge the power of moral emotions to generate aversive reactions which may be difficult for learners to manage. The discussion above is not intended to deny the important role of agency in becoming an L2 speaker but is rather to acknowledge that decisions about how to interact are informed by learners' felt experience of language use and are likely to be particularly mediated by moral emotions which can lead to defensive or ethnocentric reactions. This means that there is work to be done in the classroom to help learners identify and understand the nature of such emotions and how they inform their judgments about pragmatic features and practices.

Addressing Pragmatic Resistance and Moral Emotions in Language Learning

In the next part of the chapter, I discuss how language teachers might help their learners explore pragmatic resistance as an embodied phenomenon. The premise in doing so is that devoting attention to the nature of pragmatic evaluations and moral emotions has the potential to contribute to a foundation of self-awareness that promotes wellbeing and more mindful evaluations of others. Indeed, the field has seen increased interest in promoting wellbeing as an explicit goal in language teaching, particularly with the aim of encouraging self-awareness, more effective emotional regulation, and inner peace (e.g., Mercer 2021; Oxford et al. 2021; also see Chapters 1 and 9, this volume).

The idea that language learners should be encouraged to become conscious of their evaluative reactions to linguistic and cultural difference is not new. In fact, it is central to thinking about the goals of learning within interculturally oriented language learning, and is visible in Byram, Nichols and Stevens' (2001) definition of the intercultural speaker as "someone who has an ability to interact with 'others', to accept other perspectives and perceptions of the world, to mediate between different perspectives, *to be conscious of their evaluations of difference*" (p. 5, italics added). Such awareness of conscious evaluations of difference is closely aligned with the goal of decentering, explained by Byram (2021) as "a willingness to relativise one's own values, beliefs and behaviours, not to assume that they are the only possible and naturally correct ones, and to be able to see how they might look from the perspective of an outsider who has a different set of values, beliefs and behaviours" (p. 5). Such processes engage relatively advanced cognitive capacities such as the ability to make meaningful comparisons, to identify abstract cultural elements, and to actively shift frames of reference, as well as engage in explicit reasoning.

The literature on developing learners' (meta)pragmatic awareness similarly emphasizes analytical and reflective processes, such as interpreting pragmatic norms according to context, making cross-linguistic comparisons, exploring how perceptions of social roles and relationships influence pragmatic judgments, and reflecting on one's personalized reactions to different pragmatic phenomena (e.g., Liddicoat 2006; McConachy 2018; McConachy & Liddicoat 2016). This work tends to take a view of meaning as "subjective and intersubjective, growing out of not only the language in which meaning is communicated but also from the memories, emotions, perceptions, experiences, and life worlds of those who participate in the communication" (Liddicoat & Scarino 2013: 2). The focus here on the reciprocal nature of meaning making foregrounds the importance not only of being able to take up the perspective of the other but also the ability to become more deeply attuned to one's own reactions.

Whilst much of the literature above tends to focus on analytical engagement in relation to the self and other, it is worth considering the extent to which analytical thinking about assumptions, beliefs, and values will be enough to become attuned to the moral emotions that trigger negative judgments of linguistic and cultural difference. After all, whilst values and beliefs do give rise to emotions (Schwartz 2012), they are also abstractions which might seem quite removed from the concrete felt reality of a communicative encounter and the immediacy of embodied reactions. As highlighted in the work of Haidt (2012) and others, conscious analysis aimed at explaining one's own evaluative judgments can lead to ad hoc rationalizations which do not necessarily accord with actual intuitive reactions. In other words, analytical thinking may not be enough, as the analytical mind may seek to divert attention away from immediate emotional and somatic experience. Thus, we need to consider the following: if aversive reactions to difference are emotional in nature, do we not need to target emotions directly? If so, how?

I will argue that mindfulness allows for exploration of emotional reactions in a direct, non-judgmental way that is useful for learners to develop insights into their own reactions to L2 pragmatics. In this sense, it can be a useful complement to more abstract and rational analysis of situations and reactions.

Applying Mindfulness

With its roots in several Eastern religious and philosophical traditions, including Buddhism and Hinduism, mindfulness has attracted increasing attention in scholarly, clinical, and educational domains. Although mindfulness is currently interpreted in different ways, it is fundamentally linked to contemplative practices which take an embodied approach to human perception and human wellbeing (Feldman & Kuyken 2019). That is, mindfulness is associated with an integrated view of body and mind which recognizes that perception of reality is filtered through the whole being and is subject to distortions produced by the analytical mind (i.e., Haidt's elephant or Kahneman's "system 2" thinking). In this sense, Žegarac, Spencer-Oatey and Ushioda (2014: 77) explain that "mindfulness is best defined as active attention, a controlled heightened level of sensory awareness to potentially relevant inputs to cognitive processes which inform and guide our actions."

The practice of mindfulness aims to center attention on present-moment experience and to help regulate perception by observing thoughts, feelings, and bodily sensations. As Feldman and Kuyken (2019) explain, "[b]odily sensations, feelings, mental states, and present-moment experience are perceived and held in awareness where they can be explored with attitudes of curiosity, patience, and kindness" (pp. 12–3). This is designed to counteract the tendency of the analytical mind to divert attention away from the present moment and the immediacy of embodied experience. The aim is not to judge the analytical mind for doing so, but rather to observe its tendencies and to gradually bring it back to the present moment of experience within an overall spirit of kindness toward oneself and others.

Feldman and Kuyken (2019) present a four-component model of experience that is useful for promoting mindfulness practice. They suggest it is useful for individuals to draw attention to the following: bodily sensations, emotions, thoughts, and conscious appraisals, behavioral impulses, and behaviors. The purpose in doing so is not to recognize these elements as separate but to gradually realize their interconnectedness. They explain:

> We can see how our thoughts shape our emotions and bodily sensations; we can see how our bodily states, particularly fatigue, shape our thinking and emotions; we can see how behavioural impulses are associated with emotion and body states; we can see how emotion shapes our thoughts and behavior.
>
> (p. 47)

In connection to pragmatics, McConachy (2018) has also argued for the importance of learners becoming mindful of their own emotional reactions when experiencing a sense of resistance or dissonance.

> … one of the important ways in which reflection works is by helping learners focus on the nature of their own emotional reactions, to identify the reaction, and to attempt to identify where the reaction is coming from. The initial object of noticing is an emotional charge—such as experience of "discomfort" or "strangeness"—and the act of reflection helps the learner more consciously recognize—i.e. notice—the emotion, label it, and thereby bring it under more conscious attentional control so that external triggers can be explored.
>
> (p. 157)

In this formulation, thus, the goal is to first of all become aware of one's own internal emotional experience—even if it is barely perceptible initially—then work to more clearly perceive the emotional experience and explore its origins.

Although it is not indicated in the quote above, this should be understood as a non-judgmental "observing" of one's own internal experience that seeks to accept the experience as it is, with any bodily sensations (Feldman & Kuyken 2019). This focus and awareness on the reality of inner experience provides a foundation of self-awareness that can then be extended to a consideration of the inner experiences of others. Here, mindfulness shifts from an intrapersonal to an interpersonal focus. This is broadly similar to Ting-Toomey's (2015) understanding of mindfulness as applied to intercultural interaction, which places emphasis not only on attending to internal experience but also to the necessity of openness, flexibility, and empathy toward the emotional states and perceptions of others. Similarly, McConachy and Spencer-Oatey (2020) suggest that "mindfulness entails noticing, attending, being aware, seeking out, creating, and using empathy in relation to (a) the situational context and (b) the assumptions, ideas, mental categories and emotions of self and others" (p. 411).

It is within such a conception that there are clear parallels between mindfulness and metapragmatic awareness, and it is indeed unlikely to be fruitful to suggest a clear division. As a general understanding it might be said that whereas metapragmatic awareness is frequently associated with analytical understanding of pragmatic norms and sociocultural assumptions, mindfulness is anchored most fundamentally in immediate, pre-analytical internal reactions of the individual. It is a non-judgmental observing of the "what" in order to understand its nature before turning toward the "why." Mindfulness may be considered a more grounded observing and noticing of internal experience that acts as a helpful complement to the more analytical and abstract thinking characteristic of metapragmatic awareness, though there are points of overlap.

In the next section, I outline a number of pedagogical suggestions that teachers could use to engage their learners in mindful exploration of their own pragmatic judgments.

Pedagogical Strategies for Exploring Embodied Reactions and Evaluative Judgments

Whilst language learners are liable to encounter a wide range of emotions in learning and using the pragmatics of a foreign language, the focus of the pedagogical suggestions here is on exploring moral emotions through mindfulness (see Chapter 9 for applications of mindfulness in teacher education). It is important to note that in the suggestions below, mindfulness is first exercised in relation to the learner's own internal experience and is oriented toward non-judgmental observation. This is used as a foundation of self-awareness that allows for a gradual broadening out of attention toward communicative scenarios and the potential viewpoints of other speakers.

Exercising Mindfulness in Pragmatic Judgment Tasks

One useful way of helping learners explore their evaluative reactions toward aspects of L2 pragmatics is by setting simple pragmatic judgment tasks. Pragmatic judgment tasks have long been in the toolkit of language teachers and L2 pragmatics researchers who aim to help learners think about the in/appropriateness of linguistic choices in particular contexts. In contrast to discourse completion tasks, which usually require some form of production on behalf of the learner, pragmatic judgment tasks usually just require that learners consider the scenario that is presented to them. Below, I present a number of scenarios that would potentially tap into learners' other-condemning emotions (i.e., anger, disgust, condemnation) or self-conscious emotions (i.e., shame, guilt), though this of course depends on the backgrounds of the learners and their individual personalities to some extent. Whereas Scenarios A and B are constructed in the third person and might allow for a degree of detachment, Scenarios C and D are written in a way to foreground the imagined involvement of the individual reading/listening to the scenario.

Scenario A

Upon being complimented by a teacher for achieving the highest score in a class test, Student X responds to the news by saying, "Excellent! I guess I worked harder than everyone else."

Scenario B

A student experiences influenza in the week leading up to an assignment deadline and sends a polite email to the teacher asking for an extension. The teacher rejects the request by saying, "You should always anticipate that these things might happen. It's your responsibility to submit your work on time."

Scenario C

You are sitting on a crowded train and decide to offer your seat to an elderly passenger who has just boarded. You say, "Hi, please have a seat. I don't need to sit." The elderly passenger says, "Actually, I don't need to sit either. Do I look that old?!"

Scenario D

You arrive late for an important work meeting. After the meeting, you approach your boss to explain. You briefly apologize and then try to explain in as much detail as possible why you were late and that you really didn't mean to be late. Your boss says, "You spend too much time explaining. I don't like excuses."

In working with such scenarios (or similar ones constructed by the class teacher), one challenge is not jumping immediately into an analysis of the scenario itself. Rather, the initial aim here is for learners to mindfully observe their own embodied reactions to being presented to the scenarios. Students could be told that they will be presented with a scenario and that they are encouraged to direct attention to their immediate internal reactions to the scenario, particularly emotions and bodily sensations. They can be encouraged to simply observe their own reactions. After a while, students could be asked to individually consider questions as follows, even if they don't voice an answer or are encouraged to write something down privately. This helps bring reflective attention to aspects of their experience.

Q) What did you <u>feel</u> when you heard this scenario?
Q) Did you feel this sensation in any particular part of your body?
Q) What thoughts accompanied this feeling?

Once learners have spent some time tuning into their individual reactions, the teacher may wish to then help learners turn their attention more toward the scenario itself and the relationship with their own internal reactions. These are sample questions which might be conducive to this aim, and which could be provided for individual consideration or discussion with other students.

Q) What do you think about (character)'s reaction in this scenario?
Q) Do you think it is reasonable? Why? Why not?
Q) What thoughts and feelings do you think the people had in this situation? Why?
Q) What adjectives would you use to describe the people in this situation? Why?
Q) How would you react in this situation? Why?

In the questions above, attention shifts to incorporate more of a focus on others' reactions, and learners are also encouraged to take a personal stance on what has happened in the scenario. They are encouraged to explicitly evaluate actions or attitudes and to consider what they themselves would do in this situation. Thus, there is a transition from mindful observation of one's own reactions to more analytical and evaluative engagement. A final sequence of questioning might then encourage learners to explore the interface between their own immediate reactions and their evaluation of the scenarios.

Q) When you heard/read the scenario, how long did it take you to have an emotional reaction to it?
Q) Did this reaction change as you paid attention to it? What happened?
Q) How did analyzing the scenario affect the way you felt?

Although such questioning might initially be difficult for learners to answer, they can help draw attention to the embodied nature of pragmatic judgments and the fact that we are very quick to generate evaluative reactions to communicative scenarios.

In presenting these suggestions for engaging students in mindful observation and reflection, it is not assumed that learners' consideration of these scenarios would necessarily end here. As argued in much of the previous work on (meta) pragmatic awareness, there is an important role for questioning which helps learners think more explicitly about pragmatic strategies across languages and cultures (e.g., requesting, thanking, complimenting) and for digging deeper into their own contextual expectations, assumptions about social relationships, and values (see McConachy & Spencer-Oatey 2020). The initial work to tune in to one's own embodied reactions is an essential complement to this more analytically oriented work and abstract thinking.

Pragmatic Resistance Exploration Task

Whereas pragmatic judgment tasks allow for evaluation of scenarios and learners' exploration of their own reactions from a relatively "distanced" perspective, what I suggest below would aim to help learners identify and explore aspects of L2 pragmatics they are uncomfortable adopting. Students' exploration of their own pragmatic resistance is something that could be encouraged right from early stages of learning but is particularly relevant when learners begin engaging in productive use of language—i.e., using the language to represent their own subjectivity and accomplish relational tasks. What I mean here is that it is important to explore any feelings of discomfort or identity dissonance that arise when engaging in new communicative practices or exploring relatively unfamiliar pragmatic features. This is especially important for those learners who spend time immersed in an L2 environment, such as study abroad. During periods of study abroad, it is highly likely that learners will experience pragmatic differences as more intense in terms of their own embodied experience of foreignness and more consequential from an identity point of view (e.g., Devlin 2018; McConachy & Fujino 2022).

Here, again, the initial aim is for learners to engage in mindful exploration of their own reactions as a starting point. I present a sequence of processes by which learners can begin to explore their own embodied experience of particular L2 pragmatic features. The process starts from *identification* of the particular pragmatic feature that a learner feels uncomfortable about (e.g., compliment responses, refusal strategies, pronouns). This part of the process is particularly important, and some time can be spent silently bringing aspects of emotional experience to attention and mapping them onto a particular linguistic feature or interactional behavior. As it might be difficult for learners to explain in detail, the next *description* stage involves them in labelling their own emotion and the context in which they experience it. The use of adjectives (e.g., angry, disappointed) helps to signal emotional valence. This is then followed by *description* of the intensity of emotional arousal. Finally, there is exploration of two main interfaces: feeling/thought and feeling/body. Examples are given below in italics.

–Identifying the pragmatic trigger (object of pragmatic resistance)
I don't feel positive about the pronoun "watashi" in Japanese.

–Describing the emotion and context
I feel angry/disappointed when I see people using honorifics to others who are only slightly older.

–Describing the intensity of the feeling
It makes me <u>really</u> uncomfortable.

–Exploring the feeling/thought interface
When I have these feelings, I tend to think that I don't want to learn Japanese.

–Exploring the feeling/body interface
I feel a sense of disappointment in my chest/throat/whole body.

It is important when following the sequence of processes above that the focus remains as much as possible on the learners' internal experience and the aim of developing insight into their own patterns of reactivity. In other words, this is a non-judgmental process aimed at developing self-awareness. Once some time has been spent developing this foundation, teachers might wish to move onto analytical and reflective questions or tasks that help learners interpret their thoughts and feelings and why they might react this way. As suggested above, learners can also be encouraged to extend the attitude of non-judgment to other L2 speakers and to consider the logic behind different pragmatic behaviors.

Conclusion

In this chapter, I have argued for the need to more explicitly theorize the emotional dimensions of pragmatic resistance and pragmatic judgments more broadly. In line with recent research at the intersections of pragmatics and moral psychology, I have argued that the learning of pragmatics can present a challenge to the learners' felt sense of right behavior—whether that means "right" in terms of personal fit or "right" in terms of deeper social and moral judgments. Whereas much of the existing work on pragmatic resistance tends to place emphasis on rational decision-making and learners' agency to determine their own courses of communicative action and ways of constructing a symbolic self, it is crucial to acknowledge that the pragmatic decision making that helps constitute agency is mediated by learners' embodied reactions to difference. That is, it is not a rational process of "selection" but is rather a psychologically consequential process that is tied up with how learners perceive and react to challenges to their felt sense of "appropriate" language use. From a theoretical viewpoint, it is important for more interdisciplinary investigation into the emotional and somatic aspects of learning pragmatics and how learners' evaluations of pragmatics shape their learning trajectory and potential. From a practical viewpoint, acknowledging that the learning of pragmatics engages learners at deep levels of self and can trigger aversive reactions necessitates a turn toward a humanistic pedagogy of wellbeing. As teachers, our aim is not simply to help our learners become more effective communicators, it is also to help them become more mindful of their evaluations of self and others and more adept at regulating their own reactions.

References

Al-Issa, A. (2003), "Sociocultural Transfer in L2 Speech Behaviors: Evidence and Motivating Factors." *International Journal of Intercultural Relations*, 27 (5): 581–601.

Bhabha, H. K. (1994), *The Location of Culture*. London: Routledge.

Byram, M. (2021), *Teaching and Assessing Intercultural Communicative Competence: Revisited*. Blue Ridge Summit, PA: Multilingual Matters.

Byram, M., Nichols, A. & Stevens, D. (2001), "Introduction." In M. Byram, A. Nichols & D. Stevens (eds), *Developing Intercultural Competence in Practice*, 1–8, Clevedon: Multilingual Matters.

Chapman, H. A. (2018), "A Component Process Model of Disgust, Anger, and Moral Judgment." In K. Gray & J. Graham (eds), *Atlas of Moral Psychology*, 70–80, New York and London: The Guildford Press.

Culpeper, J., Schauer, G., Marti, L., Mei, M. & Nevala, M. (2014), "Impoliteness and Emotions in a Cross-cultural Perspective." *SPELL: Swiss Papers in English Language and Literature*, 30: 67–88.

Davis, J. M. (2007), "Resistance to L2 Pragmatics in the Australian ESL Context." *Language Learning*, 57 (4): 611–49.

Devlin, A. M. (2018), "Becoming Me in the L2: Sociopragmatic Development as an Index of Emerging Core Identity in a Study Abroad Context." In A. Sánchez-Hernández & A. Herraiz-Martínez (eds), *Learning Second Language Pragmatics beyond Traditional Contexts*, 255–85, Berlin: Peter Lang.

Eslami, Z. R., Kim, H., Wright, K. L. & Burlbaw, L. M. (2014), "The Role of Learner Subjectivity and Korean English Language Learners' Pragmatic Choices." *Lodz Papers in Pragmatics*, 10 (1): 117–45.

Feldman, C. & Kuyken, W. (2019), *Mindfulness: Ancient Wisdom Meets Modern Psychology*. New York: The Guildford Press.

Ford, M. T., Agosta, J. P., Huang, J. & Shannon, C. (2018), "Moral Emotions towards Others at Work and Implications for Employee Behavior: A Qualitative Analysis Using Critical Incidents." *Journal of Business and Psychology*, 33 (1): 155–90.

Garcés-Conejos Blitvich, P. & Kádár, D. Z. (2021), "Morality in Sociopragmatics." In M. Haugh, D. Z. Kádár & M. Terfourafi (eds), *The Cambridge Handbook of Sociopragmatics*, 385–407, Cambridge: Cambridge University Press.

Gomez-Laich, M. P. (2016), "Second Language Learners' Divergence from Target Language Pragmatic Norms." *Studies in Second Language Learning and Teaching*, 6 (2): 249–69.

Haidt, J. (2003), "The Moral Emotions." In R. J. Davidson, K. R. Scherer & H. H. Goldsmith (eds), *Handbook of Affective Sciences*, 852–70, New York: Oxford University Press.

Haidt, J. (2012), *The Righteous Mind: Why Good People Are Divided by Politics and Religion*. New York: Pantheon Books.

House, J. (2008), "What Is An 'Intercultural Speaker'?" In E. Alcón Soler & M. P. Safont Jorda (eds), *Intercultural Language Use and Language Learning*, 7–22, Dordrecht: Springer.

Hutcherson, C. A. & Gross, J. J. (2011), "The Moral Emotions: A Social-functionalist Account of Anger, Disgust, and Contempt." *Journal of Personality and Social Psychology*, 100 (4): 719–37.

Ishihara, N. (2009), "Transforming Community Norms: Potentials of L2 Speakers' Pragmatic Resistance." In M. Hood (ed.), *Proceedings of the 2008 Temple University Japan Colloquium on Language Learning*, 1–10, Tokyo: Temple University Japan.

Ishihara, N. (2010), "Maintaining an Optimal Distance: Nonnative Speakers' Pragmatic Choice." In A. Mahboob (ed.), *The NNEST Lens: Nonnative English Speakers in TESOL*, 35–53, Newcastle upon Tyne: Cambridge Scholars Press.

Ishihara, N. (2017), "Teaching Pragmatics in Support of Learner Subjectivity and Global Communicative Needs: A Peace Linguistics Perspective." *Idee in form@zione*, 6 (5): 17–32.

Ishihara, N. (2019a), "Understanding English Language Learners' Pragmatic Resistance." In X. Gao (ed.), *Second Handbook of English Language Teaching*, 621–41, Cham: Springer Nature.

Ishihara, N. (2019b), "Identity and Agency in L2 Pragmatics." In N. Taguchi (ed.), *The Routledge Handbook of Second Language Acquisition and Pragmatics*, 161–75, New York: Routledge.

Ishihara, N. & Porcellato, A. M. (2022), "Co-constructing Nonessentialist Pedagogy: Supporting Teachers to Support Learners' Translingual Agency through L2 Pragmatics Instruction." In T. McConachy & A. J. Liddicoat (eds), *Teaching and Learning Second Language Pragmatics for Intercultural Understanding*, 151–72, New York and London: Routledge.

Ishihara, N. & Tarone, E. (2009), "Subjectivity and Pragmatic Choice in L2 Japanese: Emulating and Resisting Pragmatic Norms." In N. Taguchi (ed.), *Pragmatic Competence in Japanese as a Second Language*, 101–28, Berlin: Mouton de Gruyter.

Kádár, D. Z. (2020), "Capturing Injunctive Norm in Pragmatics: Meta-reflective Evaluations and the Moral Order." *Lingua*, 237: 102814.

Kádár, D. Z. & Haugh, M. (2013), *Understanding Politeness*. Cambridge: Cambridge University Press.

Kahneman, D. (2011), *Thinking, Fast and Slow*. New York: Farrar, Straus and Giroux.

Koutlaki, S. A. & Eslami, Z. R. (2018), "Critical Intercultural Communication Education: Cultural Analysis and Pedagogical Applications." *Intercultural Communication Education*, 1 (3): 100–9.

Kramsch, C. (2009), *The Multilingual Subject: What Foreign Language Learners Say about Their Experience and Why it Matters*. Oxford: Oxford University Press.

Kramsch, C. (2011), "The Symbolic Dimensions of the Intercultural." *Language Teaching*, 44 (3): 354–67.

Liddicoat, A. J. (2006), "Learning the Culture of Interpersonal Relationships: Students' Understandings of Personal Address Forms in French." *Intercultural Pragmatics*, 3 (1): 55–80.

Liddicoat, A. J. & McConachy, T. (2019), "Meta-pragmatic Awareness and Agency in Language Learners' Constructions of Politeness." In T. Szende & G. Alao (eds), *Pragmatic and Cross-cultural Competences: Focus on Politeness*, 11–26, Brussels: Peter Lang.

Liddicoat, A. J. & Scarino, A. (2013), *Intercultural Language Teaching and Learning*. Chichester: Wiley-Blackwell.

McConachy, T. (2018), *Developing Intercultural Perspectives on Language Use: Exploring Pragmatics and Culture in Foreign Language Learning*. Bristol: Multilingual Matters.

McConachy, T. (2021), *Exploring Intercultural Dimensions of L2 Pragmatics Learning in a Japanese EFL Context*. Abingdon and New York: Routledge.

McConachy, T. & Fujino, H. (2022), "Negotiating Politeness Practices and Interpersonal Connections in L2 Japanese: Insights from Study Abroad Narratives." In T. McConachy & A. J. Liddicoat (eds), *Teaching and Learning Second Language Pragmatics for Intercultural Understanding*, 19–39, New York and London: Routledge.

McConachy, T. & Liddicoat, A.J. (2016), "Meta-Pragmatic Awareness and Intercultural Competence: The Role of Reflection and Interpretation in Intercultural Mediation." In F. Dervin & Z. Gross (eds), *Intercultural Competence in Education: Alternative Approaches for Different Times*, 13–30, London: Palgrave Macmillan.

McConachy, T. & Liddicoat, A. J. (eds). (2022), *Teaching and Learning Second Language Pragmatics for Intercultural Understanding*. New York and London: Routledge.

McConachy, T. & Spencer-Oatey, H. (2020), "Developing Pragmatic Awareness." In K.P. Schneider & E. Ifantidou (eds), *Developmental and Clinical Pragmatics*, 393–428, Berlin and Boston: De Gruyter Mouton.

Mercer, S. (2021), "An Agenda for Well-being in ELT: An Ecological Perspective." *ELT Journal*, 75 (1): 14–21.

Myers, D. G. (2004), *Theories of Emotion in Psychology*, 7th edn. New York: Worth.

Oxford, R. L., Olivero, M. M., Harrison, M. & Gregersen, T. (eds). (2021), *Peacebuilding in Language Education: Innovations in Theory and Practice*. Bristol & Blue Ridge Summit: Multilingual Matters.

Schwartz, S. H. (2012), "An Overview of the Schwartz Theory of Basic Values." *Online Readings in Psychology and Culture*, 2 (1). doi: https://doi.org/10.9707/2307-0919.1116

Sharifian, F. & Tayebi, T. (2017b), "Perception of (Im)politeness and the Underlying Cultural Conceptualisations: A Study of Persian." *Pragmatics and Society*, 8 (2): 231–53.

Siegal, M. S. (1996), "The Role of Learner Subjectivity in Second Language Sociolinguistic Competency: Western Women Learning Japanese." *Applied Linguistics*, 17 (3): 56–382.

Spencer-Oatey, H. & Kádár, D. Z. (2021), *Intercultural Politeness: Managing Relations across Cultures*. Cambridge: Cambridge University Press.

Spencer-Oatey, H. & Xing, J. (2019), "Interdisciplinary Perspectives on Interpersonal Relations and the Evaluation Process: Culture, Norms, and the Moral Order." *Journal of Pragmatics*, 151: 141–54.

Ting-Toomey, S. (2015), "Mindfulness." In J. M. Bennett (ed.), *The SAGE Encyclopedia of Intercultural Competence*, Vol. 2, 620–6, Los Angeles, CA: SAGE.

Turner, J. H. & Stets, J. E. (2006), "Moral Emotions." In J. E. Stets & J. H. Turner (eds), *Handbook of the Sociology of Emotions*, 544–66, Boston, MA: Springer.

van Compernolle, R. A. (2016), "Sociolinguistic Authenticity and Classroom L2 Learners: Production, Perception and Metapragmatics." In R. A. van Compernolle & J. McGregor (eds), *Authenticity, Language and Interaction in Second Language Contexts*, 61–81, Bristol: Multilingual Matters.

van Compernolle, R. A. & Williams, L. (2013), "Reconceptualizing Sociolinguistic Competence as Mediated Action: Identity, Meaning-making, Agency." *The Modern Language Journal*, 96 (2): 234–50.

Žegarac, V., Spencer-Oatey, H. & Ushioda, E. (2014), "Conceptualising Mindfulness-Mindlessness in Intercultural Interaction." *International Journal of Language and Culture*, 1 (1): 75–97.

Positive Psychology Activities for Promoting Emotion Regulation and Wellbeing in Language Teacher Education

María Matilde Olivero, María Celina Barbeito, and
Adelina Sánchez Centeno

Introduction

Research has documented that being a (pre-service) language teacher is a highly emotional experience (e.g., Dewaele et al. 2019; Hiver 2016; Gkonou & Mercer 2017; Kostoulas & Lämmerer 2020; MacIntyre et al. 2020). For example, it has been shown that negative emotions are often experienced due to heavy workload, poor interpersonal relationships among members in an institution, insecurities related to language and teaching techniques, and differences between what (pre-service) teachers envision and reality, among other things. Such conditions tend to trigger unpleasant emotions that, if not properly regulated, might lead to unfavorable outcomes, such as high levels of stress and job dissatisfaction. However, (pre-service) teachers can also experience positive emotions as a result of joyful experiences related to their work, often accompanied by the use of conscious strategies to enhance positivity (Gkonou et al. 2020).

In recognition of the emotional nature of language teaching, the field of language teacher education has started to pay closer attention to the role of emotions. Although language teacher education has traditionally been largely cognitive in nature, there is increasing interest in holistic approaches that aim to develop the cognitive, emotional, and social aspects of the person in an integrated way (e.g., Barbeito & Sánchez Centeno 2021; Burns 2017; Helgesen 2017; Olivero et al. 2021; Olivero 2017; Olivero & Oxford 2019; Oxford 2017). In other words, holistic approaches aim to strategically engage multiple dimensions of the self and promote holistic learning that enhances the wellbeing of student teachers. Holistic approaches that integrate positive psychology-based pedagogy, for example, can help future teachers increase positivity and regulate unpleasant emotions, resulting in greater optimism as well as the development of resilience and empathy, among other attributes (e.g., Mercer 2016; Olivero 2017). Positive psychology-based practices are also intended to enhance participants' wellbeing (Gregersen & MacIntyre 2021), which can lead to helping future teachers flourish and have a more meaningful journey in their teacher education programs.

In this chapter we highlight the value of incorporating positive psychology activities based on holistic learning approaches into language teacher education programs as a way of enhancing emotion regulation and wellbeing. The chapter first presents the theoretical background on wellbeing and emotion regulation in language education as well as on holistic learning, which serves to frame the activities that are described next and to elucidate their underlying principles. The chapter offers a sample of positive psychology-based activities that have been used in language teacher education courses with the purpose of helping future teachers regulate their emotions and enhance their wellbeing while learning to teach a foreign language. In closing, the chapter discusses implications for second language teacher education (SLTE) that relate to the need to prepare future teachers to flourish.

Wellbeing and Positive Psychology

Wellbeing entails being satisfied with one's life, and is influenced by interrelated factors at personal, professional, and contextual levels (Mercer & Gregersen 2020). According to Holmes (2005), individuals experience four interrelated kinds of wellbeing: physical (being in good physical health); emotional (being able to produce positive emotions and thoughts and adapt in stressful situations); mental (being able to realize one's own potential and cope with normal stresses); and spiritual (finding a sense of deep purpose and meaning in life).

Positive psychology is a well-known subfield of psychology for understanding wellbeing. It is the study of human strengths and virtues that lead people to flourish (Seligman & Csikszentmihalyi 2000). Unlike traditional psychology, which focuses on the root causes of mental disorders and emotional distress, positive psychology centers on the positives that help people increase their wellbeing. This relatively new subfield of psychology, whose origins date back to 1998, is closely linked to humanistic psychology but with greater emphasis on empirical research (MacIntyre & Mercer 2014).

Positive psychology intends to enhance individuals' wellbeing. One influential approach to doing so is the PERMA model (Seligman 2011), which emphasizes the notion of *flourishing* by increasing positive emotion (P), engagement (E), positive relationships (R), meaning (M), and accomplishment (A). *Positive emotion* is associated with the importance of feeling well, and it involves a wide variety of pleasant emotions, such as pride, hope, joy, serenity, among others. As understood in the PERMA model, *engagement* refers to reaching a state of flow by being fully immersed in a task. *Relationships* relates to having and maintaining quality relationships. Another key component within positive psychology is *Meaning*, which entails living a purposeful life and doing relevant activities. *Accomplishment*, the last factor of the PERMA model, emphasizes the importance of experiencing and recognizing our achievements and successes. Based on this model, the interaction of positivity within positive emotion, engagement, relationships, meaning, and accomplishment leads to wellbeing (Mercer & Gregersen 2020). From its origin, positive psychology has aimed at addressing three main areas, including the function of emotions, positive individual characteristics, and the institutions that influence people's wellbeing (MacIntyre & Mercer 2014).

In the last decade, positive psychology has had an increasing influence in the field of foreign language education. The pioneering work by MacIntyre and Gregersen (2012) on the broadening and narrowing functions of positive and negative emotions has led the way to various theoretical, empirical, and intervention-based works that have appeared in the following years (e.g., Dewaele et al. 2019; Fresacher 2016; Gabryś-Barker 2016; Gregersen et al. 2020; Helgesen 2019; MacIntyre & Ayers-Glassey 2021; MacIntyre & Mercer 2014; MacIntyre et al. 2019; Oxford 2016).

Positive Psychology in Language Teacher Education

The key positive psychology components of the PERMA model have been explored in the field of language education to increase the wellbeing of learners, teachers, and student teachers. Among the plethora of reasons why it is important to develop positivity in language teacher education courses is that it can help increase optimism in pre-service teachers, foster resilience and hope (Hiver 2016), and increase inner peace (Barbeito & Sanchez Centeno 2021; Olivero 2017). Moreover, the development of positive emotion can lead to better reasoning and performance by promoting innovative thought and action

(Oxford 2015). Positivity can also help relieve tensions and teachers' ability to cope with anxiety (Gregersen et al. 2016; Mercer & Gregersen 2020), as well as establish a harmonious learning atmosphere by fostering quality relationships between teacher and students and among students (Gkonou & Mercer 2017; Mercer 2016).

Engagement is a construct that is gaining increased attention in the field of language education (e.g., Edstrom 2015; Hiver et al. 2021; Mercer & Dörnyei 2020; Svalberg 2018). Whereas the PERMA model defines engagement with achieving a state of flow, scholars in the field of language education have related engagement more specifically to commitment and active participation in learning. Mercer (2019) states that there are key psychological aspects that are important for learner engagement to take place, including developing a sense of competence for mastering goals and succeeding; enhancing self-regulation and agency; helping learners identify the meaningful purpose of learning a language and engaging in tasks; and promoting a sense of belonging to the classroom, based on quality relationships with the teacher and peers.

Because of increasing recognition that quality relationships between teacher and students are highly beneficial for learning to take place, this construct has also been a matter of investigation in language education. Although studies are still scarce, a growing interest in quality relationships can be observed in the second language acquisition (SLA) literature. Gkonou and Mercer (2018), for example, found that socio-emotionally competent language teachers work hard at developing quality relationships with their students, and do so by being empathetic, sensitive to students' needs and emotions, establishing a relationship of mutual respect, and by creating an atmosphere of trust. In addition, a study has indicated that language teachers construct positive relationships with their students with the purpose of helping them cope with language anxiety (Gkonou & Miller 2019).

Meaning, the extent to which people find a purpose and make sense of their life, has been emphasized in humanistic teaching approaches within the field of language teaching (Stevick 1990). For Stevick, it is paramount to embrace teaching approaches that focus on learners' attributes and through which language learners can relate what they learn with real life. Oxford and Cuéllar (2014) have used learner narratives to help language learners make meaning of their learning experiences. Holistic approaches, which will be discussed in depth later in this chapter, have been found to be highly meaningful and transformative in the context of language teacher education (Olivero 2017; Olivero & Oxford 2019; also Chapter 1, this volume) as they have led to a change in future teachers' emotions, beliefs, and identities, thereby facilitating teacher development.

In their recent book on teacher wellbeing, Mercer and Gregersen (2020) claim that ways in which language teachers can get a sense of accomplishment include engaging in a new project, innovating in the classroom, celebrating (small) work-related successes, and being involved in professional development activities. Moreover, they state that in order to be able to experience the positive emotions that emerge from accomplishing tasks, teachers can engage in *savoring*, which means being aware of the good things that happen to us (positive experiences, feelings, among others). Savoring helps teachers not only be conscious of the accomplishments in the present but also in the past as a way of generating positivity toward the future.

As has been described above, positive psychology has gained prominence in foreign language pedagogy intended to enhance language learners' and teachers' wellbeing. An important aspect to highlight is that in order for teachers to experience wellbeing throughout their careers and to care for the wellbeing of their language learners, it seems paramount to incorporate content and approaches that focus on wellbeing in language teacher education programs. In addition, it seems sensible to incorporate wellbeing during language teacher preparation due to the complexities involved in learning to teach a foreign language. An important part of addressing wellbeing in language teacher education is emotion regulation, which is discussed in the next section of this chapter.

Emotion Regulation in Language Teacher Education

Teaching is an experience loaded with emotions, often unpleasant and difficult to manage. It is known to be a stressful job due to, among other aspects, the difficulty in achieving balance between private and professional life, low-paid jobs, and new demands as education becomes complex (Day & Gu 2010). In addition, it seems clear that teachers' emotions, together with their beliefs and attitudes, tend to have a direct impact on the classroom. In recognition of the important role that emotions play in teachers' performance and wellbeing, there has been an increased interest in emotions and emotion regulation in the field of teacher education in the last decades.

Apart from the general reasons stated above that illustrate the need to focus on emotions in teacher education, there are stressors that are specific to language learning and teaching, which highlight the need to pay attention to emotion in the context of language teacher education. Such stressors include insecurity related to language ability; having to cope with language learners' emotional struggles; varied levels of proficiency within the same group of learners; and difficulties associated with the intercultural aspects of teaching, among others (MacIntyre et al. 2020).

One way in which language teachers can better cope with the emotional challenges of their profession and experience greater wellbeing is by learning to regulate their emotions. Emotion regulation occurs when "emotions are felt to be undesirable, and therefore individuals consciously try to avoid painful feelings and seek out pleasant ones, protect the feelings of others, and feign an emotion" (Gkonou et al. 2021: 33). Gross's (2014) theory of emotion regulation describes the process through which a person tries to upregulate positive emotions in order to increase their strength and duration and downregulate negative ones to reduce the effects of unpleasant experiences and the reactions that can result from such events.

Due to the multidimensional nature of emotions, Gross (2002: 282) states that emotion regulation involves changes in the "latency, rise time, magnitude, duration, and offset of responses in behavioral, experiential, or physiological domains." Gross (2014) proposes different types of emotion regulation. *Situation selection* implies taking actions that would be conducive to experiencing a situation that might trigger positive emotions. Another broad type of emotion regulation is *situation modification*, which implies modifying an external situation to change its emotional effect. *Attentional deployment* implies distracting one's attention and directing it toward a specific situation to manage often unpleasant emotions. A fourth type of emotion regulation is referred to as *cognitive change* or reappraisal, which means reframing, modifying the way one thinks about a situation. Finally, *response modulation* implies trying to regulate the reactions that result from emotionally charged situations, including deep breathing, counting to ten before reacting, among others.

Different scholars in the field of language teacher education have emphasized the value of emotion regulation strategies when learning to teach and teaching a second language. Gregersen, MacIntyre, and Macmillan (2020), for example, explored language teachers' workplace stress when working abroad. Through a case study, they investigated the effects of a positive psychology cognitive reappraisal strategy (*Finding Silver Linings*) that is intended to reduce the often-unpleasant impact of stress. The *Finding Silver Linings* intervention has been shown to function as a useful type of emotion regulation for language teachers. Moreover, in their model of teacher resilience used to study pre-service teachers at an Austrian university, Kostoulas and Lämmerer (2020) explain how emotion regulation strategies, among other factors, help pre-service teachers develop an adaptive resilience system, which could lead to positive professional outcomes.

Gkonou, Olivero, and Oxford (2021) have proposed a framework for teaching important competencies to enhance peacebuilding, which include emotion regulation. They argue that language teacher education programs should prepare future teachers to develop ethnocultural empathy, intercultural understanding, cognitive flexibility, and emotion regulation, which can be done through specific activities based on holistic teaching approaches, including positive psychology-based interventions.

We, the authors of this chapter, have worked on different projects that involve the use of emotion regulation strategies in the context of language teacher education and acknowledge the difficulties student teachers face when attempting to regulate their emotions. Such projects have consisted of pedagogical interventions carried out in phonetics, teaching methods, and practicum courses of a foreign language teacher education program with the aim of helping future language teachers develop tools to regulate their emotions associated with learning to teach a foreign language. Olivero (2017) has found that *inner peace activities*, which are language activities intended to increase inner harmony, have helped pre-service teachers downregulate unpleasant emotions, such as fear and insecurity, experienced during the practicum. At the same time, *inner peace activities* have allowed practicum students to increase their positivity during their teaching practices, which has led them to be more innovative and strengthen the relationships with their students (Olivero 2017; Olivero & Oxford 2019). Barbeito and Sánchez Centeno (2021) highlight the importance of teaching emotion regulation strategies in the initial stages of teacher preparation. More specifically, they emphasize the value of incorporating positive psychology-based activities to help future teachers cope with the difficulties encountered when having to produce orally in the phonetics class and to have a more joyful experience throughout the course.

As we have discussed, emotion regulation is paramount for cultivating wellbeing. Having conceptualized emotion regulation and discussed its importance in the field of language teacher education, let us now turn our attention to a teaching approach that is useful for addressing wellbeing in language teacher education.

Holistic Learning in Language (Teacher) Education

Holistic learning refers to an educational approach that intends to develop the whole person. In other words, it focuses on the cognitive, emotional, social, cultural, and spiritual aspects of the learner (Olivero & Oxford 2019; Oxford, this volume). Holistic learning approaches are based on deep reflection and inner work, they engage the learner in personally meaningful experience, they are embodied, contextualized, intuitive, creative (Oxford et al. 2021), and they focus on a concern for love, peace, and justice (Miller et al. 2018).

There are various forms of holistic education, such as contemplative, embodied, transformative, experiential, and deep learning (Oxford & Olivero 2019). Through contemplative learning the learner develops the inner self through contemplation and deep reflection. Common techniques in contemplative learning are yoga, meditation, and journaling, among others. Embodied learning aims at enhancing learning through emotional work and practical experiences. Embodied practices involve not only intellectual work but also learning with one's body and spirit. Transformative learning also intends to develop the learner's whole self and does so by helping learners reflect on and modify their beliefs, emotions, and behaviors. Experiential learning offers opportunities to learn through concrete experiences and by reflecting on them.

Another form of learning that centers on learning holistically is deep learning (Shaules 2019: 60). In his recent book, he defines deep learning as "the integration of complex skills into the intuitive mind in a process that is meaningful and engaging for learners." Deep learning is based on personally meaningful experience, it is a whole person approach intended to foster development and growth. Shaules (2019) claims that language pedagogy should be based on the recognition that learning a language involves both attentive and intuitive mental processes that must work in tandem. Deep learning is seen as an embodied process that can facilitate engagement, a state of flow, and transformation of the self.

In the field of language education, research on holistic learning is still scarce. One of the reasons is that language teacher education has traditionally neglected holistic practices (Olivero & Oxford 2019), in spite of the fact that holistic learning has been established in the field for decades (Stevick 1990). This is an issue not unique to language teacher education but also exists in general higher education, which has tended to embrace mainly cognitive approaches, often not recognizing the important role that other aspects of the self (such as emotional and social) play in education (Bai et al. 2013; London 2013). The strong focus on cognition has characterized language teacher programs around the world, which has led language teachers to replicate similar practices in their own classroom once they become in-service teachers (Johnson & Golombek 2016). Given that language teaching involves cognitive, social, and emotional aspects, incorporating holistic approaches into language teacher education seems highly reasonable.

The incorporation of holistic forms of education in language teacher education has recently grown (e.g., Barbeito & Sánchez Centeno 2021; Burns 2017; Helgesen 2017; Olivero 2017; Olivero et al 2021; Olivero & Oxford 2019; Oxford 2017). It has been demonstrated that holistic language education enhances wellbeing, positivity, creativity, teacher development, and helps strengthen important human virtues (Olivero & Oxford 2019). In language (teacher) education, holistic approaches can be used to develop learners' (and future teachers') cognitions, emotions, and identities together with their language competencies. For example, holistic learning techniques such as journaling and creative writing involve reflecting with words. Non-verbal forms of reflection can also be fostered in the classroom through techniques such as visualization and meditation. Moreover, various forms of art can be used in the classroom including singing, painting, drawing, and dancing with the purpose of reflecting on different aspects of the self. Non-verbal language activities can be combined with verbal language ones.

When future teachers experience holistic learning activities throughout their language teacher education programs in a gradual and systematic way, it is likely that the content, the competencies, and the techniques involved in such activities will become part of their pedagogical content knowledge (Shulman 1986), which would help them incorporate similar practices in their own classrooms once they start teaching. In the next section of this chapter, we describe a sample of positive psychology activities based on holistic learning approaches that can be used in language (teacher) education. Such activities are intended to foster wellbeing and emotion regulation and help future teachers thrive throughout their programs and in their profession.

Positive Psychology Activities for Language (Teacher) Education

The positive psychology activities described in this section aim at helping future language teachers enhance their wellbeing and emotion regulation while learning to teach a foreign language. The activities were designed to be integrated into regular coursework of language teacher education courses. In recent years, we have used the activities in practicum courses of the undergraduate English as a Foreign Language teacher education program at the National University of Río

Cuarto, in Argentina. It is important to note that the empirical evidence of the effectiveness of such activities in this program is still under investigation.

The activities involve learning through reflection on experience, and aim at developing the cognitive, emotional, and social aspects of the self. When learning experientially student teachers are given the possibility to undergo personally meaningful experiences related to wellbeing and emotion regulation through embodiment, that is by having concrete opportunities to employ strategies for self-regulation and ways of enhancing their wellbeing, which they can later incorporate into their teaching practice. Through reflection student teachers can confirm, shape, modify their beliefs and emotions, as well as identify how the activities proposed relate to their actions as future teachers and to their overall professional identities. Reflecting on experience facilitates the transformation of the self.

In order to better guide the reader, the four activities proposed follow the same organizational pattern. Each activity begins with (a) a brief introduction with the theoretical rationale, followed by (b) the main purpose of the activity, and (c) a detailed description of the procedures. We have also included optional (d) follow-up tasks that teacher educators can incorporate in order to extend learning opportunities as well as (e) tasks that involve the use of technology.

Although these activities were used with student teachers taking practicum courses, they can be adapted to other language teacher education courses, including literature, teaching methodology, phonetics, and foreign language, among others. Moreover, these activities can be easily adjusted to other contexts, such as language classrooms or professional development courses. We trust that the readers of this chapter who are interested in the activities proposed below will employ their creativity and take a critical stance in order to adjust them to the different variables of their specific teaching contexts.

Activity 1: Building Positive Relationships

Relationships are vital to successful classrooms (Gkonou & Mercer 2018). Building quality relationships and a sense of community in the language classroom mostly depends on the teachers' willingness to build connections with their students. Much of the interaction that takes place in a classroom occurs nonverbally. Gregersen and McIntyre (2021: 44) state that "many of the cues that enrich meaning, convey emotion and augment learning in the target language are embedded in nonverbal communication." An effective way of establishing deep connections with students is by engaging in small talk, listening attentively and making eye contact, if culturally appropriate.

In the authors' experience, during their teaching practice student teachers are so concerned with following the planned stages of their lessons, that they tend to overlook taking the time to generate a positive, caring environment and bond with their students, which can certainly be a common practice for many educators. Experiencing a deep connection between teacher educator and student teachers in the practicum lessons, and later reflecting on how this is achieved, can lead to a more natural and effortless implementation of these valuable procedures once they start teaching.

Purpose: To develop quality relationships with students and strengthen mutual respect.

Procedures: In this activity, we encourage student teachers to acknowledge that both verbal and non-verbal communication are essential to establish deep connections in the classroom.

1. Enter the classroom and take five minutes to engage in genuine and mindful conversation with the student teachers, responding with interest to what they say, through both verbal and non-verbal language. As a teacher educator, you should aim at creating a sense of community and a safe place for students, characteristic of positive and healthy interpersonal relationships.
2. After some weeks of incorporating these actions as a routine when starting the lesson, prompt discussion of what you do when you start the lesson every day. Ask student teachers to express how they feel about that classroom routine. Tell them they will take turns to start the following lessons in the same way so as to see whether they feel confident to proceed in such a way, and whether it suits their teaching style. Invite student teachers to try this activity in their own classrooms when practicing teaching.
3. When student teachers plan their lessons, encourage them to include a section at the beginning of their lesson plan to incorporate this routine.
4. After student teachers teach their practice lessons in their assigned settings, ask them to reflect on their own emotions and students' responses to this routine, and share with the whole class.

Follow-up: Ask student teachers to write about their experiences in a journal. Ideas for prompts include: a) a specific description of the routine they implemented to start their lessons; b) their own emotions experienced during the implementation; c) the effect it had on students, among others.

Techy option: Building quality relationships with students can be more difficult in virtual classrooms. Taking time to chat with students and listen attentively to what they say is very important and can help both teachers and students transcend the screen and feel connected. In order to strengthen your relationships with students you can also pretend to shake hands, use the chat box to send greeting emojis, count down and make a hi five to the camera, and send virtual hugs.

Activity 2: Deadlines and *Lifelines*

"All the domains of your life, both inside and outside the workplace, are integral to how satisfied, content and happy you are" (Mercer & Gregersen 2020: 12). When teachers intentionally seek to be in a positive state, their minds will "broaden" (Fredrickson 2001) and their wellbeing will increase; they will be more creative, open-minded and able to connect with themselves and others.

Student teachers often feel overwhelmed by their everyday routine and cannot find the occasion to have a self-care moment. One reason why this might happen is because self-care does not have a place in their schedule, which is often packed with deadlines. The word deadline formerly referred to 'a boundary around a military prison beyond which a prisoner could not venture without risk of being shot by the guards' (collinsdictionary.com). This historical meaning might depict the frantic lives teachers have. Even though teachers cannot omit deadlines, they can deliberately assign an opening and add a *lifeline* right after a deadline.

What do we mean by *lifelines*? They are self-care moments, i.e., activities we enjoy doing and which remind us that we should try to keep or reestablish a healthy balance between academic and personal life. It is important to treasure these self-care moments and to commit to them as we do with deadlines. Enjoying self-care moments after meeting deadlines also serves as a way of celebrating accomplishments, which is an important aspect for understanding wellbeing.

Purpose: to focus on reestablishing academic and personal balance and celebrating academic successes.

Procedures: In this activity we encourage student teachers to consciously plan mindful self-care moments during busy times and reflect on the importance of keeping a healthy academic/personal balance.

1. Ask student teachers to take a screen capture or a picture of their schedules and to share them with the rest of the class. You can also participate in this activity as a practicum teacher and show your own schedule.
2. Ask student teachers about their daily routines. Then, discuss what deadlines mean and imply.
3. Introduce the concept *lifelines*: Tell student teachers they are self-care moments that can be done after they accomplish tasks and meet deadlines. For example, taking a fifteen-minute break with no phones or laptop and drinking a glass of water mindfully, in complete silence. Focus on the fact that balance is conceived differently by each person and that the frequency and type of self-care moment selected should work for each person (Mercer & Gregersen 2020).
4. With the whole class, create a self-care checklist with activities that the student teachers would like to do and that are feasible. Ask student teachers to share their choices to inspire their classmates.
5. Get student teachers to reflect on the importance of finding openings in their calendars to schedule brief conscious activities to reestablish academic and personal balance and celebrate academic successes. Invite student teachers to take action by inserting these self-care activities into their schedules and meeting the *lifelines*.

Follow-up: The following week, ask student teachers whether they were able to take their self-care moments and how they felt. Encourage them to savor the positive, relaxing moments they could experience during their breaks and to "protect them just as if they were important meetings" (Mercer & Gregersen 2020: 155).

Techy option: If student teachers express difficulties in remembering to take self-care moments, they suggest setting a lifeline alarm in their cellphones. In this way, they will eventually get used to incorporating these breaks into their routine. You can also encourage them to make a self-care schedule for a specific week or month using their favorite app and to share it with the rest of the class or on social media among their friends.

Activity 3: My Self-confidence Booster Anthem

Music has the power to transport our souls to unimagined places. Music and songs have helped language teachers to present vocabulary and grammar, to build classroom routines, to break the ice, to develop intercultural competence, among others. Likewise, as Prado et al. (2021: 113) have expressed "environments rich with symbols, images, art, music, poetry and stories […] enable a connection between our conscious world and unconscious self."

Music and lyrics accompany us at all times, it helps generate pleasant emotions and boosts wellbeing (Murphey 2014 in Gregersen 2016); more so when we need inspiration to accomplish our aims. Student teachers in the practicum can benefit from music, as it can act as a transmitter or catalyst of message and emotions (Fonseca-Mora & Machancoses 2016).

Purpose: To downregulate student teachers' unpleasant emotions and increase positivity by boosting self-confidence and experiencing joy.

Procedures: This activity involves the use of music and art to create an inspirational anthem based on a selection of already published songs and to design an art collage (see pictures below).

1. Discuss with student teachers the role of music in their lives, if they have favorite songs, when they listen to those songs, what they are about, if they can sing or play an instrument, etc. Announce there will be a project related to music the following class. For that purpose, ask them to select between three and five lyrics of their favorite motivational songs at home, and to save them on their phones (or make sure they have access to them) and print the lyrics in colored paper to take them to class.
2. Once back in class, engage student teachers in a discussion about the value of music as a source of inspiration and how music can help us in the midst of stressful times.
   Ask student teachers which songs they selected and why. Play instrumental music in the background while student teachers read the lyrics for themselves.
3. Once they have read all their songs, tell student teachers to create their own inspirational anthem (Figure 9.1) based on the lyrics from the songs they have just read. They should choose lines or stanzas from each song to create their own inspirational anthem. They can work individually, in pairs or groups and they should feel free to modify the lyrics to suit the message they wish to convey.

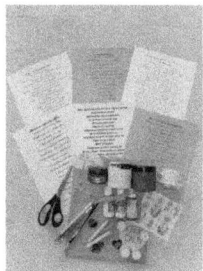   

Figure 9.1 Creation Process of the Self-confidence Booster Anthem

4. Once the anthem is ready, provide student teachers with color pencils, brushes, scissors and all the materials needed to create a collage.
5. a. Ask student teachers to share their productions with the whole class and display their works of art on the wall.
   b. Get student teachers to tell the rest about some of the lines in their inspirational anthem and what they mean to them.

Follow-up: Show student teachers' work on social media and invite everybody in class to *like* each other's' publications and comment on them.

Techy option: Tell student teachers to propose one inspirational song each, create a Spotify open playlist for the course and name it. Each year new songs are added by the teacher educators and student teachers to be used in class for activities as the ones proposed.

For this activity we suggest student teachers listen to the following songs for inspiration: "Fireworks" by K. Perry, "Born This Way" by Lady Gaga, "Brave" by S. Bareilles, "Know Your Worth" by D. Khalid, "When You Believe" by W. Houston and "Adventure of a Lifetime" by Coldplay.

Activity 4: Look Back, You've Made It so Far…

Focusing on what we have accomplished and on our successes can empower us and help us strengthen our wellbeing. A large body of research has shown that students' appraisal of past accomplishments and the amount of satisfaction they experience will significantly determine how they approach future learning (Dörnyei & Muir 2019). Encouraging positive retrospective reflection upon accomplishments can play an important role in increasing positivity (Helgesen 2016).

In general, students do not take the time to reflect on their successes and tend to lose sight of them as they move from one task to another in their academic lives. Taking the time to savor one's accomplishments could stimulate students to increase pleasant emotions such as optimism and pride.

Purpose: to focus on accomplishments and to savor them.

Procedures: In this activity, student teachers have the opportunity to acknowledge and reflect on their successes and share them with the whole class.

1. As student teachers enter the classroom, give them a warm welcome playing an audio file with the sound effects of applause and cheer. See how they react.
2. Explain to student teachers that you organized such a welcome to congratulate them on their academic accomplishments so far. Open the floor for discussion on the power of taking the time to focus on achievements as it can help them enhance motivation, and a sense of control and pride, among other aspects.
3. Draw a chart on the board and ask student teachers to write down what they see as their main academic accomplishments to date. Guide student teachers to include successes related to different aspects, including academic, emotional, and social.
4. Get student teachers to reflect on how much they have accomplished and how this makes them feel. Ask them about the processes they have followed to reach their goals. Then, discuss the idea that it is the means by which they arrive at those goals that is of paramount importance.
5. Invite student teachers to congratulate each other face to face or in writing. In this way you will give every student teacher in the class the chance to savor their accomplishments.

Follow-up: Talk about the future achievements student teachers would like to accomplish. Prompt them to focus on concrete, feasible actions they can do to achieve them. Encourage student teachers to be positive, optimistic, and hopeful.

Techy option: At the end of the activity, student teachers can congratulate each other through text messages, make a phone call or video call, or write a nice message on social media.

Those readers interested in more positive psychology-based activities for language teacher education might find the following sources useful. For book chapters with sequences of positive psychology-based activities that can be used in language, phonetics, or other language teacher education courses, see Barbeito and Sánchez Centeno (2021), Fresacher (2016), and Helgesen (2016). For activities that include positive psychology as part of holistic approaches for peacebuilding in language teacher education, see Gkonou et al. (2021); Gregersen and MacIntyre (2021); Olivero (2017); Olivero et al. (2021); and Oxford (2017).

Conclusion

Our experience as language teacher educators and recent researches that have included similar pedagogical interventions in the field of language education (e.g., Gregersen et al. 2020; Gregersen et al. 2016; Olivero 2017) indicate that positive psychology-based activities can serve as a powerful means for emotion regulation and wellbeing. Activities such as the ones described above can help future teachers increase their self-confidence, downregulate unpleasant emotions, be more optimistic, experience joy in the course, improve relationships with peers, students, and mentors, and care about their emotional wellbeing, among other aspects. Although the literature on wellbeing in language teacher education has shown an increased interest in applying pedagogical interventions based on positive psychology, there is still need for more empirical evidence of the particular impact of such interventions.

It has been argued that teaching and learning to teach a language is a highly emotional and often stressful experience. In this light, positive psychology activities based on holistic approaches should be further incorporated into language teacher education programs with the purpose of helping pre-service teachers regulate their emotions and enhance their wellbeing throughout their programs of study and their careers. By incorporating positive psychology-based activities in an experiential way, future teachers can embody what they learn and better integrate theory and practice, which will allow them to incorporate the new knowledge and competencies into their knowledge base of teaching. The activities presented in this chapter are intended to enhance transformation and teacher development. However, it should be noted that in order for transformations to be profound and long lasting, the mere incorporation of activities into language teacher education courses might not be enough. Wellbeing should become a priority in language teacher education programs, and it should involve a joint effort of all the members in the institutions that offer such programs, including curriculum designers, authorities, administrators, teacher educators, and students. May such ideas find their way into the hands of those committed to the wellbeing of language teachers around the world.

References

Bai, H., Cohen, A. & Scott, C. (2013), "Re-envisioning Higher Education: The Three-Fold Relationality Framework." In J. Lin, R. L. Oxford & E. J. Brantmeier (eds), *Re-envisioning Higher Education: Embodied Pathways to Wisdom and Social Transformation*, 3–22, Charlotte: Information Age Publishing.

Barbeito, M. C. & Sánchez Centeno, A. (2021), "Inner Peace and Emotion Regulation during Oral Production in ESL/EFL Teacher Education." In R. L. Oxford, M. M. Olivero, M. Harrison & T. Gregersen (eds), *Peacebuilding in Language Education. Innovations in Theory and Practice*, 63–79, Bristol: Multilingual Matters.

Burns, A. (2017), "Innovating Teacher Development: Transformative Teacher Education through Classroom Inquiry." In T. Gregersen & P. D. MacIntyre (eds), *Innovative Practices in Language Teacher Education*, 187–203, Switzerland: Springer.

Day, C. & Gu, Q., (eds). (2010), *The New Lives of Teachers*. Abingdon: Routledge.

Dewaele, J. M., Chen, X., Padilla, A. M. & Lake, J. (2019), "The Flowering of Positive Psychology in Foreign Language Teaching and Acquisition Research." *Frontiers in Psychology*, 10.

Dörnyei, Z. & Muir, C. (2019), "Creating a Motivating Classroom Environment." In X. Gao (ed.), *Second Handbook of English Language Teaching*, 719–36, Sydney: Springer.

Edstrom, A. (2015), "Triads in the L2 Classroom: Interaction Patterns and Engagement During a Collaborative Task." *System*, 52: 26–37.

Fonseca-Mora, M. C. & Machancoses, H. (2016), "Music and Language Learning: Emotions and Engaging Memory Pathways." In P. D. MacIntyre, T. Gregersen & S. Mercer (eds), *Positive Psychology in SLA*, 359–73, Bristol: Multilingual Matters.

Fredrickson, B. L. (2001), "The Role of Positive Emotions in Positive Psychology: The Broaden-and-build Theory of Positive Emotions." *American Psychologist*, 56: 218–26.

Fresacher, C. (2016), "Why and How to Use Positive Psychology Activities in the Second Language Classroom." In P.D. MacIntyre, T. Gregersen & S. Mercer (eds), *Positive Psychology in SLA*, 344–58, Bristol: Multilingual Matters.

Gabryś-Barker, D. (2016), "Caring and Sharing in the Foreign Language Class: On a Positive Classroom Climate." In D. Gabryś-Barker & D. Gałajda (eds), *Positive Psychology Perspectives on Foreign Language Learning and Teaching*, 155–74, New York: Springer.

Gkonou, C., Dewaele, J. M. & King, J. (2020), "Introduction to the Emotional Rollercoaster of Language Teaching." In C. Gkonou, J. M. Dewaele & J. King (eds), *Language Teaching: An Emotional Rollercoaster*, 43–77, Bristol: Multilingual Matters.

Gkonou, C. & Mercer, S. (eds). (2017), *Understanding Social and Emotional Intelligence among English Language Teachers*. London: British Council.

Gkonou, C. & Mercer, S. (2018), "The Relational Beliefs and Practices of Highly Socio-emotionally Competent Language Teachers." In S. Mercer and A. Kostoulas (eds), *Language Teacher Psychology*, 158–77, Bristol: Multilingual Matters.

Gkonou, C. & Miller, E. R. (2019), "Caring and Emotional Labour: Language Teachers' Engagement with Anxious Learners in Private Language School Classroom." *Language Teaching Research*, 23: 372–87.

Gkonou, C., Olivero, M. M., & Oxford, R. L. (2021), "Preparing Language Teachers to Be Influential Peacebuilders: Knowledge, Competencies, and Activities." In R. L. Oxford, M. M. Olivero, M. Harrison & T. Gregersen (eds), *Peacebuilding in Language Education. Innovations in Theory and Practice*, 29–42, Bristol: Multilingual Matters.

Gregersen, T. (2016), "The Positive Broadening Power of a Focus on Well-being in the Language Classroom." In D. Gabryś-Barker & D. Gałajda (eds), *Positive Psychology Perspectives on Foreign Language Learning and Teaching*, 59–73, Cham: Springer.

Gregersen, T. & MacIntyre, P. D (2021), "Acting Locally to Integrate Positive Psychology and Peace: Practical Applications for Language Teaching and Learning." In R. L. Oxford, M. M. Olivero, M. Harrison & T. Gregersen (eds), *Peacebuilding in Language* Education. *Innovations in Theory and Practice*, 179–95, Bristol: Multilingual Matters.

Gregersen, T., MacIntyre, P. D. & Macmillan, N. (2020), "Dealing with the Emotions of Teaching Abroad: Searching for Silver Linings in a Difficult Context." In C. Gkonou, M. Daubney & J. M. Dewaele (eds), *The Emotional Rollercoaster of Language Teaching*, 228–46, Bristol: Multilingual Matters.

Gregersen, T., MacIntyre, P. D. & Meza, M. (2016), "Positive Psychology Exercises Build Social Capital for Language Learners: Preliminary Evidence." In P. D. MacIntyre, T. Gregersen & S. Mercer (eds), *Positive Psychology in SLA*, 147–67, Bristol: Multilingual Matters.

Griffiths, C. (2021), "What about the Teacher?." *Language Teaching*: 1–13.

Gross, J. J. (2002), "Emotion Regulation: Affective, Cognitive, and Social Consequences." *Psychophysiology*, 39: 281–91.

Gross, J. J. (ed.). (2014), *Handbook of Emotion Regulation*, 2nd edn. New York: Guilford Press.

Helgesen, M. (2016), "Happiness in ESL/EFL: Bringing Positive Psychology to the Classroom." In P. D. MacIntyre, T. Gregersen & S. Mercer (eds), *Positive Psychology in SLA*, 305–23, Bristol: Multilingual Matters.

Helgesen, M. (2017). "Jobs, Careers, and Callings. Adapting Positive Psychology Tasks for Use in ESL/EFL and Other Language Classes and Teacher Education." In T. Gregersen & P. D. MacIntyre (eds), *Innovative Practices in Language Teacher Education*, 165–83, New York: Springer.

Helgesen, M. (2019), *English Teaching and the Science of Happiness: Positive Psychology Communication Activities for Language Learning*. Tokyo: Abax ELT Publishing.

Hiver, P. (2016), "The Triumph over Experience: Hope and Hardiness in Novice L2 Teachers." In P. D. MacIntyre, T. Gregersen & S. Mercer (eds), *Positive Psychology in SLA*, 168–92, Bristol: Multilingual Matters.

Hiver, P., Al-Hoorie, A. & Mercer, S. (eds). (2021), *Student Engagement in the Language Classroom*. Bristol: Multilingual Matters.

Holmes, E. (ed.). (2005), *Teacher Wellbeing. Looking after Yourself and Your Career in Your Classroom*. London: Taylor and Francis.

Johnson, K. E. & Golombek, P. R. (2016), *Mindful L2 Teacher Education*. New York: Routledge.

Kostoulas, A. & Lämmerer, A. (2020), "Resilience in Language Teaching: Adaptive and Maladaptive Outcomes in Pre-service Teachers." In C. Gkonou, J. M. Dewaele & J. King (eds), *The Emotional Rollercoaster of Language Teaching*, 206–47, Bristol: Multilingual Matters.

London, R. (2013), "Transformative Approaches to Teacher Education. Becoming Holistic Educators in 'Unholistic' Settings." In J. Lin, R. L. Oxford & E. J. Brantmeier (eds), *Re-envisioning Higher Education: Embodied Pathways to Wisdom and Social Transformation*, 77–94, Charlotte: Information Age Publishing.

MacIntyre, P. D. & Ayers-Glassey, S. (2021), "Positive Psychology." In T. Gregersen & S. Mercer (eds), *The Routledge Handbook of the Psychology Language Learning and Teaching*, 61–73, London: Routledge.

MacIntyre, P. D. & Gregersen, T. (2012), "Emotions that Facilitate Language Learning: The Positive-Broadening Power of the Imagination." *Studies in Second Language Learning and Teaching*, 2 (2): 193–213.

Macintyre, P. D., Gregersen, T. & Mercer, S. (2019), "Setting an Agenda for Positive Psychology in SLA: Theory, Practice, and Research." *The Modern Language Journal*, 103 (1): 262–74.

MacIntyre, P. D., Gregersen, T. & Mercer, S. (2020), "Language Teachers' Coping Strategies During the Covid-19 Conversion to Online Teaching: Correlations with Stress, Wellbeing and Negative Emotions." *System*, 94: 1–13.

MacIntyre, P. D. & Mercer, S. (2014), "Introducing Positive Psychology to SLA." *Studies in Second Language Learning and Teaching*, 4 (2): 153–72.

Mercer, S. (2016), "Seeing the World through Your Eyes: Empathy in Language Learning and Teaching." In P. D. MacIntyre, T. Gregersen & S. Mercer (eds), *Positive Psychology in SLA*, 91–111, Bristol: Multilingual Matters.

Mercer, S. (2019), "Language Learner Engagement: Setting the Scene." In X. Gao (ed.), *Second Handbook of English Language Teaching*, 643–60, Cham: Springer.

Mercer, S. & Dörnyei, Z. (2020), *Engaging Language Learners in Contemporary Classrooms*. Cambridge: Cambridge University Press.

Mercer, S. & Gregersen, T. (eds). (2020), *Teacher Wellbeing*. Oxford: Oxford University Press.

Miller, J. P., Nigh, K., Binder, M. J., Novak, B. & Crowell, S. (eds). (2018), *International Handbook of Holistic Education*. New York: Routledge.

Murphey, T. (2014), "Singing Well-becoming: Student Musical Therapy Case Studies." *Studies in Second Language Learning and Teaching*, 2: 205–35.

Olivero, M. M. (2017), "Cultivating Peace via Language Teaching: Pre-service Beliefs and Emotions in an Argentine EFL Practicum." Doctoral diss, College of Arts and Sciences, University of South Florida, Tampa.

Olivero, M. M., Harrison, M. & Oxford, R. L. (2021), "Peacebuilding through Classroom Activities: Inner, Interpersonal, Intergroup, Intercultural, International, and Ecological Peace." In R. L. Oxford, M. M. Olivero, M. Harrison & T. Gregersen (eds), *Peacebuilding in Language Education: Innovations in Theory and Practice*, 245–71, Bristol: Multilingual Matters.

Olivero, M. M. & Oxford, R. L. (2019), "Educating for Peace: Implementing and Assessing Transformative, Multidimensional Peace Language Activities Designed for Future Teachers and Their Students." In L. Walid Lofty & C. Toffolo (eds), *Promoting Peace through Practice, Academia, and the Arts*, 184–206, Hershey: IGI Global.

Oxford, R. L. (2015), Integrating Innovative Peace Activities into Language Teacher Education Courses. Paper presented at the Annual Meeting of the American Association for Applied Linguistics, Canada.

Oxford, R. L. (2016), "Toward a Psychology of Well-being for Language Learners: The 'EMPATHICS' Vision." In P. D. MacIntyre, T. Gregersen & S. Mercer (eds), *Positive Psychology in SLA*, 10–90, Bristol: Multilingual Matters.

Oxford, R. L. (2017), "Peace through Understanding: Peace Activities as Innovations in Language Teacher Education." In T. Gregersen & P. D. MacIntyre (eds), *Innovative Practices in Language Teacher Education*, 125–63, New York: Springer.

Oxford, R. L. (2021), "Emotions." In T. Gregersen & S. Mercer (eds), *The Routledge Handbook of the Psychology Language Learning and Teaching*, 178–90, London: Routledge.

Oxford, R. L. & Cuéllar, L. (2014), "Positive Psychology in Cross-cultural Learner Narratives: Mexican Students Discover themselves while Learning Chinese." *Special Issue, Studies in Second Language Learning and Teaching*, 4 (2): 173–203.

Oxford, R. L. & Olivero, M. M. (2019), "Expanding the Ripples of Peace and Thinking of New Metaphors. Employing Transformational Peace Language Activities in Teacher Education and the Schools." In J. Lin, S. Edwards & T. Culham (eds), *Contemplative Pedagogies for Transformative Teaching, Learning, and Being*, 101–19, Charlotte: Information Age Publishing.

Oxford, R., Olivero, M. M. & Gregersen, T. (2021), "Promoting Peace in Cultural and Language Studies." In N. Johnson (ed.), *Humanities Perspectives in Peace Education: Re-engaging the Heart of Peace Studies*, 55–78, Charlotte: Information Age Publishing.

Prado, J., Uguralp-Cannon, G., Harrison, M. & Fratz Smith, L. (2021), "Seeking Connection through Difference: Finding Nexus of Transformative Learning,

Peacebuilding and Language Teaching." In R. L. Oxford, M. M. Olivero, M. Harrison & T. Gregersen (eds), *Peacebuilding in Language Education. Innovations in Theory and Practice*, 80–109, Bristol: Multilingual matters.

Seligman, M. (ed.). (2011), *Flourish: A Visionary New Understanding of Happiness and Well-being.* New York: Atria.

Seligman, M. E. P. (2011), *Flourish: A Visionary New Understanding of Happiness and Well-being.* New York: Atria.

Seligman, M. E. P. & Csikszentmihalyi, M. (2000), "Positive Psychology: An Introduction." *American Psychologist*, 55 (1): 5–14.

Shaules, J. (ed.). (2019), *Language, Culture, and the Embodied Mind: A Developmental Model of Linguaculture Learning.* Singapore: Springer.

Shulman, L. S. (1986), "Those who Understand: Knowledge Growth in Teaching." *Educational Researcher*, 15 (2): 4–14.

Stevick, E. (ed.). (1990), *Humanism in Language Teaching: A Critical Perspective.* New York: Oxford University Press.

Svalberg, A. M. L. (2018), "Researching Language Engagement; Current Trends and Future Directions." *Language Awareness*, 27 (1–2): 21–39.

Index

Abbott, *Shakespearian Grammar* 131
action chain 111–12, 118–19
active methods 134, 138
active reflection 30. *See also* contemplative/reflective learning
adaptive demands 7–9, 18, 40–1, 45, 48–51, 182
adjustment perspective 40–1, 43–4, 47–9, 51–2, 54–5
  and transformation 50–1
aesthetic reading 7, 10, 154–9, 168
appraisal 47, 183, 189, 206, 215
assumptions 5, 10, 21, 41, 48, 52, 64, 157
  inter-cultural approach 131–2, 139, 142–3
  pragmatic resistance 175, 177–8, 181–2, 184, 188, 193
attitude 17, 28–9, 48, 62, 71, 135, 150, 156–7, 175, 189, 193, 195, 205
  humanistic motivation 89, 92, 95–7

Bakhtin 87
beauty
  language teaching 74, 76
  learning through 137–8, 150
  rehearsal room approach 135
  of spaces 32
behaviour 6, 11, 28, 30, 40–2, 45, 74–6, 157, 206, 208
  pragmatic resistance 175–7, 182–7, 189, 194–5
belief 21, 28, 32, 41, 43, 61, 64–6, 71, 88, 134, 187–8, 204–5, 208, 210
Boud Reflection Model 30

case study, adjustment and transformation 50–1
causative constructions 9–10
  action chain 113, 119
  CAUSER and CAUSEE 114
  CL 111–18, 125
  concept 109–10, 115, 120

definition 110
  embodied learning activities 118–24
  L1 speakers 124
  passive 111, 122
  periphrastic 110–13, 116, 123
  structural difference 121
  target 108
  types 118–19
Chinese
  English learners 9, 62, 74
  Japanese learning 88, 90, 93, 97–8
  journey and travel metaphor 69, 71–2, 79, 81, 87
  learning culture 64–6, 70–1, 77, 96
  teachers 67
  university workshops 133
cognition 5, 8, 16, 20, 23, 26–7, 42, 68–9, 78, 81, 107, 109, 183, 208
cognitive linguistics (CL)
  dual process models 183–4
  embodied views 108–9
  English causative constructions 111–15
  grammar teaching 115–18
contemplative learning 30–2
contemplative/reflective learning 6, 8, 15
  experiential learning 27
  freer forms 31
  meditation 30–2
  purpose 30–2
creativity 26, 79, 209–10
cross-cultural adjustment (CCA) 8, 40, 45, 47–9, 53

deep learning. *See also* German language; Shakespeare's language
  adjustment psychology 40
  definition 17
  Dewey's view 26–8
  foundational principles 3–7
  L2 classroom 108
  language and culture, role of 25

language learning motivation 2–3
notion of embodiment 4–6
pedagogical approaches 2, 8–11
theoretical perspectives 8–11, 17–19
transformative potentials 6–7
wellbeing process 7, 16
deep linguaculture learning. *See also* contemplative/reflective learning
adjustment and adaptive demands 18
concepts 18–19
Dirkx's "emotional soul work" 23–4
Mezirow's approach 20–2
overlapping approaches 19
wellbeing 8, 15–16, 18–19, 33
Dewey, John 32, 137
Experience and Education 26
experiential approach 26–7
view on education 28
Dirkx, J. M.
debriefing steps 23
deep linguaculture learning 23
educational concepts 24
teaching books 23
views of transformative learning 20, 22–4

embodied approach
causative constructions 118–24
Cognitive Linguistics 108–9
deep learning 2–7
grammar teaching 108–9, 115–19, 122–5
moral emotions 183–4
pragmatic resistance 181–4
transformation 6–7, 42–3
emotions. *See also* Dirkx, J. M.; moral emotions
cognition 20, 42
contemplation-reflection 27, 30–1
intuitions and 21, 40
learner well-being 39, 44
lift-off 3
moral 11
personal transformation 6
positive 7, 16
resistance 52
shifting views of language 5
teacher's role 29
types 11

English as a Foreign Language (EFL)
challenges 130, 133
using Shakespeare 131–2
rudimentary interactions 51

foreign language learning (FLL)
learner anxiety 44
learning process 53–4
motivational system 49–50
personal growth 1, 4, 6, 9, 45, 47, 55
psychologically challenging aspects 44–7, 53
resistance and engagement 47–9, 52
transformative elements 42–7, 52–3, 55
well-being concept 7
Foucault, Michel 87

German language
aesthetic dialogue 168–9
Klara's Story, reader response 160–6
reader response 10, 154–62
social nature 153
transactional reading 153–4
grammar teaching
action chain 111–13
CAUSER and CAUSEE 112–15
Cognitive Linguistics (CL) 108–9
concept of causation 109–15
deep approach to learning 115–18
descriptive pedagogy 108–9, 123–4
embodied approach 108–9, 115–19, 122–5
English simple past tense 107–8
generative approach 107
L1 classroom 110
L2 classroom 107–10
passive causatives 111
pedagogical practice 115–18
periphrastic causative 110
rules and exceptions 107–8
social and physical basis, example 108–10
usage-based approach 108–9

holistic learning 8, 11, 26–8, 32. *See also* metaphoric conceptualizations
integrate positive psychology 202, 207
language (teacher) education 207–10

Index

humanistic learning 26
  Dewey, John on 26–8
  Rogers, Carl on 28–30
humanistic motivation
  Bakhtin's ideology 87
  boosting self-confidence 89–92
  enhancing self-understanding 92–5
  ethical self-formation 87
  formal environment 99–100
  investment concept 86–7
  Japanese example 87–99
  key concepts 87
  language education 85–6
  learner's experience, research 88–9
  multiple dimensions 85–6
  pedagogical implications 86
  person-in-context relational view 86
  reshaping social identity 95–8
  transformative experience 101–3

informative learning 41
intercultural perspectives
  adaptive processes 53–5
  emotion regulation 207
  evaluative reactions 187
  interpersonal relations 175, 178
  language teaching and learning 139–43, 159
  mindfulness 190
  music and lyrics 214
  psychological dynamics 45
  transformative learning 42–3

Japanese
  humanistic motivation 87–99
  "Tim" an Anglo-American learner, example 180–1
  watashi, first person pronoun 179–80
journaling 30–1

language education
  active construction 140
  "efferent" and "aesthetic" reading 155–6
  five areas of learning 135–8
  intercultural perspective 139–43
  learning together 136
  making connections 140
  pedagogical approach 135–8

  positive psychology activities for teachers 209–17
  reflection and responsibility 140–1
  social interaction 140
  through beauty 137–8
  through experience 137
  through physical conception 136–7
  through playing 135–6
language learning
  challenges 53–4
  contextual analysis 141–2
  cultural dimension 139–43
  ecological approaches 155–6
  experience of 2
  five principles 140–1
  learners' (meta) pragmatic awareness 187–8
  meta-functions 62–3
  psychological adjustment 45–6, 52–3
  transformative experience 41–3
leap into the unknown 43, 47, 51
L1 (first language) 110, 124, 177
L2 (second language) 99, 107–10, 116–17, 123, 125
  pragmatic resistance 176–9, 181–4, 186, 188, 191, 193–5

McConachy, Troy 5, 10, 18, 47, 130, 139, 141–2
  on FLL's pragmatic resistance and moral emotions 175–8, 182, 186–7, 189–90, 193–4
mediator 24–5
metaphoric conceptualizations
  Chinese teachers and students 62, 64–7, 69–74, 77, 79, 81
  classroom engagement 61, 64
  cognitive linguistics 62, 67–70, 76–7, 80–1
  cultural synergy 62–3, 65, 78–9, 81
  cultures of learning 61–5, 67, 76–81
  diversity contexts 64–5
  goal attainment 68–70
  holistic model 76–8
  indigenous pedagogies 64
  journey of language learning 65–70
  learner centered approach 78
  learners' transformation of the self and growth 72–4

pedagogical suggestions 79–81
reaching destination 71–2
socio-cultural status 70–1
students' perspectives 62–3
teacher discussions 67
teachers' caring for learner wellbeing 74–5
top-down and bottom-up view 61–2
Mezirow, Jack
cognitive-analytic approach 21
deep linguaculture learning 20, 22
transformative learning 21–2
women's education 41
mindfulness 188–90
definition 188
educational domains 188
four-component model 189
intercultural interaction 190
metapragmatic awareness 190
pragmatic judgment tasks 191–3
present-moment experience 189
mixed states 49
moral emotions
embodied perspectives 183–4
four main types 184
learner's subjective experience 175–6
phenomenological perspective 179–80
pragmatic resistance 176–86
Moskowitz, Gertrude 29–30, 32–3
motivation 2, 5–6, 8–9, 18, 43, 47–9, 53–4, 56
definition 86

pedagogical suggestions
"active" approaches to Shakespeare 134–8
evaluative judgments 190–5
grammar teaching 115–18
metaphoric conceptualizations 79–81
transformative experience 53–4
PERMA model 16, 203–4
personal growth 1, 4, 6, 9, 45, 47, 55, 85–7, 91, 102–3
positive psychology activities
building positive relationships 210–12
music and lyrics 214–15
self-care moment 212–13
students' appraisal of past accomplishments 215–17

pragmatic resistance
embodies perspectives 181–4
exploration task 193–5
illustrative examples 179–81
language learners 176
mindfulness 188–93
pedagogical strategies 190–5
phenomenon 176–8
role of moral emotions 187–8
pragmatics, foreign language
learner's subjective experience 175–6, 181–2
L2 classroom 184, 188, 193
mindfulness 191
moral psychology 178, 183
pedagogical strategies 190–1
psychology of FL learning
adjustment and transformation 50–1, 56

reflection, definition 30
resistance. *See also* pragmatic resistance
adaptive demands 9, 18, 41
adjustment perspective 40, 47–52, 54
engagement and 52, 55
to foreignness 45, 53
narrative inquiry 26
negative outcomes, language learning 7
pragmatism 10
psychological trauma 4
Rogers, Carl 32, 44
humanistic psychology and humanistic education 28–30
principles of humanistic learning 29
Rosenblatt, Louise 10, 154–60, 167
RSC model 134–6, 144, 149–50

second language and literacy studies 155–60
Shakespeare's language
active methods 134
classroom as rehearsal room 135
contextual analysis 142
historical terms 132
intercultural perspective 142–3
King John, example 143–9
linguistic and cultural assumptions 130–1
literary perspectives 131

Index

pedagogical approach 132-3, 135-8
practical examples 130-1
Queen Katherine in English court 129-30
"rehearsal room" or "creative" approaches 134-5
syntax or vocabulary 132-3
Shaules, Joseph 3-4, 7-8, 15, 17-20, 25-6, 33, 78, 85, 208
  on FLL's transformative experience 39-40, 45-9
solipsism or hyper-personalization 156
Stevick, Earl 2, 20, 23-4, 29-30, 32, 44, 204, 208

teacher education
  emotion regulation 205-7
  holistic learning 207-9
  PERMA model 203-5
  positive psychology activities 209-17
transactional reading 154, 156, 159-60, 169
transformation
  adjustment perspectives 40, 43, 50-1, 56
  aesthetic reading 10
  contemplative learning 30-2
  creativity 26
  curriculum design 42
  deep forms 8
  deep linguaculture learning 3-7, 15, 18-19
  different aspects 42
  Dirkx's approach 22-4
  embodies process 6-7, 42-3
  emerging paradigm 41
  language use 52-3
  learner identity 43

learner well-being 7
Mezirow's ten phases 21-2
negative experience 39
pedagogical reflections 53-4
personal growth and 55
scaffolding 25
Vygotsky's link 24-5
ZPD metaphor 24-5
transformative learning (TL) theory 8-9, 17, 19-22, 24-6, 29, 31-2, 41-3, 51, 54, 78, 154, 156, 208

unconscious 22-3, 56, 175, 214
university workshops 133
Ushioda, E. 1-2, 43, 85-6, 188

Vygotsky, Lev
  contemplative learning 32
  horticultural metaphor 24
  speech metaphor 24
  transformative learning 24-5, 31

wellbeing
  adjustment psychology 40, 44
  aesthetic reading 10
  deep learning perspective 3-7
  deep linguaculture learning 15-16, 18-19, 33
  definition 16
  holistic perspectives 80
  learners and teachers 2, 8, 39
  and positive psychology 202-17
  teacher's emotion regulation 11, 74-5, 201-17

zone of proximal development (ZPD) 24-5

www.ingramcontent.com/pod-product-compliance
Lightning Source LLC
Chambersburg PA
CBHW062216300426
44115CB00012BA/2087